THOMAS AQUINAS

Great Theologians Series

Series Editors: Reverend Professor John Webster,
Professor Trevor Hart and Professor Douglas Farrow

The Ashgate series, Great Theologians, presents a cluster of high profile titles focusing on individual theologians from the ancients through to the contemporary. The series includes a balance between important new perspectives on major figures who have already received much research attention in the past, and lesser-known theologians or those on whom there has been little published to date. Offering a fresh approach to in-depth theological studies, each book presents an accessible, stimulating new study and comprehensive overview of the theologian and their writing, whilst providing a detailed survey of the historic and contemporary international research already undertaken from a range of different perspectives, and analysing important trends of interpretation and research. This series is intended to provide an invaluable and lasting resource at the upper level of study and academic research.

Thomas Aquinas
Theologian of the Christian Life

NICHOLAS M. HEALY
St John's University, New York

ASHGATE

Published by
Ashgate Publishing Limited
Gower House
Croft Road
Aldershot
Hants GU11 3HR
England

Ashgate Publishing Company
Suite 420
101 Cherry Street
Burlington, VT 05401–4405 USA

Ashgate website: http://www.ashgate.com

British Library Cataloguing in Publication Data
Healy, Nicholas M.
  Thomas Aquinas: Theologian of the Christian Life.
  1. Thomas Aquinas, Saint, 1225?–1274. 2. Theology, Doctrinal—Middle Ages, 600–1500.
  I. Title
  230.2

Library of Congress Cataloging in Publication Data
Healy, Nicholas M.
  Thomas Aquinas: Theologian of the Christian Life/Nicholas M. Healy.
     p.   cm. (Great Theologians Series)
  1. Thomas Aquinas, Saint 1225?–1274. 2. Christian life—Catholic authors.
  I. Title. II. Series.
  BX4700.T6H43   2003
  230'.2'092–dc21   200206240

ISBN 0 7546 1471 9 (hbk)
ISBN 0 7546 1472 7 (pbk)

Typeset by Manton Typesetters, Louth, Lincolnshire, UK.
Printed and bound in Great Britain by MPG Books Ltd, Bodmin, Cornwall.

Contents

Preface

Why Read Thomas?

There are two basic questions that should be addressed by everyone who writes a book about Thomas Aquinas. The first asks why anyone should find it worthwhile to read about the work of this Dominican *magister in sacra pagina* (master of the sacred page) who lived so long ago – in the middle years of the thirteenth century (1224–75). There were many other medieval friars and monks, many of whom were *magistri*, and not a few of whom wrote theological and philosophical works that were regarded as significant in their day. Few of them are read nowadays, even by theologians and philosophers. Thomas, though, has been read ever since his death, and recently as much as ever. So what is it that distinguishes his work?

One reason for Thomas's perduring popularity, and thus one possible reason for devoting time and energy to him today, may lie in the experience of many of his readers who have found that the more his thought informs their own thought and action, the more coherent, profound and, so to say, *livable* it appears. Thomas seems to have an unusual ability to display the richness, the glorious complexity yet profound simplicity of the Christian way of life. Immersing oneself within his work, one may come to see that being a Christian can be thoroughly exciting, even something of an adventure.[1] No doubt the theology of Thomas's great Franciscan contemporary, St Bonaventure (1217–74) is livable, too, but it seems that considerably more people over the years have found Thomas's thought livable, or at least of interest, than they have Bonaventure's.

However, the fact that Thomas has enjoyed a relatively large readership raises the second question. Many books have been written about his work, some of which are very good, so why write yet another? My answer is no doubt much the same as many others who think that they, too, have something worth saying about Thomas. That is, I think that my perspective on his work, though certainly not original, is one that should be better known. As with any great thinker, people have appreciated Thomas for various reasons, depending in part upon their own agendas and contexts. My own more particular reasons for thinking that his work is worth careful study today have shaped my account of it here, so it is only fair to state them at the outset. They can be reduced to three.

Three Reasons

First, I read Thomas as a theologian. Thomas was a Christian theologian, as I am, too, though, to be sure, he and I are by no means in the same league. I find Thomas worth reading because he was an extremely good theologian and an extraordinarily skilled Christian. His theological judgment, acuity and imagination are among the best in the tradition. Faced with a choice between two more or less reasonable yet apparently unappealing theological alternatives, Thomas will find a third that combines the best of the other two, or rework one of them to recover some little-noticed aspect of the tradition, or bypass the problem altogether by some ingenious move. Certainly there are many areas where one might pose critical questions, especially in light of the differences between his and our intellectual contexts and concerns. But many of his theological judgments and proposals have held up well over time, so that they may still be brought to bear in contemporary theological inquiry.

Second, I read Thomas as an evangelical and Catholic Christian.[2] Thomas's thought is grounded in Scripture, and his reading of Scripture is structured by the doctrine of the Trinity and centered upon Jesus Christ. This, in combination with his good judgment and insight, suggests that his theology may offer resources for those Christians who are concerned to recover a similar orientation within an ecumenical context. Put another way, I think one can make the case that, when read on his own terms, Thomas's theology can be made to respond to the concerns of the Reformers in a more convincing way than some might suppose. While the thirteenth-century Thomas does not always agree with his colleagues of the sixteenth century, his and their respective positions evidently reflect the same fundamental concerns.

My third reason for thinking Thomas worth another book has to do with what would now be called his theological method. According to a now popular periodization (itself not unproblematic), Thomas lived in that era some call the premodern. The era ended with the onset of the modern period sometime about the middle of the seventeenth century. Now we seem to be moving into a post- or late-modern period. This is not the place to expand upon the characteristics of modernity or modern theological methodology, which are difficult to formulate without appearing tendentious.[3] And what may be in store for us in the new period, if indeed we are in such, can only be guessed at. But it has been quite reasonably suggested that the decline of the dominance of modern theological methods, a decline linked perhaps to recent challenges to certain of the presuppositions and norms of modernity, may permit the recovery of some elements of premodern theological method for postmodern use. I think Thomas's method offers one of the best hopes for such a recovery.

One or two of my reasons for reading Thomas are already largely taken for granted among a growing number of Thomas scholars, and I am fortunate indeed to be able to draw upon their work. To learn of Thomas's wise judgments and evangelical orientation, one cannot do better than to consult the work of some of the contemporary French Dominicans, particularly Jean-Pierre Torrell and Gilles Emery. I am indebted, too, to experts in the USA, including David Burrell, Thomas Hibbs, Mark Jordan and Joseph Wawrykow. And there are a number of others whom I will gratefully acknowledge in due course.

Alternatives

However, such interpreters of Thomas are still a minority. Until recently, the premodern Thomas was read and taught almost everywhere as if he were a modern Neo-Scholastic *avant le temps*. His manifestly scriptural, Christoform and theocentric premodern theology had been transformed into something more like a modern philosophical system or, more accurately, an anti-modern system of religious philosophy that shared many of the principles of modernity. One reason for this transformation may have been that for many centuries Thomas was the most authoritative theologian of the Roman Catholic church, so later commentators used his work to deal with issues he did not consider. They made him support proposals sometimes quite foreign to his own views and for which his theology was neither intended nor suitable. The relocation of Thomas's work on to alien ground has guaranteed that certain parts of it were widely read, especially during the heyday of Neo-Scholasticism in the first half of the twentieth century. But this has been at the cost of considerable distortion of his work.

Thomas is still often read as if his significance lies primarily in his philosophy. Among such interpreters are some who are not at all Neo-Scholastic and to whom I am indebted for help in understanding this aspect of his thought. An outstanding contribution is that of John F. Wippel, who believes that Thomas had a 'well-worked-out metaphysics in his own mind [which] can be recovered from his various writings'. On this basis, Wippel puts together a comprehensive Thomistic philosophy as if Thomas had written, as Wippel puts it, a *Summa Metaphysica* (Wippel, 2000, pp. xvii, xxvii). The founding members of the self-described Radical Orthodoxy group, John Milbank and Catherine Pickstock, have argued that Thomas's work represents the supreme Christian metaphysical synthesis before the decline into modernity ushered in by Duns Scotus and William of Ockham. In at least one of their works they seem to read Thomas's *Summa Theologiae* (henceforth ST) as a system, the culmination of which is its concluding Christology, wherein the synthesis of the divine and the human is achieved (see, e.g., Milbank and Pickstock, 2001, pp. 59, 68f.). Their analysis is often brilliant and penetrating. Yet I cannot but think that their focus on philosophical issues, however sympathetic they are to more strictly theological matters, leads them and Wippel to bypass the main thrust of Thomas's project. A similar focus can be seen in the work of Thomas scholars in other areas, in my view, such as the lucid studies of Thomas's ethics by Ralph McInerny, who seems to privilege the perspective of 'moral philosophy' over that of Christian theology (e.g., McInerny, 1982/1997).

There is considerable truth in the pervasive assumption that Thomas's thought, broadly viewed, presents us with an internally coherent and cohesive system. His work is indeed so 'enormously systematic' (Davies, 1992, p. viii) that the boundaries between philosophy, morality and theology tend to break down under the pressure of Thomas's synthetic genius. In my view, though, his more philosophically minded readers have tended to overlook the way in which Thomas engages in imaginative, flexible and often anti-systematic and dialectical forms of inquiry. These are a vital part of his method because they reflect, indeed, they grow out of, his fundamental concern, which is theological. Thomas's theology is evangelical. That is, his method depends upon Scripture, and not upon philosophical principles that could stand apart from Scripture, even if they were once derived from it. The purpose of his theology is to help preachers preach on Scripture better and Christians to live the Gospel more truly. Thus his chief concern was not to develop a complete system – a Christian Theory of Everything or Grand Totalizing Narrative, to use some modern and postmodern expressions. Rather, he sought to display Christianity as a way of life that always and with good reason accords the primacy to Scripture and thus to Jesus Christ.

An Outline

My primary goal throughout what follows is to present a clear account of Thomas's mature theology. I make some effort at placing his work within its historical and cultural context, but I do not have enough space to discuss the many theological and ecclesiastical controversies of his time, except those that bear most significantly upon his work. Nor can I discuss the development of Thomas's theology except, again, when it is particularly relevant. I do not offer any criticism of Thomas, but neither, I believe, do I avoid or hide those aspects of his work that are likely to strike the reader as needing further critical reflection. My main concern is to display the evangelical, pastoral and theocentric character of his premodern theology, a concern that has required me to make choices about what to emphasize, and what to treat more summarily. Naturally, I do not expect everyone to agree with my decisions, but I am sure all will agree that they have to be made if I am to reduce so complex and voluminous a thinker to the confines of this little book. I have centered my account on the *Summa Theologiae*, since that work is his most mature and broadest in scope. It often lives up to its title, however, in its summary style, so I draw upon parallel passages in the *Summa contra Gentiles*, the Commentaries on Scripture and other works when it is useful to do so. I have tended to be brief in my account of the more philosophical aspects of Thomas's thought, focusing only upon what is necessary to understand his theology.

Organizing Thomas's theology into a clear yet sufficiently detailed presentation is extraordinarily difficult. Thomas's own order of exposition in such works as the *Summa Theologiae* is brilliantly conceived, yet in my view it is best not to replicate it since it so easily leads to misunderstanding for contemporary readers. My account here is arranged in six chapters. The first chapter is introductory and historical, and begins with a brief overview of Thomas's life and career. In the seven hundred years since his death, his writings have been subjected to a range of interpretations, culminating in Neo-Scholasticism and the various Neo-Thomisms of the twentieth century. To grasp what is involved in interpreting Thomas today one needs at least a passing acquaintance with these developments, which I present in a brief overview in the remainder of the chapter.

The main body of the book – Chapters 2 through 6 – begins and ends with Thomas's treatment of the Christian life. Chapter 2 describes the key elements of Thomas's formation as a Dominican and his later understanding of the purpose and goals of the Order. The Order was thoroughly Christocentric in its orientation and in the formation of its members, stressing preaching and obedient following of Christ in poverty. The remainder of the chapter explores the bearing of Dominican (and scriptural) principles upon Thomas's theological method and his hermeneutics.

According to Thomas, the Dominican life, like that of Christians generally, is an active one, lived with others in the world. The Dominicans are to serve the needs of Christians by their preaching and teaching. They are to engage with the world by bringing to it the fruits of their contemplation, following the example of Christ. The next three chapters discuss the 'fruits' of Thomas's theological contemplation. Chapter 3 begins the contemplative ascent that Christian theological inquiry requires. My reading of this movement is in part intended to counter the notion, pervasive among his Neo-Scholastic interpreters and those they have influenced, that Thomas works out his doctrine of God in a linear and deductive fashion. On the contrary, because Thomas's inquiry is undertaken in obedience to Christ, he moves dialectically from (and away from) ordinary and philosophical talk about God's existence to the Christ-revealed doctrine of the Trinity. Throughout this 'ascent' he is guided by Scripture and the church's doctrines, with the goal of arriving somewhere near to the 'high, full and perfect' vision of the triune God required of the Christian theologian, following John the Evangelist.

Chapter 4 continues on with that same perspective as Thomas makes the link between God as such and God's work as creator and redeemer. Again, the logic of Thomas's theology in these doctrines is more flexible and complex – and more scriptural – than some of his critics have suggested. The 'link', of course, is the second person, the Son of God, God's wisdom and Word revealed and active: Jesus Christ. Here, then, I discuss Thomas's Trinitarian understanding of creation and its purpose before turning to his

Christology. Chapter 5 considers the link between Christ's person and work and ourselves. Thomas makes that link with the concept of grace. Grace refers to the salvific work of Christ brought to us through the infusion of the theological virtues and the gifts and operations of the Holy Spirit. Here, too, I treat matters associated with the Reformation controversies, including faith and works, merit and election. Finally, Chapter 6 returns to Thomas's conception of the Christian life, considered now in light of its ground in the Trinity and in the work of Jesus Christ. I have developed this in terms of Thomas's understanding of law, primarily the eternal law and the new law of the Gospel. Under this rubric I discuss Thomas's understanding of human action, sin, Israel and the church. The church serves, and is a product of, the new law of freedom in Christ. So I conclude with a brief look at Thomas's sacramental theology and the place of the cardinal virtues within the Christian life.

A Note on Translations

English translations of some of Thomas's works are sometimes difficult to find. My citations from the Commentaries on Scripture are from the Marietti edition and are my own translations.[4] I have used the translation of the *Summa Theologiae* by the Fathers of the English Dominican Province for its convenient size, availability and its fairly literal rendering of the Latin. Though somewhat torn over the matter, I thought it best to replace the 'Holy Ghost' of my childhood with the now more familiar 'Holy Spirit'. For the *Summa contra Gentiles*, I have used the translation by Anton Pegis and others. I have altered both translations slightly and without comment in order to conform to the publisher's requirement that I use inclusive language. Throughout, I have avoided male forms when talking about God as such and the Holy Spirit, even though it makes for awkwardness at times. For theological reasons, though, I have retained male terms when referring to the Son and the Father.

Notes

1 I believe it was Stanley Hauerwas who taught me to think of the Christian life as an 'adventure'.

2 I do not mean 'evangelical' in the sense often, though confusedly, associated with Protestant fundamentalism. That kind of evangelicalism seems to trade on modernistic hermeneutical assumptions that are no longer reasonable, nor would they have seemed reasonable to Thomas. Rather, I mean 'evangelical' in the sense, say, of the first article of the Barmen confession, i.e., concerned to maintain or recover the primary of Scripture and its witness to Jesus Christ within the church. I mean 'catholic' in the sense of ecumenical, along the lines of Augustine's usage which, for me, includes Catholic in the more restricted sense.

3   One good attempt to do so can be found in the opening essay by George Schner, in *Theology After Liberalism: A Reader*, John Webster and George P. Schner eds, Oxford: Blackwell, 2000.
4   See the References section at the end of the book.

Chapter 1

Introduction: Life and Interpretation

Too much can certainly be made of the bearing of lived experience upon a thinker's work. Knowing a little or a lot about the author's personal experience and social situation cannot fully explain a text, yet it may well help us to understand it better. Thomas Aquinas lived so long ago and in a context so very different from our own that his readers need some idea of his life and career if they are to avoid even the most elementary misunderstandings. Moreover, Thomas's writings have been subjected to various and often conflicting interpretations from his time to ours, interpretations that not infrequently reflect a failure to acknowledge his historical and social context. So some acquaintance with the history of the reception of Thomas's texts is vital to reading his work well today. Any interpretation of Thomas is controversial, including the one that I will present here, and best presented with such alternative readings in mind. Thus this chapter is introductory; it provides some of the background for the more detailed consideration of Thomas's texts that follows. The first section begins with a biographical sketch and then, in the second section, I offer a brief account of the history of Thomism.

Thomas's Life and Career

Thomas Aquinas was born into a minor aristocratic family in Italy in 1224 or 1225 at the family castle of Roccasecca, located not far from Naples on the road to Rome.[1] As was the custom with the younger sons of the nobility, he was destined for a career in the church. He was sent as a child to the nearby Benedictine monastery of Monte Cassino to be an oblate, perhaps with the idea that he would eventually become the abbot there. In 1239, the Benedictines sent him to Naples to begin his studies in the liberal arts. At Naples he came into contact with the Dominicans, who had recently established a priory there. Their influence seems to have been decisive, for when the time came to make a decision about his future, Thomas chose to become neither a Benedictine monk nor a regular priest, but a friar in the order founded less than thirty years before (in 1217) by St Dominic. His decision to join this less than socially acceptable order – he took the habit in April 1244 – upset his relatives, particularly his mother. The story is told of how she arranged for Thomas to be taken by force and kept in the family castle at Roccasecca for a little over a year, during which his family tried various strategies to change his mind.

His family's concern was understandable, for the friars dedicated them-selves to what was then a somewhat countercultural way of life. Unlike priests, they did not settle in a parish under the authority of a bishop, nor, unlike the various orders of monks, did they devote themselves to contem-plation and manual labor within the walls of a monastery. Instead they dedicated themselves to a more itinerant and unusually independent life of 'preaching in poverty'. Thomas's decision for the Dominicans reflects the radical nature of his conception of Christianity, 'radical' Christian in the original sense of having a deeply rooted desire to follow Jesus Christ what-ever the cost, but also in the contemporary colloquial sense of innovative and going against cultural norms and assumptions.[2]

Realizing that Thomas was not going to change his mind, the family returned him to the Dominicans at Naples. In 1245 he was sent to Paris, where he probably studied in the Faculty of Arts of the University with the Dominican scholar, Albert the Great (1206–80) (see Torrell, 1996a, pp. 19–24). In 1248, Albert was asked by his superiors to teach at a new *studium generale* (a college for members of the Order) at Cologne, and he took Thomas along with him. It is likely that Thomas was ordained a priest there. He began to teach as a bachelor – a kind of apprentice professor – by taking students through some books of the Old Testament. In 1252 he was sent back to the University of Paris to teach, even though he had not yet reached the canonical age. There he began what was required of any aspiring teacher of theology at the time, namely to write a commentary on the *Sentences* of Peter Lombard. The resulting book, the *Commentary on the Sentences (Scriptum super libros Sententiarum)*, was his first large work. Peter's *Sentences* – so called because they were a collection of brief opinions *(sententiae)* on different theological issues drawn from patristic writers – had been arranged into four books about a century earlier. The authoritative texts of the *Sentences* provided a common basis for debate among the range of theological positions of the time (Buckley, 1987, p. 43). They prompted commentators to engage with the main issues in Christian theology, but were flexible enough to permit them to introduce their own concerns. And Thomas did so, as Torrell says, 'most resolutely' (Torrell, 1996a, p. 41), adding considerable material from Aristotle and substantially changing the principle of organization.[3]

In 1256 he became a master, roughly the equivalent of a professor of theology, though the word 'theology' is not quite right, since Thomas's discipline was not divided into specialties, as it is now customarily divided into systematics, ethics, biblical studies and history. It is perhaps better to retain his full title, namely *magister in sacra pagina*, master of the sacred page (sacred page = Scripture). The title appropriately draws attention to the master's focus upon the Bible. For Thomas and those of his time, theologi-cal inquiry was not as easily distinguishable from commentary upon Scrip-ture as it is today. Scripture itself is theology or *sacra doctrina* – sacred teaching in the sense both of something taught and the action of teaching, too – and so theology is largely the explication of Scripture. One might say that Scripture displays God's 'theology', God's own self-understanding, in a form appropriate for us, upon which, of course, our theology must depend.[4] To be sure, the two terms were never synonymous. Scripture is the norm over all its theological interpretations. Theology serves Scripture by relating it to everything else we know in order to show that it makes sense and that it can reasonably be held to be true.

As a doctor of Scripture (another contemporary title), Thomas's function was threefold: to 'preach' upon scriptural texts (*praedicatio*); to 'read' Scripture (*lectio*), i.e., to analyze books of the Bible in the form of commentaries; and to engage in 'disputation' (*disputatio*), to argue for and against rival interpretations of Scripture and their doctrinal and moral consequences. Thomas wrote many commentaries upon Old Testament books: Isaiah, Jeremiah, Job, the Psalms; as well as upon the New Testament: the gospels of Matthew and John and some of the letters of Paul. This area of Thomas's work has been too often ignored, perhaps in part because of the commentaries' dry, scholastic style, with its sometimes laborious concern for noting distinctions and categories that seem to have little significance. Yet these works are of vital importance in properly interpreting Thomas's thought, for hidden within them are a multitude of insights that enable a better reading of his more obviously 'theological' works. They give us some idea of which texts he drew upon in treating particular doctrinal issues. They make it clear how much his theology depends upon his reading of Scripture, and how his reading is oriented throughout to Jesus Christ.

Thomas sometimes notes that theology's concern is not only the right interpretation of Scripture and doctrine, but also the correction of errors and the removal of stumbling-blocks to the faith, among which are mistaken philosophical principles and concepts. Thomas made a life-long habit of writing treatises and commentaries upon philosophical works, although this was never a part of his official duties; nor did he ever teach philosophy. While still a bachelor, he wrote a significant work, *De Ente et Essentia* (*On Being and Essence*), in which he worked out certain metaphysical distinctions which became fundamental for his doctrine of God and creation. While at Paris he wrote a commentary on Boethius's *De Trinitate* (*On the Trinity*), which addresses questions to do with scientific inquiry and how we may know God. In later years he wrote a number of commentaries on works by Aristotle, on the *Nicomachean Ethics*, for example, written while Thomas was working on his own moral theology in the second part of his *Summa Theologiae*. As Torrell puts it, 'he undertook these commentaries in an apostolic perspective in order better to carry out his job as a theologian, and better to accomplish his labor of wisdom … : to proclaim the truth and refute error' (Torrell, 1996a, p. 239).

The University curriculum required one's understanding and use of authoritative texts to be tested by engaging in debate. The bachelor learned the art of public disputation by arguing for his own resolution of a question and by responding to objections from his audience. The master would then give his determination orally, followed later by a written version, in which he would set out his resolution of the question, together with possible objections and his responses to them. Thomas's disputations were collected and written down as *Quaestiones Disputatae*. Once or twice a year, the audience for such debates could present a question they wanted discussed. These were collected into Thomas's twelve *Quaestiones Quodlibetales*, questions on freely chosen topics. Many of the texts of the period, though composed independently of any debate, preserved the format of the disputation, as is the case with Peter Lombard's *Sentences* and commentaries thereon, as well as Thomas's larger theological works, the *Summa contra Gentiles* and the *Summa Theologiae*, which I will discuss in a moment.

Thomas left Paris after about four years, returning to Italy probably in late 1259. He went back (perhaps) to Naples for a couple of years (Torrell, 1996a, pp. 98–101), before arriving in Orvieto by September 1261. There he was appointed conventual lector, the prior in charge of the education of friars who were unable to study at a *studium generale*. One of the more significant works from this time was the *Catena Aurea* (*The Golden Chain*), a collection of texts from the Latin and Greek Fathers discussing each verse of the four gospels. It is likely that at Orvieto he largely completed the great work he had started in Paris, his *Summa contra Gentiles*. It was here, too, that he wrote the Office for the feast of Corpus Christi. Thomas then moved to Rome in late 1265 to start another *studium* for specially selected Dominicans. He conducted a series of disputations, collected in the *De Potentia* (*On Power*), and wrote, among much else, a commentary on Aristotle's *On the Soul*, and the *Compendium Theologiae*, a book-length treatment of the Christian faith organized according to the three theological virtues, faith, hope and charity (the work remained unfinished, stopping half-way through hope). It was while in Rome that he began the first part of what would be his most widely read work, the *Summa Theologiae*. At this point it will be helpful to make some preliminary remarks about the two *summae*.

The Summae

It used to be thought that the *Summa contra Gentiles* (abbreviated henceforth as 'ScG') was an occasional work, written at the request of a Dominican master general, Raymond of Peñafort, to aid missionaries in converting the Muslims of Spain. This now seems unlikely. There is no dedication to Raymond, nor is there any discussion of Muslim doctrines, so some contend that the book has a more general purpose, namely to display the relationship between philosophical wisdom, i.e., the knowledge of the *gentiles* or pagans, and Christian wisdom (Hibbs, 1995, pp. 11f.). In line with this purpose, Thomas focuses upon the philosophical or metaphysical aspects of whatever is being discussed. As there is no expressed occasion for Thomas to write the work, it has been suggested that it is 'an essay in personal reflection' (René-Antoine Gauthier, cited in Torrell, 1996a, p. 108). That is, while it was obviously written for others to read, it examines a set of issues that were of particular concern to Thomas.

The ScG consists of four books, each of which is divided into 'chapters', often only a page or so long, which are further divided into paragraphs. (Thus the reference ScG 3.6.2 is to the third book, sixth chapter, second paragraph.) Book One begins with a methodological introduction (chapters 1–9), and then examines what may be known about God apart from Christian revelation (chapters 10–102). The second book discusses creation, the third, providence, the divine ordering of things by which they are drawn into relation to God by grace. Only with the final book does Thomas turn explicitly to what is known about God through the Scriptures, namely the doctrines of the Trinity and the Incarnation, as well as the Sacraments and the Eschaton. So Thomas's organization of his material has led some to believe that the first three books are philosophical in nature or an exercise in natural theology, while it is only with the fourth book that the discourse becomes properly theological.

This is far too simple, however (see Hibbs, 1995, pp. 1–34). A key passage is ScG 2.4, which defines the different tasks and orientations of philosophy and theology. The philosopher discusses things as they are, apart from their relation to God, and only then, as it may be, moves on to consider their relation to God. The theologian begins from the opposite perspective, from God to creatures, which is the order followed by the 'doctrine of faith'. Thomas expressly notes that he follows that latter order, beginning in Book One with 'God as such' and then in the remainder of the work discussing all that derives from God. Thus while he may treat what may be known of God apart from revelation, this does not mean that he abandons theology. The discussion of the first three books is clearly dependent upon and oriented towards revealed knowledge for, as Thomas says elsewhere, it is only with revelation that we know about God's providence and omnipotence (ST 2/2.1.8 ad 1 – see page 6 for an explanation of this reference style). Thus the work is better read as a special kind of theological discourse, the aim of which is to enact the dialectic between the wisdom of the ancient pagan philosophers (the *gentiles* of the title) and Christian wisdom. The latter is the 'highest wisdom'. It may sometimes make use of philosophical concepts and some of its 'likely arguments' (ScG 1.9.2) as its 'first wisdom', as a convenient starting-point within ordinary human inquiry. But that wisdom must be placed within a properly theological framework, and assessed by theological wisdom. Thomas's theological examination of philosophical knowledge in all four books displays both the value and the incompleteness of what can be known apart from Scripture. ScG amounts in effect to a demonstration of our need for revelation.

The *Summa Theologiae* (abbreviated henceforth as 'ST') is also dialectical, though in a different way since its purpose is rather different. Thomas's opening remarks as to its purpose are somewhat ambiguous. He seems to say that he wrote the work for those new to theology: 'the Master of Catholic Truth ought *not only* to teach the proficient but also to instruct beginners' (my italics). The 'not only' is important, I think, because the sheer difficulty and often summary nature of the work suggest that Thomas would know that it would benefit experts just as much as novices (Corbin, 1972; Jenkins, 1997). One should note, too, that 'beginners' does not mean those with no previous catechesis. The ST's first readers were Dominican friars, thoroughly committed men who already had some years of intensive formation.[5] Thomas had his Dominican brethren firmly in mind when he wrote the work. He sought above all to deepen his readers' understanding and appropriation of Christian doctrine and Scripture so that they might better follow Jesus Christ in obedience and better preach him in poverty.

The ST adopts the scholastic method of inquiry throughout, and consists of 'articles' which summarize and resolve debate upon a particular topic. The question of the article is first stated (e.g., Whether God exists? Or, Whether angels know more than people can?), and then Thomas presents usually three or more classic, current or novel 'objections', arguments against an affirmative answer. Then follows the '*sed contra*' ('but, on the contrary'), a short statement of the view supporting the affirmative and opposing the objections. The *sed contra* usually takes the form of a short scriptural quotation, a point of logic or a brief summary of an opposing argument from an 'authority', i.e., a theologian or church leader whose views are accepted as largely normative within the tradition. The corpus of the article then presents Thomas's own response. There he makes logical, philosophical, doctrinal and scriptural arguments, often in such a way that he finds a third perspective on the issue that brings out the elements of truth within the opposing positions. Finally, the article concludes with 'replies' to the initial objections, often developing Thomas's solution significantly further.

The articles are grouped into questions, and the questions into three large parts, of which the second is divided into two. (Thus a text from the ST will be referred to in the following way: ST 2/2.23.4 ad 3 (the second section of the second part, 23rd question, 4th article, reply 'to' ('*ad*') objection 3).) Except for a few brief, paragraph-length prologues, there are no passages in the ST that are written without reference to a particular question. The format takes some getting used to and may become wearying at times, in spite of Thomas's intent, expressed in the prologue, to make things more accessible and less confusing for the beginner. But the approach has the benefit of summarizing the state of each question at the time Thomas addressed it. One should not, however, read an article or even a question in isolation from the rest of the ST. As Alasdair MacIntyre rightly insists, the ST should be read as a whole, for it was intended to be a comprehensive presentation of the Christian intellectual tradition for the benefit of those training to become preachers of the Gospel (MacIntyre, 1990, p. 169).

The initial question of the first part (ST 1.1) is devoted to preliminary matters, including the nature and function of theology as a discipline, comparison with other disciplines, and a brief discussion of how the Bible should be read within theology and the church. Thomas then considers the existence of God, presenting the famous 'five ways' (*quinque viae*) that draw upon philosophers' attempts to 'prove' the existence of God. He then develops his doctrine of God as One, and then as Triune, before turning to consider the creation of the angels and humanity. ST 2 examines our active response to God and what makes that response possible. ST 1/2 treats human actions in general, while 2/2 discusses those actions that more particularly relate to sin and grace and the history of salvation. ST 3 is devoted first to Jesus Christ and then to some of the sacraments. In a supplement drawn from the earlier Commentary on the Sentences – Thomas died before he completed the third part – we find his earlier teaching on the remaining sacraments and the General Resurrection.

Final Years

In 1268, Thomas returned to Paris for a second tour as master at the University. He remained there until 1272, working on the ST. Thomas had always worked very hard, but during his last ten years or so his productivity is astonishing. He had dictated his work ever since becoming a master, and stories are told of him in these last years dictating to three or even four secretaries at once. (Presumably, he would turn to another secretary when one got tired or needed to catch up on transcribing his virtually illegible notes.) Adding to the workload was the continuing need to respond to the controversies then disturbing the University of Paris. During much of the thirteenth century, the University was frequently the site not only of intellectual debate, but of genuine strife, with faculty strikes and factional fighting that sometimes became violent. The issue that most engaged Thomas was the attack on the Dominican way of life by Thomas's university colleagues. Thomas defended his chosen way of life throughout his career, in works written especially for the purpose and, usually less explicitly, in his larger theological works.[6]

Thomas moved to Naples in the spring of 1272 to found a new *studium generale* for theological studies. Here he continued to work very hard, writing the final Christological part of the ST, and commenting upon John's Gospel and some letters of Paul. In late 1273, while at Mass, he seems to have had some kind of experience, whether spiritual, psychological or physical, or some combination thereof, which made it impossible for him to continue working. He lost his strength, took to his bed, and then recovered somewhat. A couple of months later he was summoned to a council at Lyons by Gregory X. Early in the journey, lost in thought (Thomas's fits of abstraction were well known), he hit his head on the branch of a fallen tree and became ill again. He was taken to his childhood home at the Benedictine monastery of Monte Cassino, which happened to be nearby, and then on to some relatives. Feeling a little better, he set out again, but had to stop at the

Cistercian monastery of Fossanova where, after a brief illness, he died on 7 March 1274. Thomas was revered immediately upon his death, in part because one of the Cistercian monks was apparently cured of an eye disease by pressing his eyes against those of the corpse. His relics were eagerly sought after, leading to quarrels over his body, which was eventually re-buried (in 1369) at Toulouse. Thomas was canonized by Pope John XXII in 1323, and the title of Doctor of the Church was bestowed upon him by Pius V in 1567.

Thomisms

In the next chapter we will need to look more closely at how Thomas's formation and work within the Order of Preachers bears upon his theology. But we now have enough of an initial orientation to go on to consider the history of Thomas-interpretation from his death to the present. My account here is not meant to be comprehensive.[7] Instead, my aim is to introduce in a preliminary fashion certain aspects of Thomas's thought and briefly describe how they were altered by later interpreters. Their efforts removed his work from its historical, social and intellectual context, and relocated it in the thought-forms and agendas of modernity. As a consequence, it came to be reinterpreted as if it were a modern systematic philosophical theology and apologetics, rather than as a theology centered upon Scripture, Jesus Christ and the triune God. I include, too, some account of the issues involved in the twentieth-century effort to unearth the premodern Thomas, enabling me to situate the presentation here as a continuation of that effort.

Aristotle and Averroism

It took some time for Thomas to become established as one of the foremost theologians of his age. At first his work continued to be read at the University after his death, especially by the Dominicans, but questions were soon raised about its orthodoxy. Much of the concern had to do with his enthusiastic and innovative use of Aristotle's philosophy, following upon the work of his teacher, Albert the Great, who was one of the earliest to become familiar with Aristotle. Before the thirteenth century, theologians generally worked with philosophical tools that drew rather more upon Plato than upon Aristotle. In large part this was because of the great authority of Augustine, himself deeply influenced by derivative forms of Platonic thought, as well as the work of Pseudo-Dionysius, a sixth-century Neoplatonic monk, who was thought to have been a first-century follower of Paul. Augustine had shown how Platonic language could be used to help express the most profound theological matters. With some exceptions (such as Boethius), most theologians deemed Aristotle less helpful and, besides, comparatively little of his work was then available. However, during the course of the twelfth and early thirteenth centuries more of Aristotle's works entered the West through Arab philosophers and their translators. Initially, his philosophy was welcomed for the most part, especially as it was interpreted by those Muslims who maintained some connection with Neoplatonism, such as Avicenna (980–1037) and Avicebron (1020–70).

Other interpreters of Aristotle had developed his philosophy in a somewhat different direction, however. The adoption of what was understood to be the philosophy of Averroes (1126–98) by the Faculty of Arts at the University of Paris led to strife with the Faculty of Theology. The difficulty with Averroism was twofold. First, it sought to understand the world in terms of itself, ruling out any knowledge of another realm. It thereby rejected the Neoplatonic belief that this world is real and knowable only in so far as it participates in that other, more real world from which it emanates. All activity within the world can be explained as strictly determined by the movements of the stars and other heavenly bodies; hence there is no need to appeal to the actions of a free, loving God. The world, furthermore, is demonstrably eternal and thus does not require a creator to explain its existence. Second, Averroism undermined individual knowledge and freedom. According to Aristotle, a power, which he called the 'active intellect', is required to transform that which the mind receives from the senses, which is necessarily material, to the level of spirit or intellect. The active intellect turns sense data into ideas, making those data knowable. Aristotle's texts seem to leave it open to question whether every mind had its own active intellect or there is only a single active intellect. Averroes believed the latter was the better interpretation. As a consequence, he effectively denied the possibility of reasoning by each person individually. The existence of only one active intellectual substance made it difficult to argue for individual moral responsibility. Nor could people hope for an afterlife, since there could be no possible relation between this world and any other.

Thomas in fact expressly denies the tenets of Averroism. He rules out the doctrine of the single separate active intellect, contending that 'there are as many active intellects as there are souls, which are multiplied according to the number of people' (ST 1.79.5; also 1.76.2; ScG 2.76). Nor is our freedom in grace denied by celestial determinism: 'human actions are not subject to the action of heavenly bodies, save accidentally and indirectly'. Rather, 'what happens here [on earth] by accident, both in natural things and in human affairs', is the effect of divine providence. God, not something created, controls our destiny. Moreover, luck and chance are real as far as we are concerned. While everything that cannot act according to its own reason and will (i.e., freely and rationally) is caused by something else, there can be two or more chains of causes that come together in ways that are not caused, except by the providence that wills it to happen that way (ST 1.116.1). Unlike his colleagues, Thomas argued that we cannot rationally decide whether the world began in time or is eternal (ScG 2.38). Arguments for either position do not issue in necessary conclusions. Only through

Scripture do we know that the former position is the true one. And it is through Scripture that we become aware that this world can be known in its depths only as we know something about its relation to the triune God.

It now seems that Averroism may have been more an invention of antagonistic theologians than representative of Averroes's own views. Whether or not that is the case, it is likely that one reason why Thomas was suspected of Averroism was his rejection of certain aspects of Platonic philosophy. It is true that certain of Thomas's theological judgments were unusual and controversial, but this was not primarily because they smacked of Aristotle's influence, but because they sometimes – though by no means always – modified or developed received Augustinian doctrines that made use of Platonic concepts and principles. Thomas drew upon the newly available philosophy because he found it a fruitful source of concepts that could be adapted for use in theologically describing divine and creaturely reality. His innovations worried many, however, and he found himself the object of attack as one who seemed to follow the views of the Faculty of Arts, views which could reasonably be construed as leading to the distortion or even abandonment of Christian doctrines. The misreading of Thomas and the subsequent condemnation were exacerbated, too, by rivalries among the secular priests, the Dominicans and the Franciscans.

The official reaction against Thomas began with an investigation by Stephen Tempier, bishop of Paris, whose campaign against the heresies taught at the University resulted in a list of condemned heterodox propositions issued in 1270. These propositions were not drawn explicitly from Thomas works, but some do bear upon his own positions (Torrell, 1996a, p. 300). More direct moves against him were soon made by Robert Kilwardy, a fellow Dominican and archbishop of Canterbury, who drew up another list in 1277, and by a Franciscan, William de la Mare, who in 1279 wrote a *Correctorium fratris Thomae*, a 'correction' of over one hundred supposedly erroneous propositions drawn from Thomas. The perceived need for such a work suggests that Thomas's works were already widely read.

The disputes which arose over the appropriation of Aristotle's philosophy by theology cannot be reduced to the issue of the place of philosophy in theology, an issue that became problematic somewhat later. Those theological colleagues of Thomas who were less than convinced of the usefulness of Aristotle would not have disputed the notion that the concepts and principles derived from ancient philosophy may be helpful in doctrinal analysis. Where they disagreed with Thomas was over the usefulness of this particular philosophy, over whether or not it was appropriate or even possible to attempt to bring together Aristotle and the tradition of theology represented most authoritatively by Augustine. But neither can the issue be reduced simply to a question of rivalry between philosophical systems, as if one were correct, the other incorrect. The theologians of the time would all have agreed that neither philosopher could be correct before being reworked to conform to the scriptural depiction of reality. Neither side sought to conform to a philosophy. As a contemporary historical theologian puts it, the medievals sought to make the ancient philosophers reveal 'what they really sought without knowing it' (Torrell, 1996a, p. 239). When Thomas read Aristotle, he sought to discern his *intentio*, what he was trying to say, so as to bring him into the conversation among Christian thinkers. The idea was not merely to figure out exactly what Aristotle meant and then decide whether that was true or false. Rather, interpretation involved some use of the imagination so as to bring Aristotle's wisdom to bear upon contemporary issues. While Thomas is explicitly critical of Plato, he by no means rejected all Platonic thinking, because so much of it was useful for theology, as Augustine had shown. Thomas thought of Augustine as an 'authority', a vital interlocutor and exemplar of the use of ancient philosophy, one who 'makes use of the opinions of Plato, not asserting them as true, but relating them' to Christian doctrines (ST 1.77.5 ad 3). Thomas did something very similar with Aristotle's 'opinions'.

Primitive Thomism

It is customary to divide the history of the interpretation of Thomas's texts into three phases. During the first phase, which terminates around 1450, the task of the early followers of Thomas, most of whom were Dominicans, was to come to grips with the complexity of his thought and the attacks against it. The debates with those opposed to Thomas clarified the differences between his positions and the dominant alternatives. In the course of the debates, however, Thomas's thought was tidied up, as it were. The best example of early tidying up is the massive defense of Thomas by Capreolus (1380–1444), who developed arguments for Thomas's propositions against those of later rivals such as the Franciscans Duns Scotus (1264–1308) and William of Ockham (1300–49).

Capreolus's reformulation of Thomas's thought reflects more general intellectual shifts in the late medieval period. Around the turn of the fourteenth century there began a trend towards a greater concern for clarity and exactness. Scholars became focused upon questions of ever smaller scope, paying less attention to the broader view. This trend eventually shifted the meaning of the term 'scholastic' from a neutral reference to a dialectical form of inquiry to a pejorative reference to dry-as-dust and small-minded concern for the minutiae of doctrinal analysis.

This mentality is well displayed in a 1387 discussion over whether Thomas should be considered an official doctor of the church. As a doctor, he would be taken as an 'authority' in the sense of one whose standing in the church becomes official and thus much more difficult to challenge. Pierre d'Ailly argued that Thomas was merely a theologian among others. He was not a true doctor of the church because he changed his mind between his earlier and later works, there are inconsistencies within them, and he was mistaken about some things (Torrell, 1998, p. 126). It is worth noting that

Augustine changed his mind at least as frequently as Thomas, but the latter would never have denied Augustine's status as a doctor of the church on that account. Growth in understanding and the espousal of views that are later acknowledged to be erroneous were for Thomas to be expected, for theological inquiry is a task that will never be completed (ScG 1.8.2).

Second Thomism

The triumph of nominalism and then the reaction to it and against all kinds of scholasticism meant that Thomas was read less widely during the fourteenth century. The Dominicans persisted, however. They had in many places taught Thomas's theology from the very first, usually in tandem with Peter Lombard's *Sentences*. Towards the end of the fifteenth century, the ST began to replace the *Sentences* as the basic textbook. This is significant not only for the increased respect shown to Thomas. The *Sentences*, we recall, were a collection of texts organized in such a way that they provided a starting-point for inquiry; they prompted their commentators to engage with Scripture and tradition for themselves. The ST was likely read in much the same way by its first readers, but after Capreolus it was viewed more as a collection of propositions and arguments that could be understood and discussed *apart* from its sources and base in Scripture. No longer read as a lively engagement with Scripture and the tradition of its interpretation, the ST became the basic text of what amounted to a new tradition – 'Thomism'.

Further moves in this direction were made by later Dominicans, such as Cardinal Cajetan (Thomas de Vio, 1465–1534) and John of Saint Thomas (1589–1644). The former published his commentary on the ST between 1507 and 1522. This work was not so much a commentary as a reworking of what, in Thomas, are largely *ad hoc* distinctions and disparate concepts, into a more theoretically consistent form (Torrell, 1998, p. 135). One example of this is Cajetan's Thomistic theory of theological language. Thomas makes remarks now and then in the ST (1.13) and elsewhere (notably in the collection of disputed questions called *De Veritate*, *On Truth*, henceforth DV) about the force of words we use to say things about God. His concern is to avoid using words like 'good' or 'love' in ways that suggest that God's and our goodness and love are fundamentally the same. To fail to distinguish them would lead to anthropomorphism and would wrongly suggest that we could define God from what we know of created things. But Thomas also wants to be able to say true things about God. His solution is to say that sentences like 'God is good' may be true, even though the 'good' in question is something that is quite distinct from the kind of 'good' with which we are familiar, as in the sentence, 'Mary is good'. The two uses of 'good' are not at all the same, but neither are they simply equivocations: they are analogous.[8] And Thomas leaves it at that, suggesting that his remarks are simply clarifying the practice of Scripture and the church's custom. Cajetan, however, wanted more theoretical precision. In his *De nominum analogia*, he collates and reworks the details of Thomas's scattered remarks to build them into a substantial (though perhaps finally incoherent) metaphysical theory of analogy. He carefully distinguishes different kinds of analogy, and argues that all but one are incorrect. In this, he is only the first in a long line of similar theorists.

The concern with metaphysical theories of language is related to another fundamental shift initiated by Cajetan, namely the breakdown of Thomas's holistic conception of reality into a dualism of nature and grace. Thomas thought of nature as, so to speak, the created starting-point for grace, and grace is that which makes possible our movement towards our final end or goal, which is God. As he says frequently, 'grace perfects nature', where 'perfects' has the further connotation of completing what God began in creation (ST 1.8 ad 2; 1/2.3.8; DV 27.6 ad 1). Humans thus have a supernatural final end, one that, because it is supernatural, is beyond the capability of our natures to attain. Yet we desire that end, however vaguely and confusedly, because it is ours, our 'proper end', and concretely grace is always operating in us to draw us towards it. Even before the fall into sin and the subsequent need for sanctifying grace there was already 'a certain beginning of hoped-for happiness', i.e., happiness that is the supernatural end, not merely the natural happiness of self-fulfillment. Moreover, before the Fall, humanity 'possessed [through grace] manifest knowledge about certain points in the divine mysteries, which now we cannot know except by believing them' (ST 2/2.5.1). Thus reality and our place within it cannot be properly understood without some knowledge of divine activity and our supernatural goal.

In his commentary on the ST, Cajetan so separates nature from grace that humanity now has *two* ends, natural and supernatural. For Cajetan, the world of nature is self-contained, 'a closed whole', which can be described, at least hypothetically, as if there were no supernatural goal. Moreover, without the infusion of grace, we have no natural desire for our proper, supernatural end. If God had not willed to redeem us through grace, and if we had not sinned, we would have achieved, and been quite content with, the natural end for which we were created. Such a theory takes us far from Thomas's own view.[9]

Cajetan's dualism was developed further by a new set of proponents of Thomism that had arisen with the founding of the Society of Jesus in 1540. St Ignatius was an enthusiastic advocate of Thomas's theology, introducing the study of the ST into Jesuit schools, which soon developed their own interpretations of Thomas. One of the most influential Jesuit Thomists was Francisco Suarez (1548–1617). Suarez sought to bring together the thought of the great scholastics, melding Thomas's metaphysics with that of Duns Scotus and William Ockham to produce a common medieval philosophy. He interpreted Thomas as asserting that our natural desires could not include anything that could not be fulfilled by nature alone, for that would be unjust on the part of the creator. Thus we do not have a natural desire for our supernatural end; there can be no Augustinian 'Our hearts are restless till they rest in thee', for our hearts are not made to anticipate, even by a sense of loss, the possibility of supernatural beatitude. Thus there are two orders in the universe, the natural and the supernatural, without any intrinsic connection. What occurs by grace is totally gratuitous, unexpected, and comes to us extrinsically.

Assessments of Suarez are divided, with some seeing his work as nothing but a 'Christianized Aristotelianism' (McCool, 1994, p. 19). Whether or not that is fair, the influence of the two-tier conception of reality became widespread and was understood by many theologians as a reasonable development of Thomas's thought. For example, the rival theories of grace, merit and free will, which were developed by the Dominican, Bañéz (1528–1604) and the Jesuit, Molina (1535–1600), both shared a dependency upon a dualistic conception of nature and grace. While both were largely Thomistic in conceptuality, neither was consistent with Thomas.

Relocation into Philosophy

The relocation of nature into a sphere separate from supernature was but a short step from pure naturalism. Once the separation of the two orders is made and the self-sufficiency of nature asserted, it becomes difficult to see why the higher order is necessary. Either the divine can be understood as a kind of optional extra, or it can be relocated within a single natural sphere. The development made it difficult to talk about our intrinsic need for redemption, and how we remain unfulfilled if we suffer a merely natural lot. As a result of these developments, Thomas's work was read to support a natural or biological view of humanity and human activity, while his understanding of the Christian life was reinterpreted as primarily a matter of natural law.

These interpretations of Thomas's thought both reflected and contributed to larger historical and cultural changes which we need to note briefly. The bitter quarrels among the Christian churches and the violence inflicted upon dissidents by the ecclesiastical and secular authorities during the second half of the sixteenth century undermined the legitimacy of the church as an institution, and Christianity as a way of life. Scholastic disputations on contested points of doctrine and practice were replaced by assertion and violence between competing ecclesiastical factions. The resulting loss of confidence in the church and its teaching led some to question the hitherto generally held assumption that God exists and is a necessary element in our understanding of the world. The writings of the seventeenth century document a definite turn away from Christianity in reaction to the church controversies, especially but not only among those in high culture.

The response of theologians indicates a massive (though unrecognized) loss of confidence among themselves, too. Rather than engaging with what is particular and distinctive about Christianity – its doctrinal claims – those who sought to address atheism did so in philosophical rather than theological terms. Moreover, passing over sixteen hundred years of Christian theological tradition, they argued in terms formulated by the debates over atheism made at the time of Cicero. The response to atheism was taken 'as if [atheism] were simply a matter of retrieving the philosophical positions of the past, rather than a profound and current rejection of the meaning and reality of Jesus Christ' (Buckley, 1987, p. 47). A salient example can be found in the work of the Jesuit theologian, Lessius (1554–1623), who taught at the University of Louvain. Lessius had been educated with Thomas's *Summa Theologiae* (ST) as his textbook, and it was he who introduced the ST to Louvain. He engaged contemporary atheists in his *De providentia numinis* of 1613 (translated and published in England in 1617), using arguments borrowed from pagan humanism. One argument moved from the rational structure of the universe to an intelligent designer. Another contended that God is necessary if we are to justify moral endeavor, for without God there would be no reason to do good and avoid evil. Similar arguments were made by Marin Mersenne (1588–1648), who described God as the 'grand mover' of the universe (Buckley, 1987, p. 61). For both men, the Trinitarian God of Christianity is reduced to providence, and theology is replaced by natural theology or philosophy.

The shift from theology to philosophy meant that the church's response to the challenges of the Enlightenment and later secularist movements would be made for the most part on the ground marked out by its opponents. This shift is remarkable, though because it persists in many places as the obvious approach, its oddity is still quite difficult to realize. For Thomas, the move would have been largely incomprehensible. But later readers of the ST and the ScG would assume that Thomas was engaged in similar apologetical philosophical argumentation in the opening questions of both works, which are devoted to the existence of God. They would assume that Thomas was establishing in the natural world the groundwork and structures for his subsequent theological inquiry. In the thirteenth century, however, the existence of God was not really a question. Thomas entered upon his proofs, not because God's existence was in any doubt, as later, but, on the contrary, because it is a genuine question, and a thoroughly *theological* one which is prompted by the workings of grace. That question initiates the series of questions as to *what kind* of God in whose existence we believe. The answers depend, of course, entirely upon the person and work of Jesus Christ described in the Scriptures. There can be little or no guidance from philosophy about such matters, though philosophy may well provide – as it did for Thomas – some useful conceptual tools for discussing them.

With the shift to philosophy came a shift in philosophy consequent upon the methodological developments initiated by Descartes and Newton. Buckley points out the absurdity of the notion that the Enlightenment was a battle between scientists and religionists. The scientists were as anxious to find ways of supporting religious belief as Christian apologists. They did so, however, by reinterpreting religious belief in terms of their scientific systems. Descartes, faced with the skepticism of Montaigne, sought secure arguments for the existence of God by locating God within his Universal Mathematics, much as Newton did with his Universal Mechanics (Buckley, 1987, ch. 2). Descartes, as is well known, beat the skeptics on their own ground. By making doubt into a method, he thought it was possible to bring all reality within the purview of his mind. The existence of any and all reality, including the existence of God, is known to be certain only on the basis of my own, self-evident knowledge of myself as a thinking being. It is because I know for sure that 'I think' that I can say for sure that I and anything else, including God, exist.

This is significantly different from Thomas's approach to reality. Thomas's philosophy is realist; he begins with our experience of the world out there, with the data of our senses. Nature is created in a relation of dependence upon God. As a consequence, it is sufficiently ordered and reliable that it may be trusted to give us genuine knowledge of reality, as well as the means by which to talk about God. That knowledge is best acquired as a communal endeavor, through a tradition of inquiry guided by Scripture and embodied in the Christian church. Descartes, by contrast, turns inward to his solitary subjectivity. God functions in his philosophy as the guarantor that he is not being radically misled as he builds up knowledge of the external world on the basis of his consciousness. God is part of the proof for external reality, for if God is perfect, then the thoughts Descartes is certain of thinking cannot be merely deceptions by a cruel and thus imperfect God. God guarantees that his clear and distinct ideas must be reliable, and thus supplies the warrant for the existence of the world external to his mind.

The difference between the two approaches should not be minimized. If God cannot be reasonably talked about on the basis of our knowledge of the world, and must instead support our knowledge of reality outside our mind, then the world, as far as we can know it at least, is essentially without any trace of God. Nothing in the world can bring us to any knowledge of God. The implications for Christology are far-reaching and profound. The world and its events, including those in first-century Palestine, may be examined and explained without recourse to theology (Buckley, 1987, pp. 92, 97). The Cartesian approach to reality and God thus offered a sharp alternative to the realist metaphysics of Thomas. The Cartesian approach became common as the basic philosophy taught in seminaries throughout the period until beyond the mid-nineteenth century. Once theology and apologetics turned to philosophy as the primary form of discourse, and especially with the turn to Cartesian philosophical foundations, it became difficult to recover the scriptural witness to Jesus Christ as the privileged source of knowledge for Christians. That witness was reinterpreted by both Christians and their opponents into terms that were amenable to philosophical rather than theological inquiry. For some, Jesus became a 'moral genius' or a symbol of an idea, rather than the incarnate Word.

Thomas himself could be read as a forerunner of such Christologies in that the order of his two large works, the ST and the ScG, place the Christology last. To one accustomed to the methods of liberal Christology that arose after the Enlightenment, all that precedes the treatise appears to be known independently of Jesus Christ. Jesus may then be interpreted as a kind of representation or synthesis of what has been said about God and humanity in the earlier part of the work. If that were indeed the case, it would appear that Scripture lacks any of what Bruce Marshall has termed 'material decisiveness' in Thomas's theology (Marshall, 1987, p. 55). The material details of Jesus's life would seem, at best, only to *illustrate* what we already know *apart* from the gospel narratives, at worst to be irrelevant to more significant knowledge gleaned from other sources. We will see how mistaken this is. Thomas's theology is more than consonant with Scripture; it is guided throughout by his Christology which, in turn, is guided in materially decisive ways by the gospels.

Neo-Scholasticism

It may be said that the defining characteristic of the intellectual life of the Roman Catholic church during the nineteenth century was its attempt to find a suitable response to modernity, in its philosophical form exemplified by Descartes and Kant, and in its political and social forms exemplified by the French Revolution and the triumph of the nation-state. Many efforts in the first half of the century relied upon Cartesianism of various kinds. But soon after the middle of the century, the work of Joseph Kleutgen ushered in the third phase of Thomas-interpretation, Neo-Scholasticism, a movement that would dominate Roman Catholic theology and philosophy for the next eighty years or so. Kleutgen's *Die Theologie der Vorzeit* and *Die Philosophie der Vorzeit* sought to show that medieval scholasticism (the *Vorzeit* or 'old time' of the titles) provides a better response to modernity than any contemporary effort. Kleutgen's reading of Thomas was guided by Suarez. It was therefore primarily philosophical in orientation, heavily dependent upon the two-tier conception of reality, and relegated Christology to a secondary level of inquiry.

Kleutgen and his allies managed to convince Pope Leo XIII to support their cause. In his encyclical, *Aeterni Patris* (1879), Leo called for a Christian philosophy 'according to the mind of St. Thomas Aquinas'.[10] The great benefit of Thomas's thought for Leo was its strength as an apologetics. Thomas had 'gathered together' the doctrines of earlier doctors of the church, and 'moulded them into a whole. He arranged them in so wonderful an order, and increased with such additions, that rightly and deservedly he is reckoned a singular safeguard and glory of the Catholic church' (xv). Leo saw to it that the Cartesianism of seminary philosophical studies was replaced by Thomas's realist philosophy. On that basis, he believed, philosophy, far from being a challenge to faith, would achieve 'perfect correspondence with the gift of faith' (ix) and lead to an 'improvement' in all the human sciences (xvii).

Thomas studies flourished as a result of the pope's command. Journals and institutions devoted to his thought were founded and the ST or derivative manuals of theology were taught in all seminaries. The dominance of Neo-Scholasticism persisted until the decade or so before Vatican II. Thomas's philosophical realism, which challenged the prevailing turn to the subject in modern philosophy, together with his systematic brilliance, enabled the Neo-Scholastics to construct a metaphysical system to compete with the worldviews of modernity.

Twentieth-century Neo-Thomism

Ironically, however, the very enthusiasm of such studies led to the break-up of the Neo-Scholastic consensus as to how to interpret Thomas. One of the first to move beyond Neo-Scholasticism was the French philosopher, Jacques Maritain (1882–1973). Maritain and his wife, Raissa, had sought to solve the puzzle of existence, first using the philosophy of Henri Bergson and then, when this failed them to the point that they thought of suicide, turning to Roman Catholicism (McCool, 1989, p. 115). Maritain rejected the prevailing idealist philosophies because, he believed, to start with consciousness would mean that true knowledge of the external world would remain always in doubt. Instead, he drew upon Cajetan and John of St Thomas to develop a formidable and highly influential philosophy, based upon Thomas, that sought to replace the philosophies of modernity. Maritain's philosophy is complex and it is not to our purpose to explore it here. I need only note that he believed his metaphysics was superior to that of Descartes because it could bring together matter and mind within a basically Aristotelian understanding of science, while for Descartes science can be concerned only with material reality (McCool, 1994, p. 84). Maritain's metaphysics could thus encompass all reality, including God, into one overarching view.

Maritain intended his system to be a consistent development of Thomas's metaphysics. However, the disparity between Thomas and his later interpreters, upon whom Maritain relied, became increasingly clear with the progress of the historical and textual studies encouraged by Leo's encyclical. Maritain attempted to deal with the inconsistencies in later works (e.g., Maritain, 1956, pp. 37–40) but generally failed to convince the experts. His work continued to be popular among Catholic intellectuals and general readers, who thought they were getting the genuine Thomas. Accordingly, they assumed that Thomas's thought – for many, Thomas was virtually synonymous with 'Catholicism' – is fundamentally an ahistorical metaphysics, a perennial philosophy which cannot be replaced or modified because – according to Maritain's theory – its concepts directly reflect reality (McCool, 1989, pp. 157, 223). All that remained to do was to unpack the implications of Maritainian Thomism for other fields of inquiry, which Maritain proceeded to do for everything from political theory to aesthetics. However, as Thomas O'Meara notes, 'while he addressed the wider world in some specific areas, ultimately there was only one healthy set of principles: Maritain's own neo-Thomism' (O'Meara, 1997, p. 179).[11]

It was Etienne Gilson (1884–1978) who initiated the recovery of Thomas the medieval scholastic theologian, as opposed to the timeless metaphysician. Working first in Paris and then at the Pontifical Institute of Medieval Studies, which he founded in Toronto, Gilson approached Thomas as a thinker whose philosophy cannot be understood apart from his theology. Thomas's philosophy contrasts with ancient philosophy, which did not have the benefit of Christian revelation, and it is distinct from those modern philosophies which reject religious belief. As such, Thomas's philosophy, like that of the other medieval theologians, is an advance upon the ancients and is richer than the moderns. Because his philosophy is worked out within the context of faith, to understand Thomas properly it is necessary to focus primarily upon his theological works. It was their reliance upon Thomas's commentaries on Aristotle that misled the Neo-Scholastics into assuming that Thomas is an Aristotelian thinker. Instead, Gilson argued, Thomas is a theologian who begins with God before moving to creatures, quite unlike any separated philosophy, ancient or modern.

In addition to beginning to recover Thomas's theological intent, Gilson's historical research destroyed the assumption, common to the Neo-Scholastics and Maritain, that there was a unified medieval perennial philosophy. In a series of brilliant studies, he demonstrated the depth of the philosophical differences between Bonaventure, Thomas, Duns Scotus and other medieval theologians, showing that they had too little in common for any such view to be tenable. He argued that Cajetan did not understand the distinctiveness of Thomas's philosophy of being, and that Suarez and Kleutgen mixed Thomas with incompatible elements from Scotus, leading their interpretations far astray.

Yet Gilson's own focus remained upon Thomas the Christian philosopher rather than the theologian, even as he acknowledged Thomas the commentator upon Scripture. Gilson's concern can be seen in his analysis of the proofs of God's existence near the beginning of the ST. According to Gilson, '[i]t is natural that [Thomas's] first question should be about the existence of God. On this problem, however, a theologian cannot do much more than apply to the philosophers for philosophical information. The existence of God is a philosophical problem.'[12] Not only does Gilson gloss over the first question of the ST as if it does not exist; the first question delineates theology as the context for all other questions, including that of the existence of God in the second question. For Thomas, in contrast to Gilson, the existence of God is an issue for *theologians* to take up and resolve in a distinctively theological way. Thus, as Buckley points out, Gilson still adhered to the Enlightenment belief that Christianity has no way of its own to deal with such matters (Buckley, 1987, pp. 341f.).[13]

The Recovery of Thomas the Premodern Theologian

Gilson's historical studies were a vital first step towards recovery of Thomas the premodern theologian. The research into the history of theology by the proponents of the *Resourcement* school pushed the recovery considerably further. In the 1940s, Henri Bouillard published studies showing how Thomas's understanding of nature and grace shifted from his early *Commentary on the Sentences* to his mature work in the ST. He found that Thomas's concept of grace and that of Neo-Scholasticism were significantly different. For Thomas, the grace that justifies us is an infusion by God in us of a power that Thomas calls a habit, i.e., something that is with us over time and becomes part of our character. For the Neo-Scholastics, working within the two-tier universe, justifying grace is 'actual grace', that is, a movement by God which elevates an action of ours so that it becomes supernatural. It is therefore something extrinsic to us, occasional and temporary.

Bouillard's work also raised the level of awareness among Roman Catholic theologians and philosophers of the bearing of historical and cultural contexts upon Christianity. It is not possible simply to presume the tradition is something handed on (*traditio*) unchanged and intact. Thomas himself acknowledged this. For him, in contrast to Maritain, truth lies in the mind rather than in concepts. The concept helps the mind conform to reality, making the mind true. But concepts are never quite exact and, when referring to God, directly or formally, they are always analogical at best, with a greater degree of dissimilarity than similarity. Thus the reality to which the church's doctrines refer may be unchanging, but that reality is conveyed in words and even concepts that change. As a consequence of his work, Bouillard was attacked by some Neo-Scholastics as a relativist and an advocate for a plurality of theological systems.

The work of other *Resourcement* theologians, such as Yves Congar, OP, Marie-Dominique Chenu, OP and Henri de Lubac, SJ, extended these lines of inquiry within their broad knowledge of the patristic background to the medieval theologian's work. Others, such as Cornelio Fabro, sought to recover the Platonic aspects of Thomas's thought over against the prevailing Aristotelianism of the Neo-Scholastics and Neo-Thomists. Theologians such as Karl Rahner brought some aspects of Thomas's thought within a phenomenological approach, hoping thereby to overcome the Neo-Scholastic extrinsic theology of grace and effect a *rapprochement* with more contemporary forms of philosophy.

Many of these efforts were not supported by the church authorities at the time, and a number of the *Resourcement* theologians were condemned or silenced in the decades before Vatican II. The preference of the church authorities was for the Neo-Scholastic Thomas, whose work was taught in seminaries in dull, line-by-line analysis or in derivative manuals of theology. Little love for Thomas was generated thereby, and once the movement of *aggiornamento* was begun with the second Vatican Council, Thomas was rejected along with the manualists as an outdated and useless tradition. This is understandable, but it presumed a distorted interpretation of Thomas's thought. As O'Meara remarks, '[t]o view the medieval Dominican as a logician or an ontologist is to begin in error and to end in sterility ... An overemphasis upon his philosophy is one reason why Thomas Aquinas was ignored during the Renaissance, the Reformation, the Enlightenment, and after Vatican II' (O'Meara, 1997, p. 89).

In spite of that rejection there has been something of a new beginning in interpreting Thomas in the last two decades, during which the focus has been more directly upon his theology, but without the attempt to re-present it in a more contemporary form. One of the best of these new interpretations is that of Jean-Pierre Torrell, OP. He thinks of Thomas as primarily a spiritual master. The carefully structured order of the ST is intended to reflect the way God views reality so that, as we read it, our minds become conformed to God and we progress in the spiritual life. The order of the ST is therefore the only one that is possible for theology, because it follows the 'schema [which] imposes itself on all theology that allows itself to be structured by faith and the Creed' (Torrell, 1996a, p. 153).

While I cannot agree with this particular claim – which may reflect a lingering perennialism on his part – I am greatly indebted to Torrell's work, particularly in the area of Thomas's Christology. On my view, the ST has a rather different intent. Thomas's Christology and doctrine of God are such that they rule out any perennial account of reality other than Scripture. Thomas's is an anti-systematic system, so to speak, in that its principles systematically undermine any system that does not push the reader back to Scripture and to the concreteness of a life dedicated to following Christ. His theology is best approached from his concern with the Christian life. It is not an attempt to develop an apologetics or a system that confronts and conquers all other systems. It is not concerned with mapping out the complete set of doctrines, though it covers all doctrines that Thomas thought it necessary to discuss. It is least of all concerned to construct a perennial metaphysics to counter all other worldviews. Theology, as Thomas understands and practices it, attempts to clarify what has been revealed of divine wisdom through the incarnate Word and the operation of the Holy Spirit. Theological inquiry's main function is to serve the preaching of the Gospel. And the preaching of the Gospel serves the Christian life, which is distinct from other ways of life, since it is an attempt to follow Jesus Christ obediently.

If we begin with the notion of theology as serving those who try to help others live as Christians, we begin, so I suggest, where Thomas began. And beginning there may help us to understand Thomas's theology rather better, so I hope, than his later interpreters did. Thus the next chapter begins the presentation proper with a view of the Dominican Order within which Thomas learned what it is to live as a Christian, and as a Christian theologian.

Notes

1 For the account of Thomas's life in this section I rely particularly upon Torrell (1996a) and Weisheipl (1983).
2 I discuss the Dominican Order and its influence upon Thomas in some detail in the next chapter.
3 See Gilles Emery, OP (1995), p. 322, for a useful schematic rendering of Thomas's reorganization of Peter's *Sentences*.
4 Thomas put the matter one way: 'Theology, which is called Sacred Scripture'; his slightly older contemporary, Bonaventure (1221–74), the other way: 'Sacred Scripture, which is called theology.' The passage from Thomas is from his commentary on Boethius's *De Trinitate*, 5.4; that from Bonaventure, *Breviloquia Prol.* 5, 201. Both citations are from Henri de Lubac (1998a), p. 27.
5 A much more likely candidate for a work written expressly for beginners would be the *Compendium of Theology*, written in response to a request by his companion, Brother Reginald, the style of which is evidently more straightforward.
6 This debate and Thomas's response to it will be discussed in Chapter 2.
7 I make use especially of Torrell (1996a and 1998), Buckley (1987), McCool (1989 and 1994) and John (1966).
8 I examine Thomas's discussion of analogy in some detail in Chapter 3 below.
9 See de Lubac (1998b), pp. 68–74, 140, 143–8. The quotation is from Cajetan's commentary, *In Primum*, 12.1, n. 10, cited by de Lubac (1998b, p. 140).
10 The text is included at the beginning of the translation of the ST by the Fathers of the English Dominican Province (1981); page references in parentheses are to this edition.
11 It is ironic that Maritain accuses Barth of confusing the word of Barth with the Word of God; see his *De Bergson à Thomas d'Aquin* (New York: Éditions de la maison française, 1944), p. 99.
12 Gilson, *Elements of Christian Philosophy*, p. 42, quoted in Buckley (1987), p. 341.
13 The similarities and differences between these two Neo-Thomists (Maritain and Gilson) are complex and far-reaching. It would take us far too far afield even to sketch them if, indeed, that were possible. For a good overview, see John (1966) and McCool (1989 and 1994).

Chapter 2

Nudum Christum nudus sequi

After a brief look at Thomas's life and career, the previous chapter examined some of the many interpretations of his thought developed over the course of the seven centuries or so since his death. Among the more significant moves away from what were arguably Thomas's own views were the separation of nature and grace into a two-tier universe, the relocation of his theology into more philosophical, apologetic and systematic forms of discourse, and the founding of a tradition of inquiry, later called Thomism, that could be pursued with some degree of independence of Scripture. Most of these developments were made by Roman Catholic theologians and philosophers who sought to make use of Thomas as they responded, positively or negatively, to a modern intellectual climate characterized by secularism, by the devaluation of particular traditions and by a preference for univocal language and linear argumentation.

Perhaps the root cause of these changes, evident especially in Neo-Scholasticism, was the failure to acknowledge the scriptural basis and Christological center of Thomas's theology, a basis and center he shared with many other premodern theologians. One of the aims of this book is to recover a reading of Thomas in which his theological method, his hermeneutics and metaphysics, his conception of Christian doctrine and practice and pedagogy, as well as the material claims of his theology, are seen to be guided by principles and norms that reflect the gospel accounts of Jesus Christ. This task is more difficult than it might seem. Thomas was not a theologian like Karl Barth, who sought expressly to recover the centrality of Jesus Christ over against Protestant liberalism, nor was he like Hans Urs von Balthasar, who sought to recenter Roman Catholic theology in an analogous way. In contrast, Thomas lived in an era and a community where he could reasonably presuppose that centrality. He could therefore focus his readers' attention more on other issues and leave the treatise on Christology until the final sections of the ST and the ScG, as I noted earlier. It was only as the cultural climate changed that his Christology could be misrepresented as something added on to what had already been established on other grounds, rather than as something fundamental.

To counter such misunderstandings, it will be useful to examine Thomas's conception of the nature and function of theology more closely. An effective starting-point is to situate his work as a theologian in the context of his life as a Dominican. I noted earlier that for Thomas to decide to become a member of the Dominican Order was to choose a way of life that his

society found difficult to accept. But the more significant aspect of the
Order for our purposes was its thorough and explicit orientation to Jesus
Christ. Whether Thomas joined the Dominicans because of this orientation
or whether he learned the orientation as a result of his formation is something difficult to decide upon, and is finally not important. To discuss some
aspects of his personal experience and its social context is not to fall foul of
the so-called 'intentional fallacy', the notion that one can determine the
meaning of a text by somehow discerning the intention of its author. Thomas often defended his Order against attacks, both in the ST as well as in
works written expressly for the purpose. These texts make it clear that,
whatever his original motive for becoming a member, his own Christological
orientation is explicitly and forcefully linked with that of the Dominicans.
Thus in the first section of this chapter I present an account of the Dominican Order, and how Thomas drew upon the scriptural account of Jesus
Christ to justify it before its detractors. The second section discusses his
theological method and then, since the method is oriented towards Scripture, the chapter concludes with a section on his hermeneutics.

The Order of Preachers

St Dominic

When Thomas joined the Order, the Dominicans were a relatively new
community officially founded by Dominic, a Castilian, in 1217 (see
Tugwell, 1982, for what follows). Born in 1170, St Dominic lived during a
time when Christian doctrine and practice were threatened by the failure
of the church's leadership to respond to obvious decay in the ordinary
forms of Christian life. While there were no doubt many genuine exceptions, the average parish priest of the time was often appallingly ignorant,
barely able to get through the Mass in Latin, given over to superstitions,
and often lived with a concubine. The bishops were wealthy, closely
associated with the powerful, and had little enthusiasm for Christian witness. Those who were more fervent avoided worldly activity, including
pastoral work, seeking instead to devote themselves to contemplation and
asceticism in monasteries, following Rules drawn upon by St Benedict
and later founders. Often living in out-of-the-way places, the monks had
become largely self-sufficient. They owned considerable property in common and through their manual labor – often enjoined upon them by their
Rule – they were able to grow their own food and produce. By Dominic's
time, many monasteries had become wealthy, their members highly cul-
tured and often well connected with the aristocracy, as were the leaders of
Thomas's childhood community at Monte Cassino.
    The failure of ecclesiastical leadership resulted in inadequate care of the
laity and in some places the corruption of the beliefs and practices of

Christian life. The failure was especially egregious in light of a contemporary spiritual awakening led by enthusiastic preachers whose conception of Christianity, unfortunately, was heterodox. In Dominic's region, the south of France, the Albigensians and the Cathari presented a twofold challenge to the church of the day. In terms of practice, they shamed the clergy and attracted ordinary folk by their rigorous way of life, their exacting morality, the exemplary seriousness with which they lived their beliefs, and their pastoral concern. As to their beliefs, their theology was a version of Manichean dualism, with reality reduced to the competing principles of good and evil. From this developed a complex and rationalistic ideology which proved attractive to some people.

The monks had not failed to take notice of the problem and attempted various reforms by way of response. A movement back to the Gospel and to the apostolic life of poverty and preaching had begun in various quarters early in the twelfth century (see Chenu, 1997, pp. 239–69). But entrenched cultural assumptions about what constituted the best form of the Christian life – the *status perfectionis* – made it difficult for evangelization initiatives to get off the ground. A busy life devoted to the pastoral care of others and to witness within the world seemed quite obviously not as good and holy as a life of quiet contemplation and asceticism through which one could draw closer to God in solitude. This preference was reinforced by the fairly widespread belief that the church was about to leave behind its times of struggle and obscurity to enter upon a peaceful and glorious period. Hence 'this monastic eschatological ideal withdrew into its secure fantasies, inattentive to the drama of life, to the desperate call of the church in a state of rapid expansion and in peril' (Chenu, 1997, p. 268). Attempts to get the enthusiastic involved in pastoral activity usually ended up with the best of them back in the monastery within a generation or so.

Two new Orders, the Franciscans and the Dominicans, were founded in response to the evident inability of the church's leadership to challenge such cultural assumptions and practices effectively. With the support of his bishop, Dominic advocated a radically new kind of Christian life. He argued that the lives of the monks amounted to a kind of Pharisaism, for they separated themselves from other people by their strict and supposedly holy way of life, yet remained 'inwardly unclean' (Tugwell, 1982, p. 21). In contrast, the goal of the Order of Preachers was to serve the needs of others *and thereby* to make progress in the spiritual life. Dominic did not worry too much about what has been called the 'interior life'. For him and his early followers, including Thomas, the movement of the soul towards God is not achieved by mystical prayer so much as by serving others and by strenuous intellectual activity (Tugwell, 1982, p. 4). The 'others' in question were the ordinary folk of Christendom who were going unevangelized.

Like the monks and the Franciscans, the Dominicans sought the *status perfectionis*, the best way to live as a Christian. The *status* was a church-sanctioned way of life, such as the monastic habit or the episcopacy, adopted 'with solemnity' by a vow and a ceremony. The *status* did not by any means guarantee perfection, nor were ordinary laypeople who had no such *status* thereby denied the possibility of perfection (*Sup. Matt.* 19:21, n. 1596). But it seemed obvious that devotion to a particular way of life provided extra help in achieving perfection. If one followed a church-sanctioned *status* perfectly, then one would be perfect. Unlike the monastic orders, the Dominicans did not believe that the *status perfectionis* took the form of following a strict Rule. Instead, they sought to follow a person, Jesus Christ, in total obedience (*sequela Christi*). As Dominic saw it, obedience to Christ's example meant a life of poverty and preaching. And, to support the preaching and teaching mission, it meant a life of study and intellectual inquiry. Hence the theoretical challenge of the times was to be met by preaching the Christian Gospel in an intelligent and convincing way, while the practical challenge was to be met by the preachers leading wandering lives of voluntary poverty. The friars would frequently mix with ordinary folk and beg from those to whom they preached for their daily food; hence the term 'mendicant friar' (Lat. *mendicare*, to beg).

For Dominic, these three principles – obedience, poverty and preaching – took precedence over all others. All three oriented the Order to the life and work of Jesus, the exemplar of the true Christian life, just as much as its rival Order, the Franciscans, though in a somewhat different way. For the latter, the exemplar to follow was Francis himself. For the Dominicans, Dominic himself was not particularly significant as an exemplary figure; the focus remained on Jesus. The formation and education of the friars had a similar orientation. As a recent study puts it, there is

> abundant evidence that Dominicans understood the liturgy as a continuous meditation on, and recreation of, the acts revealed in the Articles of Faith; that they read the Bible not as a secular history book, but as a multifaceted revelation of Christ; and that their devotions, and even the daily routines of their conventual life, were designed to steep the brothers in the life of Christ. (Goering, 1998, p. 135)

Stories about specific events in Jesus's and his disciples' lives which reveal particular qualities for imitation were part of a large literature within the Order. As one might expect, the specific qualities selected for such stories were usually those that warranted the Dominican conception of the Christian life (Newhauser, 1998, pp. 249f.; Schmidt, 1998, pp. 100–112).

Formation within the Order therefore had considerable influence upon Thomas's practice and his conception of the Christian life. It did not simply determine his theology, since Thomas in due course made his own massive contribution to the Order, shaping it in ways that would perdure to the present. Moreover, he was influenced by other traditions, including Aristotelian philosophy. But Thomas was a true Dominican in that his daily life and work were permeated by the desire to follow Christ obediently. And he could expect the same desire and formation in his readers, too. As he taught in the Order's *studia* and at the Order's college at the University of Paris he could presume that his pupils were familiar with the *acta et passa Christi in carne*, with the gospel accounts of what Christ did and what was done to him in the flesh. Like many of his works, the ST was written primarily for those, whether expert or novice theologians, who had undergone Dominican, and thus Christocentric, catechesis and formation (Wawrykow, 1998, p. 177).

To gain official papal approval for his work, Dominic had to follow custom and establish a Rule that set out an ordered way of life for his community to follow. He adapted the Rule of the Augustinian canons, modifying and simplifying it as necessary so that it served the primary task of preaching. The simplicity was intentional for, unusually, it was not the details of the Rule that were important to Dominic, but what the Rule sought to serve, namely the people's need for evangelization. To that end, in 1220 Dominic introduced the innovative principle of dispensation into his Order, whereby the requirements of serving people were to take precedence over the rules of the Order. There was no sin attached to breaking the Rule, not even venial sin, provided that the friars had good reason for doing so. This was in many ways a revolutionary principle, for it relied heavily upon the friars' loyalty and trustworthiness as they moved about without an ever-present supervisor. It was a salutary move, too, in that it countered the tendency of the rules of other Orders to take on an almost divine authority for their members. Dominic's dispensation reflects, one might say, a shift from legalism to the freedom of following Christ obediently.

The principle of dispensation points to a significant difference between the Dominicans and their close cousins, the Franciscans, for all their shared concern to live the apostolic life. Tugwell (a Dominican) says that whilst the Dominicans privileged the apostolic in the *vita apostolica*, the Franciscans privileged the life, remaining comparatively focused on the Rule. Their focus led to fractious debates over the details of practicing the Rule, debates from which the Dominicans remained largely free (Tugwell, 1982, p. 19). This is not to say that Dominicans could dispense themselves from vows or from following their conscience, of course. It meant that the function of the Rule was to help their conscience, not to hinder it from seeking the best form of obedient service of others' spiritual needs. (For Thomas's discussion of this issue see ST 2/2.186.9, esp. ad 1.)

Dominic began his work at Toulouse, gathering and training a community of young men whom he sent out in small groups on missionary work. Dominic trusted his preachers not to fall away from virtue as soon as they left the safety of the community. It seems that his trust was well placed, for within a short time the friars had established themselves successfully. At first secular (parish) priests and their bishops were happy to have such well-educated men to help in preaching and taking care of their parishioners. But since the friars relied upon gifts for support, less was available to give to the diocese and the parish; tithes declined and the economic well-being of the parish priest, not particularly good at the best of times, was undermined. So the very success of the friars soon resulted in attacks upon them from secular priests, who taught their flocks to distrust these vagrants who wandered into their parishes, taking away their money and subverting their authority. The Dominicans caused resentment in higher circles, too, for their wandering life upset the established order of authority. They were not subject to a bishop or an abbot, nor were they restricted to a particular location. Their wandering, mendicant way of life implicitly criticized those among the church leadership who did not lead lives of voluntary poverty. Their very existence posed the question as to whether the wealth of the church and the monasteries could be justified. The Dominicans and the Franciscans argued that poverty is enjoined upon Christians by the example of Jesus Christ himself, displayed in acute and exemplary form on the Cross. They could further claim that such was a traditional view, citing, as did Thomas, Jerome's maxim: *nudum Christum nudus sequi*: in nakedness, to follow the naked Christ (Horst, 1998, pp. 256–70).

Thomas's Defense of his Order

By the time Thomas joined the Order, he could expect critical reaction not only from his family but from society more generally. The friars were sometimes assaulted on the streets of Paris and insults were directed personally at Thomas. One such instance is known, dating from Palm Sunday, 1259, during a sermon Thomas was preaching in Paris. A student called Guillot, a Picardian, interrupted him by getting up and selling pamphlets attacking the friars (Torrell, 1996a, pp. 71f.). As one of the intellectual leaders of his Order, Thomas wrote in defense of its principles throughout his career. One of the key questions – and a good place to begin an examination of Thomas's view of his Order – had to do with the merits of the active life followed by the mendicant friars compared with the contemplative life of the monks.[1] Thomas addresses this question in the ST towards the end of 2/2 and discusses its Christological grounding in ST 3.

Thomas believes that the contemplative life is 'simply more excellent than the active' (ST 2/2.182.1), but 'on account of the needs of the present life' the active life should be added to it (ibid. ad 3). The fundamental reason why the active life, properly understood, is the more complete form of life on earth is that it was the form of Jesus's life. 'Christ's action is our instruction', he notes (ST 3.40.1 ad 3). Jesus's human activity shows us how we are to pursue our way to God (ST 1.2 prol.). The gospels present Jesus neither as a monk nor as an ascetic, but as one who engaged with the world, seeking out those who enjoyed the pleasures of life even when they were not the most moral of people. He went off by himself to pray, certainly, so he was not *merely* active in the sense of thoughtlessly busy. But after he had prayed he would return to convey the fruits of his contemplation to those around him. Nothing he did was for himself alone or ever done in secret; all he did was for the sake of his disciples or the crowds he taught (ST 3.42.3). Those who follow Jesus, then, should similarly engage with the world in the service of others, nourishing their activity with prayerful contemplation. Such an active manner of life is finally 'more excellent than simple contemplation' (ST 2/2.188.6).

Thomas characterizes Jesus's active life *vis-à-vis* his followers as that of a preacher or teacher, as one sent to 'publish the truth' (ST 3.40.1). He taught his hearers what they could not know from any other source, about the triune God and about his own divinity, for example. As the Word of God, Jesus Christ is incarnate Truth, the revelation of God. Goodness, says Thomas, is inherently self-communicative, and God is above all else good, so God communicates God, Trinitarian life and truth, in the incarnate Word (ST 3.1.1). The event of Jesus Christ is thus a pedagogical as well as salvific act: God teaches us by his Word; Jesus Christ is the teacher (ST 3.1.2). Christ 'showed us in his own person the way of truth, whereby we may attain to the bliss of eternal life' (ST 3. prol.). For 'in order for people to arrive at the perfect vision of heavenly happiness, they must first of all believe God, as a disciple believes the master who is teaching him' (ST 2/2.2.3). Accordingly, everything that Jesus said and did was in order to teach those around him (ST 3.40.2). His preaching, especially the Sermon on the Mount, contains all the information necessary for the Christian life (ST 1/2.108.3). The most concentrated and normative form of teaching occurs in the suffering on the Cross. There God's wisdom is lifted up for all to see, the laws and precepts of the Old Testament reach their fulfillment, and all the virtues of the Christian life are displayed to perfection (ST 3.46.3; Wawrykow, 1998). There the incarnate Son displays his free and loving obedience to the will of the Father most evidently.

The gospels show that the primary recipients of Jesus's teaching were his disciples. He chose that small group to continue his preaching and spread his Word through the world. The apostles had a different relation to Christ than anyone else because although they, like us, were instructed by the Word of God, his instruction was 'not according to his divinity, but according as he spoke in his human nature' (ST 1.117.2 ad 2), face to face, and thus in the most accessible and concrete way. In his *Commentary on Matthew*, Thomas writes of the apostolate as analogous to an army assembled by a king to fight a war. In this case the war is against the devil, to expel him from the world, and the weapon is preaching (*Sup. Matt.* 4:23, n. 383). And Jesus, like any good king or general, made sure his army was well trained by sending them out to preach while he was still with them (*Sup. Matt.* 10:5ff., ns. 814ff.).

Thus the warrants for an active life dedicated to preaching the Gospel are Jesus's own example and his establishment of the apostolate. To be called to preach is to be called to the highest form of human existence *in via* (ST 2/2.188.6). It is higher even than the angels, for they learned from the preaching of the apostles 'certain mysteries' they would not otherwise have known (ST 1.117.2 ad 1). Preaching is an essential task, since we cannot attain our final glory, the beatific vision, unless we are 'taught by God', and that can ordinarily happen only through apostolic preaching. But preaching is not something one merely decides to do as one might take on one job rather than another. One must be chosen by God for the task, rather as a prophet is chosen. Within the Dominican tradition, the idea was not simply to take members of the Order and train them to become preachers; one had to seek out those who could be acknowledged as having been given the gift of preaching (Tugwell, 1982, p. 24). Those so graced still needed training, of course, and their preaching activity had always to be grounded upon contemplation. The necessity of contemplation partly explains why Thomas says that theology, which ultimately serves the preacher and his hearers, is more of a speculative discipline, ordered to thinking about God, than it is a practical discipline, ordered directly to human action, though it is finally both (ST 1.1.4). In privileging the speculative aspect of theology, Thomas differed from others at the time, such as Bonaventure and Kilwardy, who thought of it as practical. The speculative aspect of theology is at root prayerful reflection upon Scripture; it is that contemplative moment upon which all fruitful activity must be based.

The apostolic life is thus characterized by engagement with the world in the form of preaching. Preaching is always preaching upon the Christian Scriptures, for these were written by the apostles as part of their obedient witness to Christ. The apostolic life is made known to us by the Gospel, and the Gospel takes primacy over any particular rule. As Thomas says to Pope Urban IV, in the Letter of Dedication for his *Catena Aurea*, 'it is chiefly in the gospel that the form of the Catholic faith is handed on, together with the rule for all aspects of the Christian life' (quoted in Torrell, 1996a, p. 263). Torrell rightly notes that with this emphasis Thomas makes a 'decided return to the Gospel' (ibid.).

The Bible was not, of course, written by Jesus himself (ST 3.42.4). It is a human document written (New Testament) or interpreted (Old Testament) by the apostles and their immediate followers. Its canonical status within the Christian church is warranted by their unique relation to Jesus. Because he taught them in the flesh, their understanding of Jesus Christ and the triune God revealed in him is normative for us. We must be taught by him through them. Therefore to follow Christ obediently, our obedience must be apostolic in form. Apostolic mediation is significant in a number of ways, not least for Thomas's understanding of the church, as we will see in a later chapter. Here we should point out it permits Thomas to note a gap between the text of Scripture and Christ's immediate teaching, a gap which permits him to avoid fundamentalist readings of Scripture.[2] In his commentary on John's Gospel, Thomas argues against John Chrysostom's interpretation of John 10:1–3, which uses the metaphor of the door or gate through which the sheep must enter. Chrysostom asserts that Scripture is the gate, but Thomas sides with Augustine to say that Christ himself is the gate, for one enters the gate towards beatitude by means of truth, and Christ alone is the truth. Scripture is the witness to that truth and it is on that account true; but it is not that truth itself (*Sup. Ioan.* 10:2, ns. 1370–71). The gap opened up here is not one that can be widened any further. We cannot go behind the apostolic writings to reconstruct a more certain or more comprehensive view of Jesus Christ. Rather, the fact of textual mediation reminds us that Christ's teaching always exceeds what can be put into words (ST 3.42.4). This suggests two things. First, there is always something more available to us through the scriptural text; it cannot be reduced to a single meaning (ST 1.1.10). Second, the work of the apostles, both their preaching and their written witness, is insufficient by itself. The operation of Christ himself is necessary if their words are to become compelling (*Sup. Matt.* 4:19, n. 370).

The Dominican understanding of the apostolic life is characterized, more specifically, as 'preaching in poverty'. It was the second term of the phrase – poverty – that was more controversial. According to the friars, poverty is a key element of the *status perfectionis*, together with obedience and celibacy. The primary warrant, once again, is Jesus's own manner of life and his teaching. Christ counseled poverty for his followers (ScG 3.130.3). Moreover, he was himself a mendicant, according to Psalm 39:20 ('As for me, I am poor and needy'), which was applied to Christ (ST 2/2.187.5, *sed contra*, not denied). Jesus displays exemplary poverty and weakness as well as obedience in his manner of life (ST 3.40.3). He 'sent poor people to preach' the Gospel, too (*Sup. Matt.* 10:8, n. 822). The apostolic life described in the gospels and in Acts is that of communal poverty. Christians seeking perfection should therefore follow Christ by giving up earthly possessions: 'those who adopt voluntary poverty in order to follow Christ renounce all things so that they may serve the common welfare, enlightening the people by their wisdom, learning, and examples, or strengthening them by prayer and intercession' (ScG 3.135.15). But there are various forms of poverty. The apostolic community's form could not be perpetuated because it relied upon selling property for communal income. Hence that form was abandoned, especially after the church expanded out from Jerusalem (ScG 3.135.2). The poverty of the monks is fine, but of all forms, it is the poverty adopted by the friars which is the best. Not everyone can work by manual labor for their bread, as the monks often did. They might be infirm or, as Thomas says, perhaps about himself, they may not have been brought up to it. Moreover, by begging for one's food one acquires the virtue of humility (ScG 3.135.22f.).

The controversy between the two mendicant Orders required more careful elaboration of the relation between poverty and obedience. If one agreed with the Franciscan belief that poverty is the defining characteristic of the *status perfectionis*, then it would seem that the bishops lived in a second-rate manner, since few of them at that time could be accused of an overemphasis upon poverty. Traditionally, though, the *status* of the bishop was held to be the most perfect. Furthermore, if poverty is the pre-eminent Christian virtue, one would think that the poorer one is, the closer one is to perfection. This raised very nice questions as to how poor one should be, and caused frequent and heated debate within the Franciscan Order over issues such as whether one can own shoes, and what kind of shoes one can wear. The difficulty of achieving consensus on the application of the poverty principle eventually resulted in the Franciscans splitting up into groups which followed more or less strict Rules on the matter.

Thomas resolved the question for the Dominicans by privileging obedience to Christ over poverty. He makes the practical point:

> a religious order established for the purpose of contemplating and giving to others the fruits of one's contemplation by teaching and preaching, requires greater care of spiritual things than one that is established for contemplation only. Wherefore it becomes a religious order of this kind to embrace a poverty that burdens one with the least amount of care. (ST 2/2.188.7)

Christ's choice of the active life excluded extreme poverty because that would make it difficult to engage with those around him. Extreme poverty would undermine anyone's ability to teach and preach, hence it was avoided by Jesus, 'the founder of poverty', as well as by his disciples. Thomas argued that the purse held in common amongst the disciples did not simply contain alms for the poor, but money for Jesus and his disciples, for they, too, are to be included among the poor (ST 2/2.188.7). But wealth is not bad of itself, provided that one does not love it for its own sake (*Sup. Matt.* 19:22, n. 1601). Thus the fact that bishops are often wealthy does not disqualify the episcopacy from being a *status perfectionis*, because bishops give themselves to active service of their flock and to those temporal affairs that concern the church, both of which require some wealth. Poverty, although indeed a vital element of the Christian life, is finally only an instrumental means by which Christians seek to follow Christ more truly. It is not a goal or a good in itself. Following Jesus obediently is the fundamental rule, as Thomas frequently remarks (ST 2/2.186.6 ad 1; 3.43.3 ad 3).

The point can be generalized: Thomas considered apostolic obedience to be something of far more account than any precept, rule, principle or system, all of which must give way to obedient following of Jesus Christ in our thinking, our action and the interpretation of our experience. Obedience to Christ is the highest point of perfection (*Sup. Matt.* 19:21, n. 1598: *Hic est finis perfectionis*). And by obedience, Thomas does not mean unwilling or unknowing actions. The fulfillment of the call of Jesus Christ does not 'consist per se in exterior perfections, such as poverty, virginity and suchlike, unless these things are instrumental to charity' (*Sup. Matt.* 4:20, n. 373), for 'the perfection of the Christian life consists radically in charity' (ST 2/2.184.1). It is the love that is a gift of the Holy Spirit which makes true obedience possible. Obedience is difficult at times, not only in that one must submit one's will to another, but in discerning the will of the Lord in a particular matter. One will face unexpected concrete situations which will require a theoretical or practical response that cannot be worked out abstractly beforehand. Certainly, principles like poverty and obedience to one's superior or to the tradition (as distinct from obedience to Christ) normally help one on such occasions. But the conclusions drawn from using such principles are never immune from further reflection in light of the more fundamental principle. Thus Thomas's ordering of principles gains him both flexibility and significant critical leverage.[3]

Thomas understood his chosen manner of life to be thoroughly Christocentric, oriented theoretically, practically and experientially by the scriptural witness to the *mystery* of Jesus Christ. We cannot be content with simply copying Jesus's human activity, since he is not simply a moral exemplar. As his eventual absence from the disciples indicates, 'the humanity of Christ is for us the way which brings us closer to God' (*Sup. Ioan.* 7:33, n. 1074). The Christocentric manner of life is, as such, thoroughly theocentric. It is ordered toward the triune God, as Christ's manner of life on earth was ordered to the Father in the Spirit. Jesus Christ thus 'implicitly contains the Trinity' (*Sup. Matt.* 28:20, n. 2467: *In Christo continetur implicite Trinitas*). Thus it is in and through his free obedience to the will of the Father, in the power and love of the Holy Spirit, that the way to life in the triune God is revealed to us and made possible for us. It is the function of theology to explicate the way of the Lord so that we may follow it more truly.

Theology

For Thomas the Dominican, theology is a practice which serves the apostolic church in its task of preaching the Gospel and forming its members into faithful followers of Jesus Christ. Theology inquires into the truth made known to us by means of Scripture and it roots out and destroys the errors that contradict that truth (ScG 1.9.1). How, then, do theologians go about their task? Most commentators rightly take the first question of the ST (1.1.1–10) as the most significant discussion of what, rather anachronistically, might be called Thomas's theological 'method'. It is a good place to begin provided one remembers that Thomas's remarks are far too concise and underdetermined to stand alone. They need to be interpreted within the context of the ST as a whole and with his other writings in mind. Moreover, his theological practice also needs to be taken into consideration since it is sometimes more revealing than his theoretical remarks. We recall, too, that theology in the modern sense is not quite what Thomas is talking about in these articles. The ST, like all Thomas's texts, is the work of a *magister in sacra pagina*. It discusses the teachings of Scripture and the church's reflection upon those teachings in a pedagogically appropriate fashion so as to display the consistency of those teachings, to refute misunderstandings and erroneous interpretations, and deepen our understanding of the Gospel in order that we may preach it more convincingly and live it more obediently.

Scientific Theology

Theology is a science, Thomas says, and a 'matter of argument'. The notion of 'science' here has little to do with contemporary scientific method, modern or postmodern, but is drawn from Aristotle. Aristotelian science sought knowledge about necessary things and principles rather than about contingent and individual things. A completely worked-out science would be constituted by chains of demonstrative reasoning from self-evident first principles to the full complement of possible conclusions. Each science has an 'object': psychology has as its object the human mind, and biology has living things. The object of theology is God, according to Thomas. Each science, furthermore, has a 'formality' according to which it inquires into its object. Thus biology will examine a person as a living organism, psychology as a conscious being, and the science of music as producer or hearer of sounds. The formality under which theology examines God is as that divine being who is revealed through Sacred Scripture (ST 1.1.3). Thus Thomas argues that the object of theology is God and everything else in so far as it is in some way related to God as revealed by Scripture. When the theologian discusses things other than God, as is often necessary, God remains the focus as their beginning and end (ST 1.1.7). Theology is therefore nobler than all other sciences because it deals with that object which transcends human reason; it has to do with our ultimate end, eternal bliss; and it brings together both practical and theoretical matters.

Thomas's description of theology as an Aristotelian science raises a number of difficulties. First, unlike the first principles of mathematics or physics, the first principles of the science of theology are not self-evident. If they were, there would be no question about whether or not God exists. But the existence of God is a genuine question for Thomas, for whom it cannot be taken as self-evident. Second, and more significantly, if we had immediate knowledge of the first principles of theology, it would be theoretically possible for us to be able to argue demonstratively from them to conclusions which we in fact know only from revelation. We could conclude that God is triune; indeed, we might be able to comprehend God and thus in some sense be greater than God. So theology cannot be a demonstrative science in quite the usual way. Thomas contends that theological knowledge comes under the rubric of faith knowledge, of that knowledge which we must *ack*nowledge rather than attempt to discover for ourselves.

To explain this further, Thomas borrows Aristotle's distinction between higher and subaltern sciences. The first principles of subaltern sciences are not self-evident but are drawn from the conclusions of the higher sciences. Thus the principles of music, in Thomas's example, are derived not self-evidently, but from the conclusions of arithmetical inquiry; music is therefore a science subordinate to and dependent upon arithmetic. Theology, likewise, is a subordinate science, but not to any other human science. Rather its first principles are derived from the conclusions of the science of God. It is dependent upon what God makes known to us of God's own self-knowledge, which Thomas calls 'God's science' or divine wisdom (*scientia Dei*). Aristotle would presumably have found the notion of theology as a subaltern science dependent upon *scientia Dei* quite unconvincing. To introduce faith at this point, right at the heart of the theological enterprise, would be, for Aristotle, to introduce uncertainty and contingency and thus to undermine the scientific nature of the inquiry. Against such assumptions Thomas insists that theology is in fact *more* scientific, and so more objectively if not subjectively certain, because it proceeds from absolutely certain first principles, namely those given us by God rather than those worked out by the efforts of independent human reason.

Those for whom Thomas wrote the ST would have quickly grasped the Christological and apostolic connotations of his discussion. It is the Word of God incarnate who mediates God's *scientia* or self-knowledge to us sufficiently for our salvation. The witness to that Word is Scripture, *sacra doctrina*. And Scripture is to be read according to the first principles of theology found therein and brought together in the Creeds of the Christian church. Thomas understands the Creeds – or the Apostles' Creed, at least – to have been formulated by the apostles themselves as normative summaries of their teaching (ST 2/2.1.9 ad 6). The fairly recent notion (in Thomas's day) of 'the articles of faith' had since its inception been associated either with the apostles or with Jesus himself. When divided up under the apostolic rubric, the Creed was found to have twelve articles, with one assigned to each apostle. When divided up under the Christological rubric, the Creed had fourteen articles. In both cases, the groups are divided into two, reflecting what Thomas considers to be the two great mysteries made known to us in Jesus Christ. The first group of six or seven concern the Godhead and speak of who God is and what God has done in creation and sanctification. The second group then speak of the other great mystery, the Incarnation, and refer to Christ's human nature and his works and sufferings in the flesh (ST 2/2.1.8; Goering, 1998, pp. 127–38).

Thus theology could reasonably be spoken of as 'the apostolic science', for it is a form of inquiry legitimated by its incorporation within the apostolic relation to Jesus Christ as determined by the first principles of the science, namely the articles of the Creed.[4] The articles describe the center of scriptural witness, Jesus Christ, and situate him within the context of the whole, namely what Christ reveals of God and God's actions in creation and redemption.

It must be admitted, however, that in spite of his Aristotelian language, in practice Thomas does not simply argue from these first principles to demonstrated conclusions; his argumentation is far more complex than that. Nor, when he does argue demonstratively, does he consider his conclusions to be logically necessary in any absolute sense. They are merely the efforts of fallible human reason and must always be tested by further inquiry. Only those conclusions that have, if practical, become the long-standing custom of the church or, if theoretical, become its defined doctrine, are to be taken as 'necessary'. The greatest of the doctors of the church may draw conclusions that are less than necessary, even quite mistaken, and Thomas is not unwilling to correct even Augustine when he must. The arguments of theologians derive their authority from the church and its eventual acceptance of their interpretation of Scripture. It is Scripture's 'conclusions' that are 'necessary'; those of theologians are only 'probable' (ST 1.1.8 ad 2). While theological authorities are to be taken with great seriousness, they can do no more than present their own conclusions which may not be able to deal with challenges raised by the circumstances or insights of a new generation. Theological inquiry, then, is always ongoing. It is a historical and communal tradition not only in the sense of something handed on as a body of knowledge and an expertise, but also in the sense of a task to be continued by every new generation. To read Thomas's theology as if he sought to construct a system sufficient for all times and places would be massively to misunderstand his conception of the theological enterprise.

Fittingness Arguments

The question of theological method is further complicated by a rather different form of theological inquiry that surfaces especially though by no means solely in Thomas's Christological texts. In ST 3.46.2 and 3, Thomas discusses the question as to whether it was necessary for Christ to suffer and die upon the Cross. Since this is to place in question a first principle (the Creed's 'he suffered, died and was buried'), one may assume that Thomas's concern here is not to draw scientific conclusions. The question had been asked by Anselm some two hundred years before. Anselm's argument in his *Cur Deus Homo* can be summarized as follows: God is both merciful *and* just. Recompense must be paid to God for sin because God cannot simply forgive without payment; that would be unjust. No finite recompense for ruining creation would be sufficient repayment. The recompense requires the divine power of re-creation, which is beyond the power of any human. Yet the debt is owed by humanity and cannot justly be taken on by someone else. Hence Anselm concluded that only someone who is both divine and human could pay the debt. On this argument, then, the Incarnation and the Cross are necessary in the *logical* sense. They *must* occur if God is to be just and to redeem creation; there is no alternative.

Thomas agrees that God's justice and mercy are shown by the suffering and death of Christ (ST 3.46.3 ad 3), but in order to maintain belief in God's freedom and transcendence he denies the logical necessity of the Cross. God is not like a human judge; there is no higher justice to which God must conform, since God is justice itself. There is no reason to say that God *must* do something; if there is necessity in God's actions, it must be of another kind. Earlier, in ST 3.1.2, the second article of his treatise on Christology, Thomas argues that the Incarnation was not absolutely necessary in order to restore human nature after the effects of sin, for God could have redeemed creation 'in many other ways'. God chose to save us through the Incarnate Son because God willed not only to restore our fallen natures but to bring us to something much greater than our original perfection, namely into 'full participation' in the life of the Trinity. God decided to save us in one way, but our salvation could have been achieved in other ways. God chose this particular way, and because God is Wisdom itself, it must be the best way. It is thus the task of the theologian to try to discern what makes it best, to show the 'fittingness' (*convenientia*) of God's decision and action. Thus Thomas adduces a number of reasons why the Incarnation was most fitting (see also *Sup. Ioan.* 1:10, n. 141).

The kind of argument Thomas makes here has often been misunderstood. Some thirty years or so after Thomas's death, Duns Scotus asserted that the Incarnation would have occurred even if humanity had not sinned. Scotus seems to have argued on logical grounds that assumed some access to God's decision-making process (Cross, 1999, p. 128). Those who supported Thomas over against Scotus read him (Thomas) as if he asserted that there is a logically necessary connection between the Incarnation and the Fall such that Christ would not have become incarnate had humanity not sinned. Thus both Thomas and Scotus were taken to be arguing according to the same meaning of 'necessity', but for diverse claims: Thomas, that God made the decision for the Incarnation *after* the Fall; Scotus, that God made the decision for the Incarnation *before* the Fall. Both groups misunderstood Thomas (leaving aside Scotus) by reading him rationalistically (see Narcisse, 1997, p. xxii).

According to Thomas, the task of theology is not to discern what makes the Incarnation necessary. Rather the necessity to be explored is that which is necessarily the case because it is described in Scripture. As Thomas says (drawing upon Aristotle), there is a kind of necessity other than the logical. If one wants to achieve something by the best possible means, those means are the necessary means. Thus if one wants to get somewhere easily and quickly, it is necessary to ride a horse rather than walk (ST 3.1.2). God freely chose to save humanity and creation by means of Jesus Christ. God did not have to save the world; nor did salvation have to occur in that way. Both salvation and the means of salvation are entirely contingent upon God's free will. But once the decision is made (loosely speaking, since God's decision is eternal rather than made within time), the means to salvation become necessary. The Incarnation is a first principle for theological science, in spite of its contingency and historicity. To show its logical necessity is as impossible as showing the logical necessity of self-evident principles in any of the higher Aristotelian sciences. Instead, the theologian should attempt to explain why these means to salvation are the best by displaying the appropriateness of God's actions as they are described in Scripture.

The argument for fittingness is therefore something like an aesthetic argument because it searches for structure and proportion. The French Dominican, Gilbert Narcisse, gives this definition:

> Theological fittingness displays the significance of the chosen means among alternative possibilities, and the reasons according to which God, in his wisdom, has effectively realized and revealed, gratuitously and through his love, the mystery of the salvation and glorification of humanity. (Narcisse, 1997, p. 572)

Fittingness arguments are found throughout Scripture where analogies are drawn, connections between things, events and people are noted, and references made back and forward. One of the most obvious examples of such arguments is figurative exegesis, such as Paul's contention that Christ is the second Adam, or the implication in Luke that the Twelve are to be linked with the people of Israel. Such connections do not depend upon deductive logic; they must appeal to one's sense of proportion or fittingness.

What prevents this kind of argument from becoming arbitrary, both in the New Testament reading of the Old Testament and in Thomas's usage, is proximately its material basis in the gospel portrayals of Jesus Christ. But more is required than careful exegesis. In the first section above, I noted how Thomas frequently appeals to Jesus's actions as exemplary and normative for our own. Undergirding Jesus's moral exemplarity is his ontological exemplarity whereby in following him we become increasingly like him. Thomas discusses this in terms of what he calls 'capital grace', grace made available for us by Christ the head of the church (*caput ecclesiae*) (ST 3.8). There is no other way to God except through Christ, since 'grace is not given us by means of human nature, but solely by the personal action of Christ Himself' (ST 3.8.5 ad 1). Grace is mediated to us by Christ's humanity, which is the 'instrument of the Godhead', the means whereby creation is drawn into full participation in the life of the triune God (ST 3.1.2). Any instrument shapes the work of the agent who uses it. So God's salvific activity – grace – bears the mark of Christ's humanity. And this is as it should be, argues Thomas, because Jesus is fittingly the mediator in his manner of life, his nature and his person. His actions are morally exemplary: when we act in obedience to him, we act fittingly. And in acting fittingly through his grace, we become fitting because we become conformed to his humanity, and so become adopted sons and daughters in the image of the Son (*Sup. Rom.* 8:29, ns. 704–706).

With regard more specifically to theological inquiry as obedient action, the link between natural knowledge and the life of grace can be made only through divine wisdom, the Word of God revealed in the humanity of Jesus Christ. It is because of the absolute fittingness of Christ's humanity that we are able to perceive the *convenientia* between the triune God and creation.

As we seek to penetrate further into the fittingness of God's action made known to us in the grace of faith, we begin to acquire some understanding of God's decisions and actions. To that extent, our minds become conformed to the mind of Jesus Christ, the Word. Through our intellectual obedience we begin to acquire theological wisdom (Narcisse, 1997, p. 573). 'A son is naturally like his father, which means that people are called sons and daughters of God in so far as they participate, by way of likeness, in him who is the Son of God by nature; and they know God in the measure that they resemble him, since all knowledge is brought about by assimilation' to him (*Sup. Ioan.* 1:18, n. 216). Therefore it is Christ's humanity which is the condition of the possibility of theology, and theology is true in so far as the theologian is transformed so as to conform to Christ.

This point is not restricted to knowledge of salvation history as such. '[T]he whole world is nothing other than a kind of representation of the divine wisdom', which can be known truly only by the light of the Word (*Sup. Ioan.* 1:10, n. 136; also 1:9, n. 128; ScG 4.13.11). The Word is 'the intelligibility of things made by God', and it is through the Word that things are maintained in their being (ScG 4.13.7f.). There is therefore a fittingness that can be discerned by us in the relation between the creator and creation and between grace and nature, a fittingness that is made evident in and is shaped for us by the incarnate Word.[5] Thus, although fittingness arguments are especially common in the Christology treatise, they are evident in many other places. One example taken at random can be found in Thomas's discussion of whether we should show greater kindness to those nearer and dearer to us or be equally kind to all. Thomas argues:

> Grace and virtue imitate the order of nature, which is established by Divine wisdom. Now the order of nature is such that every natural agent pours forth its activity first and most of all on the things which are nearest to it: thus fire heats most what is next to it. In like manner God pours forth the gifts of divine goodness first and most plentifully on the substances which are nearest to God ... but the bestowal of benefits is an act of charity towards others. Therefore we ought to be most beneficent towards those who are most closely connected with us. (ST 2/2.31.3)

It would be simple to point out the gaps in logic of such an argument, but that would be to misunderstand its force. Thomas draws analogies between vastly different things (fire, charity, God) in order to disclose to the reader a proportionality within reality. One does not penetrate God's reality by necessary arguments, since God could have done everything differently. Instead, one is to show the *convenientia* of things in relation to their exemplary source.

It may be useful to contrast Thomas's fittingness arguments with Immanuel Kant's transcendental method. They are similar in that they both begin with a given and seek reasons that would explain it – its conditions of possibility.

Kant's given is human knowledge; he sought reasons for asserting that our knowledge may be necessary and universal. The key difference is that Kant sought logically necessary conditions, so his explanation is the only possible one. That I happen to hold a true and rationally justifiable belief at this moment is made possible by the structures of my mind, structures which are the necessary condition for any and all knowing. For Thomas it is contingent events – salvation history – that function as the given to be explained and justified. But such explanations and justification cannot penetrate beyond the events. They cannot be established by appeals to more certain truths discerned through universal reason, nor by an account of their logical necessity on theological or any other grounds. Instead, Thomas's transcendental arguments are always ongoing. We try to discern the fittingness of these events so that we may be transformed into a particular kind of person – a good Christian – so that we may be better able to discern their fittingness, and be more transformed, and so on.[6]

Thomistic Dialectic

The less than fully conclusive nature of demonstrative theological arguments and the aesthetic form of argument together help to explain the presence of a third form of argument in Thomas's writings, namely dialectic. We recall that dialectical argumentation was customary in the schools in the form of the disputation, which was both a means of inquiry as well as a pedagogical tool. Thomas Hibbs (1995) has made a convincing case for reading the ScG as an exercise in dialectic whereby philosophical wisdom is corrected and transformed by theological wisdom. In the next chapter I will offer a somewhat similar reading of the early part of the ST. Thomas's dialectic seems to have been drawn more from Aristotle via Boethius than anyone else, though certainly Plato and Augustine are important influences. Recent studies have fostered greater awareness of Aristotle's reliance upon dialectic and aporia (an irresolvable philosophical conundrum) (e.g., Booth, 1983). Aristotelian dialectic is unlike scientific argumentation in that, rather than moving from self-evident first principles to demonstrated conclusions, it reverses this procedure. It is an exploratory form of philosophy which argues *towards* such principles (MacIntyre, 1990, p. 88), searching for those conditions which would seem reasonably (or fittingly) to obtain if whatever we believe is indeed true. The starting-point is therefore something that may be challenged, such as the received opinions of a culture, whether high or low, or ordinary sense data, rather than self-evident principles (Hibbs, 1995, pp. 23f.).

Thomas's use of dialectic is itself a fitting mode of discourse in light of his theological orientation to Jesus Christ, for it reflects the 'dramatic reversal in the progress of human history' (Hibbs, 1995, p. 34) brought about by the Incarnation. The wisdom of God is revealed in the life and death and resurrection, and must be allowed to judge all earthly wisdoms. The way to demonstrate and elucidate that wisdom is to engage any and all challenges to it. In Thomas's theological dialectic the starting-points are commonly held beliefs or, more usually, philosophical beliefs and arguments. By disclosing the aporias of human wisdom he indicates those places where philosophy needs to be supplemented and revised by theological wisdom. As the dialectic progresses, not only the starting-point but what has been established in the course of the inquiry must also be reconsidered in light of further reflection. Moreover, the dialectical progress must itself give way at some point to the more fundamental narrative of salvation history through the events of which God teaches us. Thus the line of argumentation is continuously broken, the form of the inquiry rendered unsystematic and reoriented toward Scripture.

Thomas draws upon all available sources to raise challenges as well as to resolve them, including logical, metaphysical and experiential arguments, and arguments from philosophers and theologians of the past. The relationship between theology and philosophy is mutually beneficial, since what is philosophically true is derived ultimately from the same source as theological truth (ST 2/2.167.1 ad 3, citing Rom. 1:19). Theology corrects philosophy, but it also makes good use of it, too. For as Thomas argued, following Augustine, philosophical proposals that can be reconciled with the faith should be appropriated by theologians (*Sup. I Cor.* 1:17, n. 43). Thomas refers to an image that appears frequently in the tradition, by which the relation between revealed truth and truths drawn from other sources was pictured. Deuteronomy 21:10–13 describes what one may do if one captures a beautiful woman from the enemy in battle. One may take her in marriage, but only after certain simple procedures have been followed. Origen understood the beautiful woman as a figure of pagan philosophy. To delight lawfully in the philosophical traditions of ancient, pagan cultures, one must purify them appropriately. Others took up the image in a similar way in a tradition that stretched to Thomas's day and beyond (see de Lubac, 1998b, pp. 211–24). Thomas puts it thus:[7]

> Doctors of Sacred Scripture take from witnesses to truth wherever they may be found. Thus the apostle Paul frequently cites the words of the Gentiles ... Not that their teachings should be appropriated as a whole; the bad parts should be rejected and the good kept. Truth from whatever source is from the Holy Spirit. Deut. 21 speaks figuratively about this where it says that if a man sees a young woman among the captives, he should trim her nails and hair; that is, cut off all that is superfluous. (*Sup. Titus* 1:15, n. 32)

Hermeneutics

Demonstrative, fittingness and dialectical arguments all depend upon our obedience and conformity to the incarnate Word. Consequently, they are equally dependent upon the material witness of Scripture, the apostolic mediation of the Word. It is Scripture which supplies the articles of faith, the first principles of scientific argumentation. Scripture displays the contingent events that, having been willed and realized by God, are now 'necessary' and require the theologian to display their fittingness. Scripture is the material witness to the truth which makes possible the judgment and revision of philosophical wisdom by theological wisdom. Demonstrative arguments begin from the apostolic teaching. Dialectical arguments may work towards it or move from it to critique knowledge from other sources. Fittingness arguments make connections within the teaching and with other knowledge. All three are materially dependent upon Scripture and upon our moral and ontological conformity to Jesus Christ as the revelation of God's wisdom.[8]

Thus the question arises as to what Thomas said about how to go about interpreting Scripture. The hermeneutical question is, of course, a pressing one for contemporary theology, to which widely diverse answers have been offered. The question arose with somewhat less urgency in Thomas's day, and the range of possible answers was far more limited. Thomas makes only a few theoretical remarks on the issue, most of which can be found in article 10 of the very first question of the ST, so they must be supplemented by considering examples of his exegetical practice.

The Four Senses

In ST 1.1.10, Thomas follows tradition in asserting that 'in Holy Scripture a word may have several senses'. The primary distinction is between the historical or literal sense (*sensus historicus vel litteralis*) and the spiritual senses, and Thomas insists that the latter are dependent upon the former. In this, Thomas reflects and extends a shift in biblical interpretation, beginning about a century before, away from sometimes fanciful allegorizing and moralizing, towards greater awareness of the need to read and respond to the text's plain sense (Smalley, 1952, ch. 6).

The spiritual senses are three and they all center upon Jesus Christ. The allegorical sense or, as we might say today, the figurative sense, reads the Old Testament in light of the Gospel in order to explicate the New Testament depiction of Christ with terms and images drawn from the Old Testament. The tropological or moral sense depicts Christ as our moral exemplar. The anagogical sense 'relates to eternal glory', once again an intrinsically Christological relation for Thomas. He quotes Dionysius: 'the new law itself is a figure of future glory' and goes on to equate the new law with exemplary acts of Jesus as the head of the church. The notion of the fourfold senses of Scripture goes back at least to Augustine and was commonly referred to among the scholastics. They believed that, because of its apostolic inspiration, Scripture, alone of all texts, may be read in all these ways (de Lubac, 1998a, p. 8).

Thomas does not develop these divisions in any theoretical detail, prompting commentators from the Neo-Scholastic period to wish that he had introduced 'a bit of logical order' and turned his few remarks into 'a kind of methodological classification' (Mandonnet, cited by de Lubac, 1998a, p. 10). In practice Thomas is quite flexible in his use of the four senses, suggesting that not too much should be made of the division. He makes other distinctions when it is helpful to do so. For example, in his commentary on John's Gospel, he notes that Scripture takes three points of view upon the reality it describes: as created, as perfected in Christ, and as sinful (*Sup. Ioan.* 1:9, n. 128). Such a division is arguably at least as significant in Thomas's reading of Scripture as that of ST 1.1.10, though it has received far less notice.

Thomas's concept of the literal is much more complex than that reflected in contemporary usage. We sometimes say that people interpret sentences literally when they fail to take into account metaphorical and imagistic modes of discourse. This restricted use of 'literal' is expressly ruled out by Thomas. What is meant literally may well be expressed by a metaphor or parable rather than the words taken according to their dictionary definition. Thus Thomas notes that when we read about God's 'arm' we should not infer that 'he' actually has an arm. It is likely, then, that any given word, interpreted 'literally', may have more than one meaning.

The key to the concept of the literal sense is its link with 'historical', for the historical–literal sense usually derives from a simple, straightforward account of things and events, such as the story of Adam and Eve, the crossing of the Red Sea or the Passion narrative. The literal reading of these stories must be allowed to control the spiritual interpretations of those who would find more complex and profound meanings in the text. Usually, too, Scripture teaches plainly what it treats elsewhere in more obscure, metaphorical ways. Thus simple people may get what is salvifically necessary from Scripture, while thoughtful people are given as much as they need to chew over, and the impious are kept from ridiculing the text (ST 1.1.9 ad 2). The literal sense of the stories provides another kind of control by means of their narrative structure. Spiritual interpretations make connections between events and things that often break up the narrative structure of revelation. That is certainly permissible, even necessary, but the diachronic structure of God's actions in the world described from Genesis to the Book of Revelation must take precedence over the synchronic explication of those actions. Individual stories, sentences and words all depend for their 'historical or literal' meaning upon their setting within the movement from creation to the eschaton. For what Scripture has to tell us can be apprehended only as we follow that story along. Hence, too, no interpretation of that story in a non-narrative system of doctrine will ever be adequate to it (Williams, 1999, pp. 47f.).

Thomas's remarks about the four senses are evidently intended to break up a flat-footed reading of Scripture on the one hand and, on the other, to avoid the excessively imaginative readings favored by some of his contemporaries. They would also rule out both those modern theories that seek to determine a single, secure meaning of a text, as well as those theories, often associated with versions of postmodernity, that would deny any privileged meaning. Another aspect of Thomas's understanding of the literal–historical sense takes the point further. The so-called intentional fallacy is the notion that the meaning of a text is secured once one has grasped what the author intended to say by it. Thomas often talks of authorial intention, but he contends that it is God who is the author of Scripture and not, say, Moses or Matthew or Paul. Because God is Truth, and because God intends to convey truth in the words of the text, there indeed is a discernible meaning in the text. However, the meaning is not (usually) reducible to just one alone, for God's intention is not always sufficiently obvious that all other possible readings are ruled out. God's intention is expressed normatively in the literal–historical sense, but it is not necessarily the case that God intends the same meaning for all the times and places in which the Scriptures are read. Matthew's own intention is secondary at most, as is his historical context in so far as it bears upon his intention in writing the Gospel. What counts is what God conveys to us by means of Matthew's words or, as we now theorize, by the words chosen by the editors of the Pentateuch or Q or the Johannine tradition. Questions about the human authors of Scripture are not ruled out since a grasp of the historical setting might enable their words to convey more of God's intention. But such questions are necessarily of secondary interest compared with the concern to discern God's intention by prayerful reading.

The matter is yet more complex, for the divine author of Scripture conveys meaning in two ways, both of which are, in the first place, literal–historical. God can convey meaning by using the words of Scripture, as we do when we write a text. In addition, God can mean in a way which we cannot, namely by 'things', i.e., by events, like the liberation of the Israelites from enslavement in Egypt, or by people, such as the figure of Elijah the prophet, or by actual things, such as the River Jordan. Each of these 'things' takes on resonances and meanings beyond its simple actuality. Such resonances are also part of its meaning, and must be elicited by spiritual interpretations. Both Testaments must be interpreted both literally and spiritually. John's Gospel focuses, Thomas says, upon Jesus's divinity rather than his humanity, unlike Matthew's, which deals more with his humanity. Thus John is more amenable to a spiritual reading. Yet it cannot be read apart from the literal sense since John must use words in their ordinary signification if, for example, he is to avoid a docetic view of Jesus as not really human. And Matthew makes connections that require the spiritual senses, for example in the nativity story, where he draws parallels between Israel and Jesus. With regard to the Old Testament, Thomas's commentary on Job is concerned with its literal sense. For him this includes, besides the events and people depicted, the theme of providence and the question of why good people are permitted to suffer. People in the Old Testament are seen as figures of Christ by spiritual interpretation, as Solomon signifies Christ, in whom are all the treasures of wisdom and recondite knowledge (*Sup. Matt.* 1:4, n. 43). Interestingly, though, when an Old Testament prophet writes of something that could be interpreted as a genuine predication of Jesus Christ, rather than a figure of him, it may be necessary to interpret in the literal sense. Thus in commenting on a passage in Matthew, Thomas notes that the reference in Isaiah 7:14 is literally to a young woman, rather than to a virgin, who will conceive a child. But, he says, against the claims of Jewish interpreters who would say that the text does not, therefore, refer 'literally' to the virgin birth, that in fact it does, since the *literal* reference is to Christ. Indeed, in this particular case, 'if someone accepts as true some sense other than the literal sense they would be a heretic' (*Sup. Matt.* 1:23, n. 148).

With regard to the historical sense as such, Thomas's usage is rather more similar to our own, though the issue is complicated by Thomas's belief that the Bible is historically accurate and describes created realities accurately, too. However, he asserts a principle that would make it possible to respond to contemporary scientific and historical claims that would challenge that accuracy. If, as he says, 'it is plain that nothing false can ever underlie the literal sense of Holy Writ' (ST 1.1.10 ad 3), then it would seem that we should not interpret a problematic text as historical or literal if doing so would result in its being untrue. Thus, for example, if we are convinced that the story of the conquest of Jericho cannot be as it is described in the book of Joshua, perhaps because the archaeological evidence indicates overwhelmingly that such an event could not have occurred at the time Scripture says it did, we would not on that account deny the truth of the story. Scripture reveals truth; truth is one, since it is from God, who is Truth itself. Hence God's intended meaning in the story of Jericho must be something other than a specific historical claim.[9]

An example of the bearing of science upon biblical interpretation is given in ST 1.68.3, where Thomas notes that the text of Genesis 1:6 seems to suggest its compatibility with the theories of certain philosophers who claimed that an infinite body of water surrounded the firmament, based on the notion that water is the primary element. Thomas notes that 'this theory can be shown to be false by true reasons', i.e., by reasons that would be convincing to other philosophers. Hence 'it cannot be held to be the sense of Holy Scripture'. So Thomas proposes that the word 'water' should be understood to refer to formless matter, so as to fit what seems to him to be a more convincing theory. When Scripture seems to say something that conflicts with what we know to be true on other grounds, it is not that Scripture is wrong; it is our reading that is wrong.

Thomas's privileging of the literal and historical sense of Scripture is best understood in terms of the text's Christological center. Thomas follows a traditional and widely held view that the key to Scripture is the person and work of Jesus Christ, who is described for us in the events of both the Old

Testament and New Testament (de Lubac, 1998a, pp. 234–40). These events are the 'realized possibilities' that constitute the 'necessary' truths for theological inquiry, and therefore they must be understood according to the historical–literal sense of the text. As such, they give rise to the principles of theological science; they delineate the form of Wisdom that must be allowed to judge all other wisdoms, including theological wisdom. That Christ died on the Cross for our salvation is the central historical–literal claim, but it should be elucidated further. This is done for us by Scripture, read according to the historical–literal sense, as a description of the history of Israel and the life of Jesus Christ. But in order to enrich one's understanding of the authorial intention of such events one should make use of the spiritual senses, with the result that multiple interpretations are often possible. One of the most striking aspects of Thomas's way of reading Scripture is that he frequently seems quite unconcerned to select one interpretation over others. Often he will present different readings of a passage, and just leave it at that. There is no reason to reject reasonable interpretations in order to arrive at 'the' reading, because that is not the point. The point of reading Scripture is to open us up to God's reality revealed in Christ, not to enclose and control that reality. One example, taken at random, is the discussion in ST 1.20.4 of whether Peter or John loved and were loved by Jesus more. Thomas notes that this question 'has been solved in various ways', and gives four or five ways, but then says that 'it may seem presumptuous to pass judgment on these matters', citing another text (Prov. 16:2) that leaves the judgment to God alone.

Scripture the Bearer of Revelation

To read Scripture well requires much beyond simply paying attention to the text and its multiple senses, as one might if one read it in a literature class in a modern university. First and foremost, it requires, as we noted earlier, the illumination of the Word. That illumination is given only as Scripture is read within the apostolic church, amidst those who participate in the life of Christ through grace and the Holy Spirit. Scripture was written or normatively interpreted by the apostles as the basis of their preaching. It is, so to speak, the church's textbook, the instrument by which we may be brought into the apostolic relation to Jesus. It reflects their teaching about his teaching and is thus as it were dictated by him to them (ST 3.42.4). To read Scripture according to its apostolic sense, one must be guided by the Creeds, for they are in origin an apostolic summary of the teaching found in Scripture (ST 2/ 2.1.9 ad 6).

It is necessary, too, to acquire the virtues appropriate for good reading. Training is vital because, while 'the truth of faith is contained in Scripture', it is there 'diffusely, under various modes of expression, and sometimes obscured, so that, in order to gather the truth of faith from Scripture, one needs long study and practice' (ST 2/2.1.9 ad 1). Failure or bad training on the part of pupil or teacher will result in false or misguided readings. It must be admitted that on occasion Thomas's own judgment is distorted by his cultural context. His views about the physical and biological world are often quite wrong, as we might expect. Nor is his understanding of the relation between men and women congenial to many today. He has some remarkably silly comments about 'little old women' whose 'venomous and hurtful' faces betray that they are 'vehemently moved to wickedness', indicating the likelihood that they are witches (ST 1.117.3 ad 2). But his remarks about reading Scripture assume that such erroneous and sinful readings occur and explain why. Reading Scripture is an ongoing task that cannot be concluded by a systematic re-presentation of its contents. It requires a dialectical form of inquiry, one 'always open to further challenge' (MacIntyre, 1990, p. 89).

For Thomas, then, Scripture is not of itself revelation so much as the bearer of revelation, rather as in a dependent way (dependent upon both God *and* Scripture), the church is the bearer of revelation, too.[10] In both church and Scripture, God remains in control of revelation. Scripture cannot be reduced to a single determinate meaning to be found either in the text or behind it in a historical reconstruction. The biblical text is instrumental but unavoidable; we must turn back to it continually. In this Thomas is a far more biblically oriented theologian than some later Roman Catholic theologians who tend to focus their attention on the church's doctrines apart from the text of Scripture. Even after Vatican II, which is often regarded as a call to return to Scripture, some theologians treat the conciliar documents as if they were a map of reality sufficiently detailed and timeless that consultation of Scripture is no longer essential. For Thomas, conciliar documents must be taken with full seriousness, but they too need interpretation, for which the text of Scripture is the necessary instrumental means and norm.

Conclusion

Thomas's formation within the Dominican Order, with its way of life informed by a Christocentric reading of Scripture, bears upon the conception and performance of his task as *magister in sacra pagina*. His theology served his community and the preaching of the church as they and he sought to follow Christ more fittingly and more obediently. Christians follow the way that is the incarnate Word of God. They come to know the truth and begin to participate in the life that Christ makes possible for them in him. The chief guide on the way is the apostolic text. But Scripture is a complex text; our interpretations must remain 'a matter of argument', of dialectic and fittingness, guided by the articles of faith. The Word illumines all who know truly, though the knowledge found through philosophical and scientific inquiry is always subordinate to the apostolic witness to the Word.

Notes

1   The issue still flares up on occasion, for example in the controversy over the supposed activism of the liberation theologians and the accusations of quietism and theoreticism made against more doctrinally focused theologians such as Rahner, Barth and Balthasar. Thomas suggests a reasonable way to move beyond the dichotomy.

2   To be sure, biblical fundamentalism is a modern phenomenon, not a premodern one. My point is that Thomas's reading of Scripture is never flat-footed and literal in the modern sense of the term. I discuss the issue in more detail in the next section.

3   As one might expect, this has a significant bearing upon Thomas's understanding of moral theology, which is discussed below in Chapter 6.

4   Thomas himself does not call theology an apostolic science. But it is clearly one of the central practices of what he calls, with the tradition, the *vita apostolica*.

5   Our ability to discern such fittingness is carefully restricted by Thomas, as Chapter 3 will make clear.

6   There are, to be sure, many other differences between Kant's method and fittingness arguments, even though they are both forms of transcendental arguments. Fittingness arguments are used in later theology, too, especially by those theologians seeking to move away from the modern paradigm. For some further discussion of transcendental arguments in Christian theology, see Tanner (1988), ch. 1, esp. pp. 20–26. Kant, of course, was faced with the kind of thinking summarized in Lessing's dictum about the great ugly ditch between the necessary truths of reason and the historical claims upon which faith relies. Thomas would have found Lessing's assertion confused, since the necessary truths of reason are for him less well established than the events of salvation history recorded in Scripture that came about contingently as a consequence of God's will.

7   I owe this and the previous citation from *Sup. I Cor.* to de Lubac (1998a, p. 421). The translation of both is my own.

8   It is my emphasis upon fittingness and dialectical arguments that perhaps most differentiates my account of Thomas's theological approach from that of Eugene F. Rogers, Jr (1995), from whose work I have learned a great deal, especially its analysis of Thomas's Christoform logic. Rogers focuses more upon demonstrative arguments, nicely developing some insights of Michel Corbin.

9   Of course, there are limits to the application of this principle, but Thomas would have had no reason to explore them. Thus today someone might say that the Resurrection cannot be historically true, given the kind of events that are accepted by historians as possibilities. But this could not mean that we should deny the scriptural account of the Resurrection. There are some non-negotiable biblical claims, as Thomas seems to assume.

10 Barth's notion of the threefold Word: Jesus Christ, Scripture and true preaching, is clearly congenial to Thomas. See Barth (1975), pp. 88ff.

Chapter 3

The Dialectic of Wisdom

With this chapter we begin to consider Thomas's theology in more detail, and we begin with the same topic as Thomas does in the ST and the ScG, namely the doctrine of God. Previously I suggested that Thomas's theological inquiries are guided by engagement with Scripture's witness to Jesus Christ, and are undertaken in order to guide the church's attempts to follow Christ obediently. However, the best interpretation of Jesus Christ is not immediately evident to faith, nor does Scripture clearly rule out misunderstandings of his person and work. So Thomas must set his Christology within the broader context of the doctrine of God (McCabe, 1987, p. 42). Scripture guides the inquiry throughout this area, too, as it must if his teaching is to be apostolic and adhere to the articles of faith. But acquiring theological knowledge of God is not merely a question of careful exegesis and argument. Good theology and truthful exegesis require the training of mind and heart. Inquiry into God is a movement towards God which involves the transformation of the inquirer. The intellectual form of that movement and transformation is exemplified in the ScG as a dialectic between philosophical and theological wisdoms. In the ST it takes the form of a dialectic in which initial attempts to talk about God, whether those of unlearned Christians or subtle philosophers, are modified, refined and reworked with a view to taking the reader further towards a truly Christian conception of the triune God.

Here I will discuss the material covered in the first forty or so questions of ST 1, together with parallels elsewhere. These questions consider the existence and knowledge of God, first as One, then as the Trinity. They conclude (at ST 1.43) with a treatment of the mission of the Son and the Holy Spirit outwards, so to speak, to creation. This reflects a shift from what is often called the 'immanent Trinity' to the 'economic Trinity', from the triune God as such, apart from God's creative and redemptive action, to the Trinity considered in light of the history (the 'economy') of salvation. I will postpone discussion of the economic Trinity to the next chapter though, for it makes a good starting-point for a further examination of Thomas's Christology, and it is not unreasonable to say that the economic Trinity is the general topic of the remainder of the ST.

Philosophy and Theological Dialectic

The early questions of the ST have been subjected to conflicting interpretations, for they bear upon what became contentious, virtually church-dividing topics during the modern period, especially the relation variously described as that between nature and grace, philosophy and theology, or faith and reason. Both Thomists and those who reject Thomas have often read the text as moving straightforwardly from a basis in premises drawn from what can be known by philosophical inquiry independent of revelation, to what can be known only through faith and revelation. Thomas himself seems to encourage such a reading. He states in the ScG that 'we must set down in the beginning that whereby God's existence is demonstrated, as the necessary foundation of the whole work' (ScG 1.9.5). He also contends that 'the existence of God and other like truths about God, which can be known by natural reason, are not articles of faith, but are preambles to the articles of faith; for faith presupposes natural knowledge, even as grace presupposes nature, and perfection presupposes something that can be perfected' (ST 1.2.2 ad 1). There is, as he says in the ScG, a 'twofold mode of truth', two ways to gain knowledge about God:

> Some truths about God exceed all the ability of the human reason. Such is the truth that God is triune. But there are some truths which the natural reason also is able to reach. Such are that God exists, that God is one, and the like. In fact, such truths about God have been proved demonstratively by the philosophers, guided by the light of the natural reason. (ScG 1.3.2)

Accordingly, the reader may be tempted to stress two things: first, the smoothness of the path from one mode of truth to the other, from reason to faith and from philosophical to theological inquiry; second, the unidirectional nature of the inquiry, as if faith had no bearing upon its initial stages. We begin with natural knowledge of God and then simply add to it what we know through supernatural means, in accordance with the two-tier conception of reality.

We should not succumb to this temptation, however. Thomas's concern in these questions is more to rule out error and idolatry in the language we use about God than to reason towards more complete descriptions of divine reality. Scripture is the primary guide as Thomas rules out false implications of early questions' conclusions and prepares language for use in talking about the triune God of Christianity. The way from the five proofs of the existence of God to the explication of God's triune existence is a dialectical movement. The way can be rough and (seemingly) wandering, rather than smooth and unidirectional, as he submits the wisdom of the world to the judgment and transformation of the Gospel. Not that the way is always rough; nor is the roughness always obvious. Often Thomas will smooth the road ahead by quietly guiding the inquiry in one direction rather than another, according to Trinitarian or Christological interests treated explicitly in other places. And on the way it often happens that philosophy helps to clarify the teaching of theology as well as to challenge it (ST 1.1.5 ad 2).

Whether God Exists?

The theological task is set up in the first question of the ST, as we have seen, and then initiated in the second, where Thomas enters upon his inquiry into the doctrine of God. We recall from question 1 that here, as everywhere, all is viewed *sub specie aeternitatis*, from God's perspective, which is the properly theological view of reality according to the formality of revelation (ST 1.1.4). The inquiry begins, as it must for theology, with God, rather than with creation, which is where philosophy begins (ScG 2.4.5).

Question 2 begins with the most preliminary issue, whether or not God exists. The question consists of three articles on issues that continue to be of interest. The first argues against the idea that God's existence is self-evident for us, even though it may seem so once we have reasoned our way to it. The second article argues against the opposing notion: that because God's existence is a matter of faith no arguments can be made for it. The third constructs five arguments for the existence of God. In each case, challenges are raised and met by more sophisticated thinking. The question repays some detailed analysis.

The first article, against the self-evident existence of God, draws upon challenges dependent upon the Platonic tradition in which appeals are made to an internal ground – the human mind – for God's existence. The first challenge, still extant today in various guises, is the notion that God is known by an innate idea. We do not need to reason discursively to know that God exists; it is a something 'we just know', naturally. Thomas agrees, but only in part. We know God in a confused and general way because we do indeed desire and naturally tend towards a good which is other than ourselves, towards that which makes us happy or – for Thomas this is the same thing – that which completes us. God is, of course, our ultimate happiness, in whom we are completely realized. But Thomas points out that the natural desire for God as our ultimate happiness and perfection is not at all the same thing as knowledge of God's existence. Many people confuse happiness with earthly pleasures and, as a consequence, they may fail to acknowledge God's existence.

The second and third objections both trade upon Platonic assumptions about the nature of language. It is sufficient to look at the second, which is Anselm's ontological argument taken as a philosophical argument.[1] According to Anselm (*Proslogion* 3), the existence of God is analytic to the concept of God. Once we understand what the word 'God' means, namely 'that than which nothing greater can be thought', we are logically required to acknowledge that God must exist. For it is evidently 'greater' for God to exist, where the word 'God' means a necessarily existent divine being, than not to exist. Therefore God must exist. Thomas replies by pointing out 'that than which nothing greater can be thought' is not everyone's concept of God. Even if it were, the 'existence' so proven is only conceptual. Just because someone can think this concept does not mean that what is thought must exist.

The second article then takes the opposing view. Not only is God's existence not self-evident; it cannot even be demonstrated. We say in the Creed that we believe in God. But faith is necessarily of things 'unseen'; it cannot be demonstrated without it becoming something other than faith. In reply, Thomas makes the observation that God's existence belongs to the 'preambles of faith' rather than to the body of faith itself. By this he does not mean to assert a non-theological basis for faith in universal reason, as if one could prove God's existence philosophically and then argue over differing beliefs about what kind of God exists. On the contrary, he does three important things here. First, he acknowledges the evident fact that many people believe in the existence of something which they call 'God', and they do so without having recourse to Christian revelation. If their belief is neither innate nor the product of a necessary relation between our minds, our speech and reality, then it can be acquired only from an external source. Their belief, as Thomas says in the body of the article, is the product of a form of discursive reasoning based upon their examination of the world, and so it is something anyone can arrive at. For example, we know through our experience something of the relation between cause and effect, and from that it is not difficult to construe the world as an effect the cause of which is God. We may reason from our experience of the world to God as its cause.

Second, by locating arguments for God's existence within the preambles of faith, Thomas rules out the use of the word 'faith' for beliefs other than those revealed in Scripture. Thomas does not use 'faith' in the sense of generic belief in God's existence; nor does he postulate a religious consciousness common to all religions and peoples, as some modern theologians have done.[2] In his theology, 'faith' is a technical term which refers to one of the theological virtues, and is therefore a gift of grace which can be had only within the context of membership in the Body of Christ.[3] Faith is belief in what is revealed about God in his Word, though, to be sure, it may include belief in God's existence for those Christians who are unable to understand the arguments for God's existence on other grounds (ST 2/ 2.2.4). The members of other 'faiths' and the philosophers are alike in making the inference to God's existence from their experience of external reality without depending upon faith in this specific sense. They use their reason unaided by revelation.

The third major point of this article is to make the distinction between knowing *what* God is, the divine nature as such, and merely knowing *that* God is. We know of God's existence only through God's effects. Causes that are not proportionate to their effects may be very unlike their effects, as, say, those who make spoons are very unlike the spoons they make. The disproportion is all the greater between God and the world; hence effects give very little indication indeed of what God is. Thomas will sharpen this distinction in the following questions.

Attempted proofs of God's existence have taken many forms. Thomas finds only a few of them convincing, mostly those originating with Aristotle. He tacitly rejects others, such as those which postulate a material god. All proofs must be able to appeal to some common ground as the context for debate. For Christians, the common ground is Scripture. But Thomas's arguments are meant to be universal in force. They cannot appeal to the witness of Scripture, since the adherents of other faiths or those who do not presently believe in God do not accept its authority. Hence it is necessary to have 'recourse to the natural reason, to which all of us are forced to give their assent' (ScG 1.2.3). But we should note Thomas's justification for that recourse. Those who make use of natural reason – the philosopher or the scientist, say – may acquire true knowledge only because they are illumined by the Word of God: 'if all people coming into this sensible world are illumined by the light of natural reason, this is by their participation in that true light' (*Sup. Ioan.* 1:9, n. 129). The knowledge of the principles by which we can argue rationally

> has been implanted in us by God; for God is the Author of our nature. These principles, therefore, are also contained by the divine Wisdom. Hence, whatever is opposed to them is opposed to the divine Wisdom, and therefore cannot come from God. That which we hold by faith as divinely revealed, therefore, cannot be contrary to our natural knowledge. (ScG 1.7.2)

The condition for the possibility of rational debate between people of diverse traditions is thus conceived theologically. Natural reason is not a neutral forum in any secularistic sense. It, too, is created and sustained by the Word and it would be misunderstood if that basis were ignored. Christians may engage with other traditions on the basis of their own quite particular account of what makes such a rational debate possible. And that account, as we will see more clearly at the end of the dialectic, depends upon the Christian doctrine of God.[4]

Quinque Viae

Thomas begins article 3 by noting two objections to the claim that God exists. The first is a version of the theodicy argument, the problem of evil. God must be good and God must be infinite; both concepts are part of what we mean by the word 'God'. If God exists, then one would think that there would be nothing but goodness, since there would be no room for anything other than goodness, whether it be finite or infinite. However, there is evil in the world, which indicates that God, as defined, could not exist. Thomas follows Augustine in rejecting this challenge on the grounds of salvation history. God permits evil to occur because good – salvation in Jesus Christ – will come from it, thus demonstrating God's infinite goodness. The second argument against God's existence employs a version of Ockham's Razor (a couple of generations before Ockham), namely that the best explanation of something is that which calls the fewest principles into play. The sufficient explanation for all 'natural things' is nature; for all 'voluntary things', it is human reason and will. There is no need to postulate a divine being to explain such things. The response to this now common argument must draw upon the main argument for the existence of God, to which we turn.

The first way (*via*), Thomas says, is the most evident one. It is obvious from our sense experience that all things in the world move or change, and all things which move other things are themselves moved by something else, and so on. There is a causal chain of mover and moved. 'Movement' here means more than a change of place. Thomas refers to what, following Aristotle, he calls 'the reduction of potentiality to act'. With regard to heat, wood is 'in potentiality'. Although it is now not hot, it may become hot by the effect of something else, namely fire. The potentiality is realized, 're-duced to act', when the wood is set on fire. The fire moves the wood in such a way that it changes. Here, then, the causal chain is not simply a linear series stretching back through time, as if it were a series of movements that could be described by a physicist. I noted in Chapter 1 that Thomas does not believe that we can demonstrate either the world's eternity or its creation in time (ST 1.46.2). That the world began at a certain point is a matter of faith. If the causal series were linear and physical there would be no reason why it could not go on indefinitely. It is thus more likely that Thomas's argument moves from observations about the physical world to metaphysical consid-erations. The series in question asserts the impossibility of an infinite chain of sources or *explanations* of movement or change. Thus to continue the wood and fire example, fire is the cause of all heat, but there must be something that enables the fire to be in act, to be what it is, beyond merely the physical fact that someone struck a match. And that something is likely to involve an explanation of how a more remote source was reduced from potentiality to act, too. But this explanatory chain cannot stretch back infi-nitely, or even very far, without one coming upon the mover that is the origin of all movement, of the chain *as a whole* (ST 1.15.2), without which it could not have started. Thomas says that it is this first mover, itself unmoved and unchanged and not explained by anything else, which 'every-one understands to be God' (Wippel, 2000, pp. 444–58).

The next two proofs are somewhat similar in their structure. The second argument replaces the first way's motion with cause. One thing is caused by another, and so on in a series. The causal chain cannot stretch back infi-nitely, hence there must be an originating cause of the series, one which is itself uncaused, to which 'everyone gives the name of God'. Again, by 'cause' Thomas does not simply mean one thing causing another to do or be something, but rather the 'why' of a thing, the explanation of what it is that is also why it is. Aristotle had argued that when one defines the cause of something, one is in fact saying what explains it, what it is and how it came to be. Such explanations cannot reasonably be pushed back to infinity. There must be something that explains why there is anything and everything at all, and that is the uncaused first cause.

The third argument notes that all the things we experience in the world need not exist. We often find that something that existed yesterday no longer exists today, and we know of many things that have come into existence. The argument then appeals to the possibility that, given enough time, it must be that *everything* would exercise this aspect of its contingency and cease to exist. And once that happened, nothing new could come into existence. That possibility has evidently not happened since contingent things presently exist. Therefore there must be something that exists necessarily, without the possibility of non-existence, so as to prevent contingent beings from entirely ceasing to be. And 'this all people speak of as God'.[5]

These three proofs support the notion that the question of God must be raised by anyone who experiences and reflects upon the world. As such, they constitute the reply to the second challenge. Nature and human freedom are insufficient explanations of reality. They change and are contingent; something necessary and unchanging is required to explain them.

The fourth argument relies upon a more Platonic view of language and reality. If one examines things in the world, one sees that, while some things are good, others are better; some are hot, others are hotter, and so on. According to Thomas, there must be a maximum of such things, the hottest, the truest, the best, the most perfectly existing, and so on. These maxima are the causes of all within their respective sets, as fire, which is maximally hot, is the cause of all other heat. But then there must be something that is the cause of the maxima, 'something which is to all beings the cause of their being, goodness, and every other perfection; and this we call God'.

Finally, the fifth way to God's existence is somewhat similar to the 'argument from design' popular today among some of those interested in a dialogue between religion and modern science. The contemporary version argues from the evident fact, supported by scientific data, that the organization of the universe is incredibly complex. Everything fits together and works so wonderfully that it seems reasonable to think that the universe was designed by an intelligent power. Thomas's version of this argument reflects his more Christian notion of creation. Rather than a one-time event that sets up the universe to run on its own, Thomas's understanding of creation includes an ongoing relation to God whereby God sustains and providentially cares for creatures. Natural things act in ways that seem appropriate for them and are usually successful in what they do, even though they cannot think about why they are acting. Worms, for example, flourish as worms without thinking and planning. This could not happen simply by chance. There must be something that directs their action in some way, a being that can think and plan for them: 'and this being we call God'.[6]

Note that Thomas's five ways appeal to our experience of ordinary, earthly realities for his proofs. None of them relies upon reports of miracles or after- or near-death experiences; he makes no appeal to empirical or quasi-empirical evidence. Rather than relying upon anecdotal evidence, he constructs demonstrative arguments. Yet with the possible exception of the argument from design it is unlikely that many people would find these arguments convincing today. Thomas anticipates this somewhat, noting elsewhere that 'many, remaining ignorant of the power of demonstration, would hold in doubt those things that have been most truly demonstrated'; this applies even to those 'reputed to be wise men' (ScG 1.4.5). But it is likely that, while these arguments are far better than naive appeals to someone else's other-worldly experience, they rely upon metaphysical principles that many of us no longer find axiomatic. We are now suspicious of the assumptions we know must lie behind such proofs. And besides, we have become used to thinking and acting as if reality needs no explanation other than its comprehensive description.

Thomas notes elsewhere that bad arguments in favor of the faith should be avoided because they expose it to the laughter of the ungodly (ST 1.46.2). Has he made such a mistake here?[7] It is important to note what the proofs seek to prove. Clearly and explicitly the arguments are not meant to establish belief in the God of Christianity. One needs faith to believe in God, not demonstrations; all that Thomas thinks he has demonstrated is the existence of something we usually name 'God'. Nicholas Lash has suggested that the arguments are not primarily intended to prove the factual existence of God. The article's question, 'Whether God exists?', is not an empirical question. Instead, Thomas's purpose is to develop a simple and very preliminary grammar for 'our handling of "existence talk" in respect of God'. This grammar enables him to show that the one who reveals God to Moses by saying 'I am Who am' (Exodus 3:14 is cited in the *sed contra*) is 'thinkable' for us who live in the ordinary world (Lash, 1996, p. 146). Put another way, Thomas seeks to prove incorrect Wittgenstein's famous dictum at the conclusion of his *Tractatus Logico-Philosophicus* ('Whereof one cannot speak, thereon one must be silent'). There *are* quite reasonable ways of speaking about the mystery of the world; silence is neither enjoined upon us, nor is it appropriate. On this view, then, Thomas's appropriation of philosophical arguments is meant to relieve us of the silence – and what for many of us would be the tedium and meaninglessness – that would be forced upon us if our only alternative to faith as an explanation of reality would be to rely upon the concept of a self-sustaining and autonomous nature.

Note that Thomas does not go outside the sphere of theology to warrant his argument. Instead he brings into that sphere sets of (properly trimmed) concepts appropriated from ancient philosophy and ordinary discourse. The commonalities are a few Aristotelian terms: God is the unmoved mover, the first efficient cause and sole necessary being. Such terms do not establish

anything; they are used because Thomas thinks they are amenable to relocation within a view of the world as created by a loving and merciful God.
Within Thomas's theological project, the arguments function as useful preliminary points of view by which to initiate theological inquiry into the
Creator who is revealed at the beginning of the Old Testament. Thomas may
have thought that they were proofs for the existence of God in the sense that
a non-believing philosopher would be forced by logical necessity to accept
them. But whether he did or not, their function here is not to provide a
secure basis for theology in empirical fact or proven concept. It is instead to
provide some reasonable notions for starting to talk about that which we
commonly name God, as the phrases at the end of each proof have it. The
'God' of the proofs is hardly the God of the Christian faith. At this stage,
that which we commonly call 'God' could easily be something like Aristotle's unmoved mover. Nothing whatsoever has been said about God's nature
or essence, about what or 'who' God is.

Some further insight into Thomas's purpose here can be gleaned from his
commentaries. In his commentary on Romans, Thomas argues that knowledge of God is available to all, citing Wis. 13:5 ('For from the greatness and
the beauty of created things, the Creator of such things can be seen in such a
way as to be known') (*Sup. Rom.* 1:20, n. 118).[8] Thomas mentions three
ways to such knowledge that are similar to the five ways and, like them,
presuppose that the creaturely realm is 'a kind of book [in which] the
knowledge of God may be read' (ibid., n. 116). Through the interior light of
reason we may come to knowledge of 'the invisible things' of God. These
things Thomas appropriates to the Persons of the Trinity: the 'perfections'
of God to the Father; God's 'power' to the Son; God's 'divinity' to the Holy
Spirit, following the traditional reading (ibid., n. 122). However, the scriptural passage which prompts Thomas's discussion indicates that he cannot
be trying to establish natural knowledge of God as a secure basis for theological inquiry. In fact, his intention must be the contrary, since the point of
Romans 1:19f. is to show the uselessness and worse of idolatrous knowledge. The Gentiles know God, indeed, but their knowledge condemns rather
than saves them. The knowledge of God acquired outside Scripture is thus
more of an obstacle to saving truth than a starting-point.[9]

With this in mind, we turn to the prologue of Thomas's commentary on
John's Gospel. There Thomas draws upon Isaiah's vision of God in the
Temple (Is. 6:1ff.) to discuss what makes John's Gospel distinctive. John's
'contemplation' is 'high, full and perfect', in accordance with the vision of
the Lord (Christ) seated on a high throne, the train of whose garment
completely and perfectly fills the temple. The 'ancient philosophers' have
also sought God in contemplation, in four ways this time (in accordance
with Thomas's spiritual reading of the Isaiah passage). John's contemplation also uses each of these four ways, though at a far higher level. If the
knowledge of the philosophers is to save rather than condemn, it must be
transformed into the knowledge available only by becoming 'high, full and

perfect'. John's contemplation is distinctive because, as the beloved friend of Christ, he was drawn up to discern 'the sovereignty, the eternity, the dignity of the Word and his incomprehensibility' (*Sup. Ioan.* prol., n. 6). What is required, then, is a 'contemplative ascent' (Levering, 2000, p. 597) which moves from pagan and idolatrous conceptions of God to the kind of 'contemplation of the nature and the essence of the divine Word' that John uniquely exemplifies (*Sup. Ioan.* prol., n. 7). It is this contemplative ascent towards the perspective of the Word that the dialectic of these questions on the doctrine of God seeks to display.[10]

Establishing language with which to talk about God's existence does not, therefore, take us very far at all; it merely provides us with some linguistic material with which to begin. To gain the kind of knowledge of God that is sufficient for salvation will require our language to be further judged by what we know of God in Jesus Christ. For it is he whose humanity 'showed us our way (*via*) to God' (ST 1.2 prol.) and 'showed unto us in his own person the way (*via*) of truth' (ST 3 prol.). Only by testing all other ways – including the five ways we have just discussed – by his way can we arrive at a true and saving understanding of God.

The Doctrine of the Unknowable God

Transcendence

As Thomas makes clear over the course of the next several questions, the first thing to say is that the kind of God in whom Christians believe is one whom we know only as one whom we cannot know. The point of the next two questions in particular is to emphasize that 'because we cannot know what God is, but rather what God is not, we have no means for considering how God is, but rather how God is not' (ST 1.1.3 prol.). This apophaticism is rather more evident in Thomas than in most of his contemporaries and seems to have come from his reading of Pseudo-Dionysius (Torrell, 1996b, p. 61).

Why is it that God is unknowable? Thomas says little here to support his assertion. On one level, we must think of God primarily as unknown because of the difficulty we have in coming to knowledge of God. We need faith to know what may seem, after we believe, to be quite obvious things. The philosophers were unable, for example, to discover God's 'providence and omnipotence, and that God alone is to be worshipped' (ST 2/2.1.8 ad 1). As Thomas says in the ScG (1.4.4): 'If the only way open to us for the knowledge of God were solely that of the reason, the human race would remain in the blackest shadows of ignorance', partly because our reason is very feeble, and partly because it has been 'clouded by the lusts of sin' (ST 2/2.22.1 ad 1). But beyond our evident feebleness, Thomas also believes that we need the apostolic witness to teach us the limits of human reason even at its best. Scripture shows us that God makes God known to us in what is other than God, so that God remains unknown as God. The Word revealed divinity in humanity, yet not in such a way that the two are mixed together, according to the Creed (ST 3.46.12). We certainly come to know God sufficiently for our salvation through faith in Jesus Christ. But Jesus is not a theophany in the etymological sense of God made visible, since God remains invisible; faith is necessarily of things that are not seen (ST 2/ 2.4.1). The apostles did not and could not see the divine Word as such except in signs which had to be in a mode suitable for us and our senses to know. Thus even at the Transfiguration and the post-Resurrection appearances, what was seen was not Christ's divinity as such, but his glorified *body* (ST 3.45.1; 3.54.2 ad 1).

At the same time, though, to say that God is unknowable is to say something – albeit quite negative – about God and our relation to God. It is an article of faith, one worked out by the church as it rejected alternative conceptions of God that could not be reconciled with Scripture, that God the Creator is transcendent, ontologically separate from what God created out of nothing. Thomas does not explicitly refer to the doctrine here, but it is presupposed by the traditional authorities he cites and it is logically necessary to justify the direction he takes next in his inquiry. Scripture and the Creed initiate and control the dialectical correctives of possible misunderstandings arising from the proofs.

In the first four proofs, various series are proposed, the first in each of which we ordinarily call God. There is nothing in the proofs themselves to indicate that, as the first of a series, God might not be included within that series. And if that were the case, we could argue back from later effects to the originating principle, and conclude to some sort of knowledge of God from the effects. Thomas must block such moves if he is to preserve the Christian doctrine of Creation. God the Creator is entirely self-sufficient and unlike any kind of created being. Hence our knowledge of God, proceeding, as it can only do, from created effects to uncreated cause, is of God as fundamentally unknown (*Sup. Ioan.* prol., n. 6). This is a methodological principle: 'then only do we know God truly when we believe God to be above everything that it is possible for humans to think about God' (ScG 1.5.3). The questions which follow are less a positive description of God than an explication of how to talk about God properly, a grammar of Christian God-talk.

Thomas blocks mistaken inferences from the proofs in question 3, in which he distinguishes between simple and composite being. Unlike any created entity, God is utterly simple or, to put what is really a negative claim in a more obviously negative form: God is not composite, not made up of parts, whether such parts are spatial, temporal or metaphysical. In effect this distinction rules out any reliance upon our imagination in thinking about God because imagination must work with created realities, and these are always composite. The most obvious example of composition is spatial:

God cannot be a body, since a body is divisible into parts. Therefore we cannot know God through our senses, for they require something physical for their operation. Scripture is thus supported in its contention that God is Spirit (John 4:24), and when it talks about God's body, or parts thereof, it must be taken metaphorically. Nor is there composition of time in God. God is, always and completely, so whatever God can do, God does, always and completely. Accordingly, we must not think of God as doing one thing (loving Israel, say) and then deciding to do something else (punishing Israel, say) as if there were some real change going on in God.

Thus the doctrine of God's simplicity makes it very difficult for us to 'think God' after all. By ruling out all ways of moving from knowledge of creatures to knowledge of what God is, Thomas severely restricts all philosophical knowledge of God, including the 'natural theology' of the ancients. The doctrine of divine simplicity also rules out any distinction between potentiality and action in God. All the things that we predicate of God – that God is loving, merciful, just, and the like – God always is, because God *is* love, mercy, justice or, better, God eternally loves and acts mercifully and justly. Created realities may be loving, merciful and just, but only 'by participation', in utter dependence upon God. They may spend considerable parts of their day *not* being actually merciful; they will then be only potentially so. God is never what God could be but is not actually so; God always is and does all that God is.

Thomas pushes this yet further. From his earliest writings he advocated a real distinction between essence and existence in created things. It is not part of the nature of any creature that it exists. Existence and essence, that a thing is and what or how that thing is, are quite different and only contingently related. *What* I am does not imply *that* I am. I am only in so far as I participate in being. I am because my *actus essendi*, the first (metaphysical) act by which I become me, is made possible as I, an effect, participate in and in some sense imitate my cause, the Creator (ST 1.44.1 and 3). The same applies to everything created. In God, however, essence and existence are identical. There can be no distinction drawn between the act by which God is what God is (God's *actus essendi*) and God's 'essential' acts of loving, creating, judging, and so on. God's nature is simply God's Being (*Esse*). There is, as Thomas puts it a bit later, 'only one real operation' in God, namely God's essence (ST 1.30.2 ad 3).[11]

From this Thomas can rule out another false inference from the proofs, namely that God may be placed within a set or class. That seems fairly obvious with regard to most things. Clearly, God as cause is quite different from effects such as animals or rocks. But neither can God be placed within a class as its principle. Principles of classes define the class of which they are the principle. Hence to say that God is the principle of any class would be to limit our understanding of God, for we would have to define God (an impossibility anyway) in a restrictive way so that God could not be the principle of all other sets. Hence God must be the cause of all classes without being a member of any one of them. But, we may ask, what of the class of everything, the set of all things that have being by participation in God's Being? Thomas rules this out, too. Being cannot be the principle of a class because every entity exists in a specific way. There is no such thing as 'existence' or 'being' as such, in the sense that it could be something that is the same everywhere and shared among diverse entities. A horse exists in a way that is quite different from a rock or a person. When we say rocks and horses and people all exist, we therefore use the word 'exist' analogically. That is, we say something different about each of them, but with the understanding that their varied existence participates in God's *Esse* as the cause of their existence.[12] Existence cannot be the defining characteristic of a class.

Because God transcends all classes, including that of being-as-such, we cannot move from knowledge of beings and their participation in being back to knowledge of God's Being. God remains unknown, because God is Being Itself (*Ipsum Esse*), beyond definition and comprehension. God therefore lies outside the sphere of metaphysics, if metaphysics is defined as the study of being (Wippel, 2000, p. 122). However, to move to the next question (ST 1.4.3), if we cannot seek knowledge of God by means of a univocal notion of being, can we not seek knowledge of God by moving *analogically* from effects to their cause? That is, instead of thinking of existence as the same in everything, as a univocal concept, perhaps there is enough of a similarity among existents to their cause that we can establish an analogy of being, an *analogia entis*. Thomas makes a brief reference here to what some Thomistic interpreters later developed into a complex metaphysical theory used to warrant philosophical inquiry into God from effects to knowledge of their cause. Creaturely effects are dependent for their existence upon their participation in the necessary Being. Participation implies imitation, so one could argue that some notion of God's being could be deduced by reasoning from created beings. But Thomas denies this, too. A concept may apply either to God or to creatures. If it applies to God, it may be applied analogically to creatures, because they participate in their cause, though they are radically different from it. But to move from creatures to God by analogy would require an analogous concept that could encompass both the created being and God. And that would be the equivalent of placing both God and a creature in the same class, which Thomas has denied (Wippel, 2000, pp. 571f.).

Hence although there is indeed some kind of analogy between divine cause and created effects, the analogy flows, so to speak, only one way, from God to creatures, but not at all the other way. One cannot establish any knowledge of God – even theological – by means of the *analogia entis* alone. On the contrary – and this is in some sense the more radical proposition – the analogy of being makes it possible to claim that only in knowing something of God can we really know *creatures* as they truly are, as created and thus as more than merely 'natural'. Clearly that is a theological claim, one not grounded upon natural reason alone. According to Thomas, Scripture tells us that created effects are like their cause, but also that their cause is not at all like them: 'Although it may be admitted that creatures are in some sort like God, it must nowise be admitted that God is like creatures' (ST 1.4.3 ad 4).

So we are left after this very forceful and careful establishment of God's transcendence with the notion that God is simple being-in-act, completely realized and utterly different from us. God 'has no genus nor difference, nor can there be any definition of God; nor, save through God's effects, a demonstration of God, for a definition is from genus and difference; and the mean of a demonstration is a definition' (ST 1.3.5). The proofs, then, say absolutely nothing about *how* God is. They demonstrate only that it is reasonable to say that God *is*; they say nothing about what 'is' might mean when said of God. Utterly transcendent, God must not be thought of as the God-particle or the world-soul or some other constitutive element of creation. God is never a part of anything; God cannot 'enter into the composition of anything, either as a formal or a material principle' (ST 1.3.8). God is beyond the reach of all our concepts and is thus best understood as that which is unknown.

Immanence

Thomas's apophatic emphasis is based upon Scripture's emphasis (in John particularly) upon our need for the self-revelation of God in the incarnate Word. We might conclude from what has been said thus far that Thomas holds that God is transcendent in the sense of Wholly Other, that God is a being radically *separate* from creation. It would follow from such a conclusion that it is the ontological gulf separating God from God's creation which prevents our knowledge of God. God's revelation would then have the function, in effect, to bridge the gap, and Jesus Christ would be understood in such terms, as the solution to a cognitive problem.[13] Such a view would lead to a number of troubling questions, not the least of which would be: first, whether creation is truly good if it is so radically separated from its cause, from the good Creator of Genesis 1; second, whether the Incarnation could indeed bridge such a gap rather than be divided by it.[14]

However, Thomas's emphasis on God's transcendence, properly understood, resolves this problem. God is so completely transcendent that God transcends any oppositional contrasts, including presence and absence, as well as ontological separation (see Tanner, 1988). God is so transcendent that God is immanent. 'As the soul is whole in every part of the body, so is God whole in all things and in each one' (ST 1.8.2 ad 3). The challenge to overly simplistic notions of transcendence is, again, fundamentally scriptural and couched here in terms of humanity's origin and goal. We may be redeemed through becoming perfect as our 'heavenly Father is perfect' (Matt. 5:48, ST 1.4.1 *sed contra*), and we are created in the 'image and likeness' of God (Gen. 1:26, ST 1.4.3 *sed contra*).

Thomas situates the discussion of God's immanence by first analyzing the concept of the good (ST 1.4–6). Is God good because God is God and thus defines what is good? Or do we know God is good because God meets our criteria of what is perfectly good? If the former, i.e., if God is simply good because God is God, then our concept of good seems arbitrary. If God is good because God conforms to our concept of goodness, then we define God. Thomas avoids this problem by defining the good neutrally and ontologically. Whatever we desire is a good, whether or not what is sought is morally or objectively good. When I desire something, that thing becomes a goal for me to achieve, causing me to act with the intention of attaining it. The object is thus what Thomas, following Aristotle, calls the final cause of my action. Since we are born with the desire for things other than ourselves, we have a natural inclination towards the good (irrespective, to repeat, of the morality of any particular good we may desire). The objective goodness of something, its goodness apart from our desire for it, is determined by the perfection of its being (ST 1.4 prol.). To ascertain the goodness of something we ask: what kind of being is it? And further: how completely itself is it? Thus a flower is better than a rock, and a living and well-made flower better than a dying or diseased one. Being and good are thus convertible: what is, is good; what is more completely itself, is better. A thing is evil to the extent that it lacks being in some way and is therefore imperfect in the sense of incomplete.

Thus far the conceptual analysis of question 5 could be done by philosophy. In the next question, though, Thomas appropriates the analysis for the doctrine of God. 'God alone is good essentially' (ST 1.6.3). As with existence, so also with goodness: all that is good, is good by participation in God's goodness. But God does not need anything other than God to be good. So God does not desire anything other than God. God is completely God, self-sufficient and fully-realized Being. God is entirely good, then, because God is perfect (the Latin, *perfectus*, draws together both being and goodness with its connotations of 'complete' and 'realized'). Created things can be good, but their goodness is dependent upon God's. There is no reversal; their goodness cannot increase the goodness of God since 'a relation of God to creatures is not a reality in God, but in the creature; for it is in God in our idea only' (ST 1.6.2 ad 1). All creatures have a natural desire for the good. God is the fullness of goodness, the most perfectly realized being, since God is essentially existing. So creatures, especially humans, naturally desire and, implicitly at least, tend towards God, who is their ultimate end. We are thus related to God not only as our origin but also as our final cause, the goal of our actions. Being is convertible with goodness, so the goodness of our being is increased the more we move towards God in our actions. Thus one's desire for the good is grounded in more than morality; it is ontologically transformative. The more we are inclined to God as our final end, i.e., the more we desire and act for the best kind of good, the more our very being is transformed and the more we become like God.

Thomas can now consider God's immanence in terms of God's infinity. If 'it belongs to the infinite to be present everywhere, and in all things' (ST 1.8 prol.), this must apply to God in an absolute and unique way. The essence of God is present in all things but never as, or part of, their essence, nor as something added, but 'as an agent is present to that upon which it acts' (ST 1.8.1). God acts to bring creatures into existence, and continues to act to maintain them in *their* act of existence. It is this action which is fundamental to the goodness of created things. Yet because God is not the being of things as such, but the ground of their being, God's presence does not exclude others from being in a place. Indeed, 'by the fact that God gives being to the things that fill every place, God fills every place' (ST 1.8.2). There is no spatial or ontological competition between God and creatures. On the contrary, it is because God is everywhere that we can truly be and act, and be good. (This, as we will see later, is a vital point when we come to Thomas's doctrine of grace and merit.)

God's Knowledge

More will need to be said later about the action of God in creatures. But already it is worth noting one consequence of Thomas's inquiry, namely that mystery lies at the heart of created being. The existence of things is not merely a puzzle to be solved as we gain more knowledge; it is essentially beyond complete explanation. Something is, and is what it is, because of its created relation to God. Creation, then, cannot be fully comprehended. Thomas takes this further in questions 14 and 15, where he considers God's own self-knowledge and how God knows what is other than God. The key theological concept here is the 'Word', which links God's self-knowledge with God's creative activity, and with the possibility of knowledge on our part both of God and of any created reality.

The term 'knowledge' must be trimmed for it to apply to God. Thomas has a complex theory of human knowledge, the later treatment of which (ST 1.84ff.) he assumes here as a starting-point in order to deny its application to God. When we see a table, we do not know the particular thing we are looking at; we only sense it. Our intellect does not know what we see – matter – as such, for it is unintelligible. Only as our active intellect abstracts the form – the idea of a 'table', its 'intelligible species' – from the colors and shapes we see, can we know what our senses bring to us. In knowing, moreover, we change, because whatever we know acts upon us in some way, upon our senses or our memory. We are therefore partly passive towards what is known. Such things cannot be said of God without denying God's simplicity as pure act, for God has no senses and cannot be acted upon or change. So it becomes difficult to talk about how God knows. For Aristotle, the problem was resolved by asserting that God has no consciousness of creatures, only self-knowledge. For Plotinus, God could have no consciousness at all because God transcends consciousness. Thomas could not accept the latter view, on the principle that God must have whatever we have if it is good, and consciousness is obviously good to a pre-eminent degree. So God has consciousness. But Thomas could not say that God knows creatures directly. Creatures are contingent, so God's knowledge would change as they changed. So God must know creatures through God's self-consciousness. We know the intelligible species or forms, but God does not. 'In God, intellect, the object understood, the intelligible species, and God's act of understanding are entirely one and the same' (ST 1.14.4).

To make sense of this Thomas relies upon concepts that he would later develop in explicitly Trinitarian language.[15] God's self-consciousness is the Word, through whom God knows created things. The Word 'is the likeness not only of God, as God's self-understanding, but also of all those things of which the divine essence is the likeness' (ScG 1.53.5). Thomas reworks the concept of 'idea' here to say that in the Word are the 'ideas' of everything. These ideas are divine and eternal. They are not the created substantial forms of Aristotle by which something is what it is and is knowable as such, since 'God does not understand things according to an idea existing outside God' (ST 1.15.1 ad 1). Furthermore, the ideas not only bear upon knowledge of created things; they also cause them because, for God, to know is the same as to act. Thus they are exemplary ideas rather than mere types of created things, divine originals which, as they are imitated by created things, cause those things to be (ST 1.15.3).

> The likeness of things in the divine intellect is one which causes things; for, whether a thing has a vigorous or a feeble share in the act of being, it has this from God above; and because each thing participates in an act of existence given by God, the likeness of each is found in God. Consequently, the immaterial likeness in God is a likeness, not only of the form, but also of the matter. (*De Veritate* (DV) 2.5)

The exemplary ideas, then, are that in God which each creature imitates analogously as they are known by God (DV 2.3 ad 4). In God's intellect, 'all the distinctions between things are predefined by God' so there is a divine idea for every single particular created thing (DV 3.2).[16] DV moves directly into Trinitarian language. The Word is the Son, the second person of the Trinity, who 'expresses all creatures' (DV 4.4). As the Word, the Son is 'not merely that by which the arrangement of all creatures takes place; [but] … the arrangement itself which the Father makes of things to be created' (DV 4.5 ad 6).

As Thomas trims more concepts for theological use in the next few questions, it becomes evident that his initial conclusion, that sense data are our only means to knowledge of an essentially unknowable God, must be understood in a somewhat different light. It is not knowledge of God that is the fundamental problem. Objectively and theologically speaking, God is utterly knowable and perfectly comprehensible, albeit only by God

(ST 1.14). Moreover, created things are fully comprehensible, but only in the same way, only as God knows them in knowing God. Full comprehension of *created* realities is therefore beyond us, too, except in so far as we are given access to God's creative self-knowledge. This is best said in its properly Trinitarian form: 'the Father, by understanding Himself, the Son, and the Holy Spirit, and all other things comprised in this knowledge, conceives the Word; so that thus the whole Trinity is spoken in the Word; and likewise also all creatures' (ST 1.34.1 ad 3). In so far as we truly know anything created, we participate in something of God's self-knowledge, God's Word.

Talking about God

It is not necessary to trace out Thomas's dialectical inquiry throughout the remaining questions leading to the doctrine of the Trinity (which begins with question 27). He continues to modify further concepts so that they may be applicable to God. These include life (question 18), will (19), love (20), justice and mercy (21), power (23–5) and finally beatitude (26). In asserting that God loves, has absolute free will, and the like, Thomas may seem to be talking quite a bit about God as known, and this raises once again the issue of theological language and our knowledge of God. Thomas discusses this in questions 12 and 13. Question 12 considers the knowledge of God possible for those who have attained eternal bliss, while 13 discusses the knowledge possible for those who are still on their journey through life but who have been united to God 'as to one unknown' through grace. The eschatological distinction is sharply drawn here (as it often is elsewhere). The blessed in heaven will find their eternal and perfect happiness in the vision of the very essence of God. Accordingly, they will be *comprehensores*, those who comprehend God, not in the strict sense of knowing God's infinity, since they remain created and thus finite, but in the sense of attaining to full knowledge of God by means of the gift of the 'light of glory'. That light enables them to go beyond their natural powers and makes them 'deiform' (ST 1.12.5). Thomas's guiding text here is 1 John 2:2: 'we shall see God as God is'.

Coming up with appropriate language by which to talk about God will obviously not be an issue for the *comprehensores*. They always contemplate God and have no need to talk of God. But for us who still journey along the way (*via*) of Jesus Christ, we who are *viatores* (wayfarers), the matter is very different, since 'God cannot be seen in God's essence by mere human beings, except they be separated from this mortal life' (ST 1.12.11). Here on earth, as we have seen, knowledge must come through our senses, either directly, or indirectly through reasoning about what we know directly. Our language must be drawn from the world around us, from the things we know through our senses. This is true even when we talk about matters of faith. Those who preach the Gospel must use earthly language. The question is, then, can we say something true about God? Can our language have any real application to the transcendent God?

Thomas's answer, as we might expect, is a very carefully limited 'Yes'. Jesus Christ is the revealed Word of God. He is Truth in his divinity, and in uniting himself to humanity he makes truth known to us (*Sup. Ioan.* 8:28, n. 1192). Jesus taught the apostles divine wisdom using human words and actions, and sent them to do likewise for others. Thus Thomas cannot accept the strong agnostic view exemplified for him particularly in the work of the Jewish theologian of the previous century, Moses Maimonides (1135–1204), according to whom we cannot know or say anything true about God because God transcends our intellectual capacities. If that were so, it would seem that a preacher's words could convey only personal or traditional opinion, not the truth of the Gospel. One could not even genuinely disagree with the preacher, because neither party could say something true or false, merely present alternative beliefs. Thomas's expressed intent, however, is to follow Christ obediently by teaching the knowledge of God. This includes refuting mistakes, but unless more than that is possible for us, we can do no more than erect a protective linguistic wall around what must remain an utter blank.

So we must after all be able to make positive claims about God. Thomas notes that certain words refer to what he calls 'perfections'. Most good things become bad if we have too much of them, such as warmth, good wine and food, shelter (houses can be too big). But we cannot have too much life; nor can something be too good or beautiful or true. These are perfections. Perfection words may be applied to God in a positive way once they have been trimmed by what Thomas calls 'remotion', so that all that applies to creatures is removed, and the words raised up (by the 'way of eminence') to the level of God. When this is done, perfection words may say something that truly signifies the divine substance. God *is* life, good, truth, wisdom and so on. We, in contrast, are 'good' only in a creaturely, composite and finite way, by participation and imitation, as we have life, beauty, will, love and so on. Thus these words are analogical concepts. The primary meaning of 'good' is that which can be attributed properly only to God. Creatures are not 'good' in the same sense, so the word 'good' cannot be applied to God and, say, to saints in a univocal way. Yet because the saints are good by participation in God's goodness, they are not good in a merely equivocal way. Nor is the similarity in the two uses of the word merely metaphorical, as when the relation is one of ideas alone. We speak metaphorically of God when we say that God is a rock, joining God and rock by the idea of solidity and strength, but with no real similarity. The usage of the word 'good' reflects a real, not merely notional, similarity, due to the ontological dependence of the saints upon God. Hence the word 'good' is used analogically of saints, properly of God.

Yet how can we apply a word 'properly' to God? We cannot, because we do not know God well enough to be able to say what the word 'is' means in a sentence such as 'God is good'. Thomas puts the matter in terms borrowed from contemporary grammarians. 'As regards what is signified by these names, they belong properly to God ... But as regards their mode of signification, they do not properly and strictly apply to God; for their mode of signification applies to creatures' (ST 1.13.3). That is, words like 'good' *do* signify something true about God, so they may be applied properly. But we cannot know *how* they apply (their mode of signification). We know how the word 'good' applies to a saint since we have a concept of the good which we use after we have assessed the saint's manner of life. But we cannot do that to God. Hence, while it is the case that '[o]ur intellect, which is led to the knowledge of God from creatures, must consider God according to the mode derived from creatures' (ST 1.39.8), this does not mean that we can move from knowledge of created effects to knowledge of their divine cause. The analogy of being still flows only one way. But it does mean that we can preach about God and say things about God with sufficient precision that we can distinguish between statements such as 'God is One' and 'God is Truth'. Theological concepts have enough meaning that they are not merely synonymous; words may be used analogously to say something true about God.

The Trinity

By question 27, Thomas is in a position to discuss the doctrine of the Trinity explicitly. The doctrine constitutes and orders the Christian doctrine of God, including the church's use of the word 'is' as it answers the question, Who is God? Thomas's treatment of the doctrine consists of only fifteen questions, about the same number as his discussion of angels (his discussion of virtues is far more expansive). He can be comparatively brief because, as we have seen, the earlier discussion has anticipated quite a bit of what he must say here. In questions 27 to 42, Thomas is still primarily concerned with theological language, with clarifying the rules for proper talk about God, though here the language is explicitly Trinitarian. As a result, his treatment is formal and tends to be rather dry. This tendency is exacerbated by Thomas's decision to begin with God as such, the immanent Trinity, before considering God the Creator and Redeemer, the economic Trinity.

Some Criticisms of Thomas

The formality of Thomas's treatment of the Trinity has led some theologians to criticize his doctrine of God as insufficiently concrete and too detached from the scriptural narrative of salvation history. Among the most prominent critics is Karl Rahner, who has argued that Thomas follows 'the Augustinian and western conception of the Trinity'. Having begun with an extended philosophical treatment of the unity of God, 'the nature common to all three persons', by the time Thomas considers the divine persons, 'it looks as though everything important about God which touches ourselves has already been said' (Rahner, 1982, pp. 83f.). Rahner contrasts this approach with that of the Greek Fathers who, he says, worked in the reverse direction, from the threeness of God to the oneness. He contends that Thomas's approach isolates the doctrine of the Trinity from the rest of his theology and results in an essentialist and static conception of God. So Rahner prefers to begin, like the Greeks, with the person of the Father rather than the divine essence.[17]

It seems likely that Rahner's criticism draws in part upon the work of Théodore de Régnon who, at the end of the nineteenth century, made the distinction between the Western and the Eastern doctrines of the Trinity. De Régnon's thesis has been challenged in recent years (e.g., Emery, 2000). We might note, for example, that John Damascene, the Greek Father whose work Thomas cites frequently later in the ST, moves in a 'Western' way in his *The Orthodox Faith*, from God's unity to God's triunity.[18]

But the more significant consideration is that criticisms like Rahner's mistakenly assume that Thomas works in a unidirectional fashion. In this and the previous chapter, I have tried to show that the logical movement of Thomas's inquiry works in at least two directions, neither of which can be reduced to the other. The doctrine of God in ST 1.2–26 is not demonstrative in the sense of moving from established principles to ever more detailed and complete conclusions. It is a dialectic guided throughout by Scripture read according to the articles of faith. Without some knowledge of those articles the inquiry cannot be properly understood. Only the most superficial reader could fail to be puzzled over Thomas's account of the relation between God's simplicity and God's self-knowledge. Moreover, God's transcendence would indicate that God is utterly solitary, as one in an absolute sense that rules out any kind of plurality. Yet, says Thomas, God's immanence requires us to think of God as somehow containing within God what is other than God. Does it really? I can find no reason within the argument to that point for thinking it should. What prompts Thomas to move in that direction rather than any other is his concern to break apart ordinary and essentialist conceptions of God's unity so that our doctrine of God conforms to Scripture and thus to the doctrine of the Trinity.[19]

For Christian readers the conclusions of the dialectic are already known. The oneness of God is emphasized throughout Scripture. The theological tradition, especially in the West, had stressed that when God operates *ad extra*, upon that which is not God, God's actions are indivisible; they are the work of the one God. Yet, as Thomas notes in the initial article of question 27, Scripture also requires us to acknowledge that there is some kind of plurality and relationality in God. Jesus's teaching about himself in John 8:42 speaks expressly of 'processions' within God (ST 1.27.1 *sed contra*: 'Our Lord says, "From God I proceeded"'). Thomas's Christian readers learn from Thomas how to think about God more profoundly by watching how he reworks ordinary and philosophical language so that it can serve the Gospel.

Thomas's discussion of the immanent Trinity in questions 27–42 is as much the starting-point for the dialectic of questions 2–26 as it is their conclusion, for it is the key to the moves he makes in the course of the dialectical inquiry. But his treatment of the immanent Trinity is not the starting-point, either. Like the doctrine of God as One, it, too, can be understood only after we have some notion of the doctrine of the economic Trinity. What God is as such can be known and talked about properly only when we consider the scriptural account of God's dealings with creation and Israel, and God's work in the person and work of Jesus Christ and his apostolic church. The dialectic of these questions is governed by a logical movement in the reverse direction. The starting-point is with Scripture. On that basis, Thomas shows that the church's use of Trinitarian language to talk of the economy of salvation is fitting. The doctrine of the economic Trinity is then the basis for a similar kind of argument showing that the church's teaching about how we should speak of God as such – the doctrine of the immanent Trinity – is fitting, too. And that in its turn makes it possible to show how we can develop fitting theological concepts and even, to a limited degree, appropriate a few things that people have said about God in their ordinary or their philosophical talk.

Why, then, does Thomas muddle the matter in this way? Why not begin the ST with Scripture and the doctrine of the economic Trinity? Simply laying out the doctrine would have required Thomas to spend far too much time ruling out linguistic misunderstandings. His dialectical procedure is a remarkably economical way of dealing clearly and summarily with an immense amount of material. More significant, though, is Thomas's evident concern to challenge and deepen his readers' ordinary understanding of God. Elsewhere he notes that there are two ways of 'acquiring knowledge: by discovery and by being taught; the way of discovery is the higher' (ST.3.9.4 ad 1). Thomas did not think that obedience to Jesus Christ is ever straightforward or easy. Even when we have the help of Scripture, we must struggle against idolatry and sin in our teaching and practice. It is thus more appropriate that Thomas's readers are not simply 'taught' the knowledge of God they need; they are led to 'discover' it as they follow the intellectual struggle displayed in Thomas's dialectic.

If this view of Thomas's method is more or less correct, and if Rahner's criticisms are misplaced, then we will expect to find that all of Thomas's theology is structured and guided by the doctrine of the Trinity, rather than by an essentialist and static conception of God. I hope to show that such is indeed the case.[20]

The Immanent Trinity

Thomas begins his inquiry into the Trinity with what he has already established, namely God's self-sufficiency. If God's oneness is to be maintained, divine processions and relations must be internal to God's being. If 'procession' means God moves outward to something other than God it would follow that, because divine processions are necessary and eternal, that into which they processed would be necessary and eternal, too. God would not be able *not* to create what is other than God. God's creative act would not be freely willed and creation itself would be necessary for God to be God; creation would be quasi-divine. But God knows and loves God with a joy that is complete (ST 1.14, 20 and 26). God is utterly self-sufficient and has no need whatsoever of creation:

> As the creature proceeds from God in diversity of nature, God is outside the order of the whole creation, nor does any relation to the creature arise from God's nature ... Therefore there is no real relation in God to the creature ... [whose] very nature entails dependence upon God. (ST 1.28.1 ad 3)

Knowledge, love and joy are therefore immanent within God; they are eternal acts that require no created being for their realization.

If we can speak of procession only within God's being as such, then we must speak of the immanent Trinity in logical – though obviously not real – distinction from the economic Trinity. Talking about the internal actions of the immanent Trinity may seem out of place for so apophatic a theologian as Thomas. But his concern is not to offer a description of God, as if he were making factual claims about what goes on 'inside' God's very being. Thomas has explicitly ruled out the possibility of speculative knowledge of the immanent Trinity. So what he says with regard to the Trinity does not follow of rational necessity. It is conceivable that other ways of talking might be possible which could support what must be said with equal or greater fittingness (ST 1.32.1 ad 2). The point of the exercise is to trim away any language with misleading connotations that could lead to error. As Thomas notes in the first article (ST 1.27.1), major heresies have arisen from misunderstandings of words such as 'procession'.

Thomas's teaching on the Trinity is traditional, but he develops the tradition in some interesting and original ways. To explicate the scriptural witness to the triune God, we have no alternative but to find suitable analogies from within creation. Following Augustine, Thomas considers the human mind to be the most fitting source of analogies. In his treatise, *On the Trinity*, Augustine had expounded his teaching using the triad of memory, intelligence and love (or will) he found within the human mind (book 9). In his earlier work, Thomas had tried to follow Augustine's lead, but he seems to have been dissatisfied with the results. This may have been because the analogy could be misleadingly interpreted (as it was by Peter Lombard) in terms of three faculties or powers of the one human soul. The three persons are then reduced to three ways by which the divine essence operates. This would introduce the notion of potentiality in God, undermining God's simplicity; it would make it difficult to make any sense of the relations between the persons; and it would make the divine essence the agent rather than the persons, potentially reducing the doctrine to monotheism.[21]

In the ST Thomas transforms Augustine's basic idea by speaking of God's acts rather than God's psychology, using an analogy drawn 'from the actions which remain in the agent' (ST 1.27.5). The internal actions of God constitute the real relations among the three persons. The Father's action is as the principle of the Son, who is Word and who, with the Father, acts as the origin of the Holy Spirit, who is Love. Word, Love and other needed terms have already been partially prepared in the earlier discussion. Now they must be fully reworked for them to take their proper place in the doctrine of the Trinity. (It is their 'proper' place because, we recall, the words 'love' and 'knowledge' are analogous words primarily signifying God, and only derivatively about created things.)

Thomas has already prepared for the analogy of the Word by reworking the notion of an internal word (ST 1.14). God knows God as the Father generates the Word. The Son is the expression of the Father in the same divine substance. This should not be misunderstood along essentialist lines, as if the Word is simply the self-knowledge of the divine substance, on the analogy of my words expressing who I am. What the Word expresses is the Trinity of persons and, in them, every other reality: 'the Father, by understanding himself, the Son, and the Holy Spirit, and all other things comprised in this knowledge, conceives the Word'. The Word is therefore the person who 'speaks' the triune God; in being spoken, 'each [divine] person understands and is understood' (ST 1.34.1 ad 3; see Williams, 2001, p. 262). God remains purely active in this self-knowledge since God is not acted upon by anything other than God; whatever God knows in the Word is God.

The Word is a proper or personal name of the Son, because a 'proper name signifies that whereby the person is distinguished from all other persons' (ST 1.33.2). 'Word' is thus not an 'essential name', because essential names apply to all three persons in so far as they together, as the three persons, constitute the divine essence. Another scripturally sanctioned way of talking about the Son is as the 'Image', which is also a personal name, since image in this case refers to the relation with the Father (ST 1.35.2).

Somewhat similar things may be said of the third person. The operative analogy here is from the will rather than (as with the Word) the intellect, in order to reflect the scriptural idea that God is Love. Scripture is rather less forthcoming about the Holy Spirit, providing us with fewer analogies. We do not even have a proper name, and must be content with Holy Spirit (ST 1.36.1). All we can say about the relations within the immanent Trinity depends upon the origins of the persons. The Father is unoriginate, so he is distinct from the other two. The Word proceeds by way of generation from the Father. What distinguishes the procession of the Holy Spirit from the Son is that, unlike the Word, who proceeds from the Father, the Spirit proceeds from both the Father *and* the Son (the *filioque* of the Western Creeds). This does not mean, though, that the procession of the second person was prior to that of the third: 'the procession of the Holy Spirit is coeternal with the Spirit's principle. Hence ... each of the operations is eternal' (ST 1.36.3 ad 3).

The Word proceeds from the Father by generation, following Scripture. We need another term to refer to the procession of the Holy Spirit, otherwise we would have no way to distinguish the relation of second and third persons to the Father. So we use the word 'spiration', breathing forth. The Love that proceeds from the Father and the Son by spiration is the proper name for the Holy Spirit. So too is 'Gift', for it is the Holy Spirit who is given to us as we are salvifically united to God by participation in God's love. Accordingly, there must be 'an aptitude' in the Holy Spirit for being given (ST 1.38.1). The Holy Spirit had been understood (by Augustine, for example) to be the medium between the Father and the Son, subsisting as their love. But this threatens to undermine the threeness of the persons, since Love can be taken as both a personal name and an essential name, applicable either to the Spirit or to God as such. Love is indeed common to all three persons and thus pertains to the divine essence. But since the Father and the Son also 'produce' love that is in a sense more and other than their relation, the Holy Spirit is said to proceed from them as a distinct person (ST 1.37.1 ad 3; 1.37.2 ad 2).

We now have words to talk about God's triunity. Thomas carefully lays out the rules for their proper use, some of which we have already seen. There are various ways to say something about God. If we need to talk about one or other of the persons, we have at least three ways. First, we can use the proper names of the persons: Love, Word, Image, Gift, Father, Son, and so on. These must be applied *only* to their respective person (except for love, as we have seen). Second, we can also distinguish each person from the others by means of what Thomas calls their 'notional acts', ideas that reflect what pertains to one or two of the persons in relation to the others (ST 1.32.2). We can apply the notion of 'innasciability' (unoriginateness, 'born from no one') and 'paternity' to the Father, but not to the other two. Unlike the Father and the Holy Spirit, we can apply 'filiation' (begottenness) to the Son. To both Father and Son we may apply 'common spiration'. Because they both breathe out the Holy Spirit, that notion is not a property in the sense of being applicable to only one of the persons. Of the Holy Spirit we may predicate 'procession' alone, since the Holy Spirit comes from others and nothing comes from it (ST 1.32.3). Clearly, these five notions, as well as the proper names, are as much negations as positive descriptions, for they do little more than deny of the others what one can say of one person; positively, they are attributes of relation only (ScG 4.14.15).

Third, we may 'appropriate' to one of the persons certain of the essential attributes or actions. Thomas defines appropriation as 'to contract something common [i.e., shared], making it something proper' (DV 7.3). Thus we may talk of the Father as Power, the Son as Wisdom and the Holy Spirit as Goodness, but in fact each attribute applies to all. This may get quite confusing. 'Love', as we have already seen, may be either a proper name or an essential attribute, and because of its dual role it may not be appropriated. In light of this discussion, Thomas goes on to clarify the usage of certain phrases or to rule them out as incorrect. One cannot say, for example, 'God begot God who is God the Father', since this confuses notional and essential attributes (ST 1.39.4).

Thomas uses linguistic clarification to avoid the classical Trinitarian heresies. The three persons' proper names and their respective notions cannot be *merely* appropriations, for the processional relations in God are real, not metaphorical. The persons are not, then, merely three ways of usefully dividing up God's various actions in salvation history, as a modalist might contend. God really exists as three persons in relation (ScG 4.14.11). A more sophisticated form of modalism, one that is a reasonable inference from Peter Lombard's interpretation of Augustine's analogy of the triad of faculties, is to assert that the three persons are subsequent to the unity. Metaphysical priority would be given to the essence, rather as if it could exist and be talked about apart from the persons. (This is, of course, the crux of Rahner's criticism.) Thomas is aware of the problem and clearly and explicitly rules this out by asserting that 'in God relation and essence do not differ from each other, but are one and the same' (ST 1.28.2). There is no substrate of essential deity from which the three persons arise (ST 1.40.3). The divine essence is not an agent apart from the agency of the three persons (ST 1.28.2 ad 2). God 'is' Trinity.

The distinction between essence and persons is necessary if we are to talk about God fittingly. We have, as it were, to maintain two perspectives upon God which cannot be synthesized. These perspectives require what Gilles Emery calls a 'redoublement of language' in our inquiry into the doctrine of the Trinity, if we wish to follow Thomas (Emery, 2000, p. 530). There are real relations within God, based upon God's actions, so we must at some point talk about the threeness, about the persons. Yet the relations constitute God's essence and God acts essentially, so we must also talk about God's action as a unity. The key is to be clear about which perspective we are taking, and make sure we balance it with the other.

Both perspectives are necessary, for the essence is the persons, and 'the persons are the subsisting relations themselves' (ST 1.40.2 ad 1). This rules out some forms of subordinationism, since it follows that the Father cannot be the Father prior to the processions. 'The Son is co-eternal with the Father, and likewise the Holy Spirit is co-eternal with both' (ST 1.42.2). On the other hand, if we talk about the persons without at some point talking about the essence they constitute, we may fall into tritheism. In part the difficulty here has to do with the word 'person'. Thomas notes that it is not found within Scripture and was appropriated and reworked in order to counter heretical notions of God. He quotes Jerome to the effect that 'a heresy arises from words wrongly used' (ST 1.31.2). Ordinary uses of 'person' must be defined so as to be applicable analogously to God, who is person in a more excellent way than we are. Thomas defines person as 'a subsistent individual of a rational nature' (ST 1.29.3). The usual understanding of person might stress the individual aspect, meaning a self-subsisting being that exists as such and thus *apart* from relations with others. This would suggest three individual gods. One could avoid the error by saying that the three persons exist as the *product* of a single essence. But this gets us back to the more sophisticated form of modalism, for the oneness of God would be metaphysically prior to the threeness.

Once again, Thomas avoids the difficulty by making careful stipulations about language. For Thomas, 'person' is *always* relational: 'it is used to express relation ... by the force of its own proper signification' (ST 1.29.4). Therefore, 'since relation, considered as really existing in God, is the divine essence itself, and the essence is the same as person, ... relation must necessarily be the same as person' (ST 1.40.1). For 'distinction in God is only by relation of origin ... Relation in God is not as an accident in a subject, but is the divine essence itself' (ST 1.29.4).

Conclusion

At ST 1.43 Thomas begins to move his focus away from the doctrine of the immanent Trinity to that for which it is the conceptual and linguistic preparation, namely the doctrine of the triune God as creator and redeemer. This I will take up in the next and subsequent chapters.

While complex and abstract, the doctrine of God covered in this chapter is far from static and essentialist. The essence of God is dynamic, relational, in act. God is truly God, in that God has no need of, or relation to, what is not God. Yet God is personal, loving and joyful. The doctrine of the immanent Trinity as Thomas develops it reflects the mystery that God is and the consequent difficulty we have in speaking of God fittingly. The complexity of the doctrine requires him to make his language as precise as possible. We must talk about God sometimes in terms of threeness and relationality, at other times in terms of oneness and essence, and at yet other times in terms of the actions of one or other of the persons. All these ways are needed to preach on, and witness to, the Christian God. Speaking truly of God as unknown requires training and hard work, for it is all too easy to misuse words. Here, then, we have seen something of the intellectual effort involved in attempting to follow the way of Jesus Christ obediently.

Notes

1   Anselm sets his argument in the context of prayer, which gives it a somewhat different force from a philosophical proof of the usual kind, since prayer presumes the existence of God. His proof may be better construed as a reflection upon theological language.

2 For example among some of those who maintain a pluralistic theory of religion or who begin with a phenomenological account of religious consciousness.

3 That said, the membership of the Body of Christ is much broader for Thomas than for some later theologians, and faith may be attached fairly loosely to the particularity of Jesus Christ. See the discussion in Chapter 6 below.

4 Accordingly, Thomas cannot be a correlationist *avant le temps*. Correlation theology understands Christian doctrine or practice as something sufficiently self-contained that it can be correlated with some other similarly self-contained body of knowledge or practice, usually that of a particular culture or society, such as 'modern man' or 'modern scientific thought'. The latter may, though it need not, claim to embody a universal and thus neutral rationality. Thomas undercuts a key premise of any correlation theology, critical or otherwise. For him, Christian theology does not move 'outside' its boundaries to engage with other forms of inquiry. On the contrary, it relocates those inquiries on to the boundary-less ground of the Gospel.

5 This argument is complex and confusing and I have offered what I think is the best reading. For discussion and literature, see Wippel (2000), pp. 462–9. Perhaps Thomas has in mind the near destruction of creation in the Flood and the preservation of contingent creatures at that time by the action of the necessary existent.

6 In an expansion of this proof later in the ST (1.103.1), the underlying fittingness aspect of this argument becomes more evident. We must decide what is appropriate and successful in the actions of natural things by judgment rather than demonstration.

7 I am assuming here that the arguments are not convincing. Some might think they are. The following points apply regardless.

8 I cite Thomas and the Vulgate here. Interestingly, the Catholic version of the New American Bible (New York: Oxford University Press, 1990) muddies the waters considerably and unwarrantably. Its version reads: 'For from the greatness and the beauty of created things their original author, *by analogy*, is seen' (my italics).

9 See Rogers (1995, chs 5 and 6) for a more detailed discussion of the *Commentary on Romans* from a slightly different perspective and agenda, though arriving at much the same reading.

10 I am indebted to Matthew Levering (2000) for this understanding of Thomas's reading of John. Levering's account is much more detailed than I have room for here and should be consulted. I can't quite follow him, though, in his assertion that 'John's contemplation, Aquinas suggests, attains and … presupposes the conclusions about God's essence reached metaphysically by the greater philosophers' (p. 615). Thomas draws a parallel, not a movement, from one to the other. Indeed, the movement would seem to be cut off by the last way he mentions, which is the acknowledgement of the incomprehensibility of divine Truth. Levering seems to agree on p. 616.

11 For the details of Thomas's metaphysics see Wippel (2000).

12 I push Thomas a bit more than he goes himself here to prepare for the point of the next paragraph. It is a temptation, usually best resisted, to fill out theoretical gaps in what Thomas says in one place with material drawn from elsewhere. Here I borrow from ST 1.13.5, where Thomas talks about analogical predication. I discuss that text below in this chapter.

13 I refer here to the kind of transcendence arguably found in early Barth.

14 That is, if humanity is on one side of the gap, and divinity on the other, it becomes very hard to make sense of Chalcedon. One or other must be downplayed and either the humanity lost in a spiritualization of Christ, or the divinity in his humanity.

15 Thomas's discussion in ST 1.14 and 15 avoids anticipating his Trinitarian doctrine as much as possible, though the doctrine is implicit throughout. To avoid an overly prolix analysis, I have supplemented the ST treatment with the parallels in ScG (which *is* explicitly though not extensively Trinitarian in its language, even in book 1) and with important material from the *De Veritate* (cited as DV). I am indebted here especially to John L. Farthing's discussion of divine ideas (Farthing, 1985).

16 Thus the ideas are not Platonic either. That said, it is evident that Thomas appropriates elements from the Platonic tradition quite heavily here.

17 See Rahner (1982). A number of theologians have come to the defense of Thomas against Rahner, including Rowan Williams (2001) and Gilles Emery (1995 and 2000).

18 Matthew Levering points this out (2000, p. 594). See John Damascene, *The Orthodox Faith*, book one. The parallel between John's book one and ST 1.2–43 is striking. John moves from proving the existence of God (ch. 3) to considering God's nature (chs 4 and 5), and then discusses the immanent Trinity (chs 6 and 7). It is likely that Rahner's criticisms of Thomas are prompted by his concern to overcome the legacy of Neo-Scholastic monotheism.

19 Not that Thomas wrote for non-Christians. My point is that, were they to read the ST, they would find it difficult to accept some of the turns in the argument as having any kind of necessity.

20 I should repeat that my case is indebted to pioneers among Thomas scholars, especially Jean-Pierre Torrell, OP, for whose account of Thomas's Trinitarian theology, see Torrell (1996a, esp. pp. 135ff. and 496ff.).

21 This is William Stevenson's thesis (2000) and it is, of course, just the kind of consequence Rahner rightly worries about.

Chapter 4

The Economy of Salvation: Jesus Christ

The previous chapter followed Thomas's 'contemplative ascent' from ordinary or philosophical ways of talking about God's existence to the 'high, full and perfect' conception of the triune God. Thomas's dialectic begins with what people ordinarily mean by 'God' and then his inquiry moves ever more deeply into the heart of the Christian understanding of God, to culminate in the doctrine of the immanent Trinity. The dialectic displays the intellectual struggle that is required of Christians if they are to know God truly as one unknown. By deepening their awareness of God's mystery, Thomas helps his readers reject the errors and idolatry that result from distorted or simplistic notions of God. The theological wisdom he seeks to inculcate in his Dominican readers is meant to help them better perform their tasks of preaching the Gospel and following Christ obediently.

After his discussion of the immanent Trinity, Thomas devotes just one question to the economic Trinity as such (ST 1.43) before he turns to creation and its relation to the triune God. In this chapter I will begin with the economic Trinity but then depart from the order of exposition in the ST (and from the somewhat similar order in the ScG). Thomas's discussion in the ST is structured historically, as it were, in that he follows the movement of salvation history through its four stages or 'states'. After a fairly brief treatment of creation in general, he considers the creation of angels and their manner of being, and then turns to humanity as it was first created in the state of innocence, before the fall into the state of sin. The remainder of ST 1 is devoted to a discussion of how humans know and will, how their souls and bodies are united and other related matters that together make up Thomas's theological anthropology. Next Thomas turns in ST 1/2 to consider how humans act as the 'principles of their actions' (ST 1/2 prol.). He considers what they have done, the consequences of their actions, the fall into sin and their need for grace. This prepares for the discussion of the workings of grace in ST 2/2. Then in the third and final part of the ST, Thomas presents an account of the one whose person and work is the sole means by which we may be raised beyond ourselves to the state of grace and, eventually, to the fourth stage, the state of glory when we shall see God 'face to face'.[1]

Thomas's order of exposition serves his pedagogical concerns very well. He organizes his material so that each section builds upon what has been dealt with earlier. In this way he can focus clearly and succinctly on the matter at hand and avoid repetition. However, because the order of the ST may be misconstrued, I will begin with Thomas's exposition of the doctrines of the economic Trinity and creation in general, and then turn directly to his Christology, to the mission of the Son for our redemption.[2] Doing so will more clearly display the role of Jesus Christ in Thomas's theology. In commenting on John 5:27 ('he gave him power to exercise judgment, because he is the Son of Man'), Thomas says that the judgment of Christ is of two kinds. The first, as we might expect, is the judgment that condemns those who have sinned by failing to respond to the Father's offer in his Son. The second is the judgment of discernment whereby we bring all before the tribunal of Christ (*Sup. Ioan.* 5:24, n. 776; also n. 483). That second kind of judgment is, as we have seen, the key to Thomas's theological method and to his conception of the Christian life both in general and in detail. All must be tested by the Son of Man, for everything – doctrines, practices, we ourselves, all things in heaven and earth – are to be made obedient to him who is the Word and wisdom of God. The dialectic of ST 1.2–42 brought Thomas's readers to the 'high, full and perfect' view of reality that has been made possible for us by Jesus Christ. From that vantage point, Thomas can employ fittingness arguments rather than dialectic, for he is concerned henceforth with showing how everything that he wants to propose as Christian doctrine conforms to the wisdom of God revealed in Jesus Christ. It is therefore best for us, his modern readers, to have on hand a fuller account of Thomas's Christology (beyond the elements mentioned in Chapter 2) before we examine the rest of his theology.

The Economic Trinity

Thomas uses the terms 'generation' and 'spiration' to talk about the eternal relations within the immanent Trinity. As God moves 'outwards' to create and redeem what is other than God, these terms are complemented by their temporal parallels, 'mission' and 'giving'. Thus the procession of the Son from the Father by generation is the basis in God's eternal being for the mission or sending forth of the Son into time and space as the creative and redeeming Word. Similarly, the spiration of the Holy Spirit from the Father and the Son is the ground of the giving of the Holy Spirit to what is other than God. The link between these two sets of divine relations is the Son, for he 'may proceed eternally as God [within the immanent Trinity]; but [also] temporally, by becoming human, according to his visible mission [the Incarnation], or likewise by dwelling in humanity according to his invisible mission [grace]' (ST 1.43.2). The Son's mission precedes and makes possible the giving of the Holy Spirit, reflecting the order of procession of the immanent Trinity.

The movement of the Son into the world should not be thought of as a new being for the second person, as if he became something different from what he was before. The Word remains the same but takes on 'a new way of existing', acting now in time as well as eternally. Similarly with regard to the Holy Spirit. Their mission in time began with the creation of time itself, but they are eternally the same persons. From the very beginning of their mission, and thus from the very beginning of creation, the Son and the Spirit have acted for our salvation. It is through their mission that God dwells in us by the sanctifying and saving grace by which 'the soul is made like to God' (ST 1.43.5 ad 2). The effects of sanctifying grace are twofold, again reflecting the distinctive work of the two persons. Through the Son, to whom matters of the intellect are appropriated, our minds are illumined; through the love of the Spirit, we are enlivened and moved to will the good and to love God, our proper end. Before becoming visible to us at the nativity of Christ and in the form of the dove at Christ's baptism, the Son and Spirit worked redemptively and invisibly among the people of the Old Testament, enabling them to participate in God's wisdom and goodness. For that is the meaning and goal of creation, namely to bring us into the life of the triune God.

Trinitarian Creation

I noted in the previous chapter how Thomas has been criticized for isolating the doctrine of the Trinity from the rest of his theology. More recent work has recovered a better sense of the way in which his understanding of creation is in fact thoroughly informed by the doctrine.[3] The criticism may stem from Thomas's way of approaching the act of creation from two perspectives. One perspective is a consequence of Augustine's rule, which states that the actions of the Trinity upon that which is not God cannot be divided up among the three persons. God acts upon creation as one and indivisible. In Thomas's terminology, creation is thus an essential act, an action done in common, rather than a notional or proper act, an action of one of the persons. It cannot be ascribed to one divine person alone as, say, the Incarnation or being spirated can. The second perspective results from Thomas's contention that, because creation is the work of the triune God, it is Trinitarian in form: 'God the Father made the creature through his Word, which is his Son; and through his love, which is the Holy Spirit' (ST 1.45.6). Hence, Thomas argues, we must follow Scripture in appropriating certain of God's essential actions to one or other of the persons, in both creation and redemption. We must say of the Father that he is the creator, because to him is appropriated divine power as the principle from which the other persons proceed. But the Father creates by the Son and the Holy Spirit, by the wisdom and the love of God.

Thus Thomas approaches the economic Trinity with the same 'redoublement of language' he used in considering the immanent Trinity. He begins by clarifying the right way of thinking about the essential act of creation, and then reconsiders creation from the perspective of the appropriations.

The theological concept of creation is more complex than contemporary usage might suggest. Sometimes we say that an artist 'creates' a sculpture, or that someone is particularly 'creative' in, say, designing a new advertizing slogan. Thomas considers such usage not entirely equivocal, but he prefers to keep the word as a purely technical term in theological discourse, since 'to create can be the action of God alone' (ST 1.45.5; ScG 2.21). This is not only because God creates in a way that is Trinitarian. It is also because the word, when properly used, refers to the act of creating out of absolutely nothing, *ex nihilo*, and that is an act of which no human or any other creature is capable. 'Nothing' here is meant absolutely. There is nothing prior to creation, not even logically prior. There is no vacuum in space which is then filled as God creates (ST 1.46.1 ad 4). Nor can there be a time when creation 'happens' since there is no 'before'.

Creation is thus a strange, unimaginable act. God creates without change in God, for the doctrine of divine simplicity rules out the notion that God could at one point be potentially a creator and then, at some other point, actually a creator. God is essentially God's acts, always and completely. Moreover, since there is nothing prior to creation, there cannot be any change involved in the act: creation simply is; it does not become (ScG 2.19). While the act of creation alters God in no way, it establishes a real relation between the creature and God because the existence of the creature depends upon the creature's participation in God's being (ST 1.44.1). Thus creation is not the event at which everything began so much as a relation, 'a relation of real dependence' upon the creator (ScG 2.18.4). It is not an event because it is not within time. Nor is creation necessarily the beginning of things, for two reasons. First, creation must be ongoing. Without the relation of dependence constituted by their participation in God's being, creatures would immediately cease to exist. Second, to say that the universe is created is not necessarily to say that it must have a beginning. That the universe is created does not rule out the logical possibility of it always having been in existence. 'Always' in such usage applies to time and thus to something created, rather than to eternity, which by definition cannot be measured. We recall that, unlike his Franciscan colleagues, Thomas believed that one cannot prove demonstratively that the world has not been always in existence. We know for sure that there is indeed a beginning only because Scripture reveals the 'newness of the world' (ST 1.46.2). But even if the contrary had been revealed to us (i.e., that the universe had always existed), it would still be created because it would always have been in a relation of dependence upon its creator for its existence.

Now we must consider creation from Thomas's other perspective. Gilles Emery has drawn attention to the way the doctrine of the Trinity bears upon Thomas's conception of created reality as a whole as it relates to God. His theology seems to be organized as a circular movement: creation moves outwards from God – *exitus* – and then is perfected as it returns to God – *reditus*. The *exitus–reditus* structure is explicit in Thomas's early *Commen-*

tary on the Sentences.[4] It is also evident in the four stages of salvation history that order the exposition of the ST. The structure is not merely a metaphysical construction. It is thoroughly Trinitarian or, as one might say, it is a Trinitarian metaphysical scheme. Creation is grounded in and, as it were, imitates the immanent procession of the Word and Spirit from the Father as it, too, comes into being as other than the Father. Creation's 'return' to God (not that it could ever actually leave God, of course) is also grounded in and made possible by the missions of the divine persons which constitute the economy of salvation (Emery, 1995, p. 520). This overarching Trinitarian dynamic pervades all of Thomas's theology. We have already seen it at work in the dialectic of the doctrine of God, where the beginning of an intellectual 'return' is brought about by the increasing conformity of our minds and language to the Word and the apostolic witness.

According to Thomas, 'the processions of the divine persons are the cause of creation' (ST 1.45.6 ad 1). There are no mediators between God and creaturely reality. The created relation is directly with the divine self-knowing, a knowing which, we recall, is also creative when God wills it to be. God creates even physical things directly by knowing them eternally in all their variety and individuality in the exemplary ideas within the divine intellect, the Word (ST 1.47.1 ad 2; DV 4.4 ad 2). From this eternal knowing in the Word, the creatures are produced in time by the Son, and through the Holy Spirit they are given their 'existence and permanence'. A significant metaphor for Thomas is that of art or craft. God is like an artist in whose mind are the ideas for what will be made. According to Genesis 1, at creation the Spirit of God hovered over the waters. This Thomas likens to 'the love of artists moving over the material of their art, that out of it they may form their work'. The art metaphor also helps to show the fittingness of God's declaration that creation is good. God is an enthusiastic creator and displays the satisfaction of an artist in the work produced (ST 1.74.3 ad 3).

More significant than the art metaphor, though, is the concept of divine wisdom. 'God produces effects according to God's wisdom' (ScG 2.24.1). God's Word, 'the concept of God's wisdom' (ST 1.47.1), divides things one from another (Gen. 1:4, 7) and orders and ranks them. This action is appro-priated to the Son so that (to move ahead for a moment to Thomas's Christology) the incarnate Word is the ground and norm of any analogy between God and creatures. Christ is the *analogia entis* in person, so to speak, the meeting place of the *exitus* and *reditus*. Creation is dependent upon its relation to the divine wisdom, so it displays what Thomas calls a 'trace' of the Trinity. Everything created has three aspects that can be explained only by their participation in unparticipate being. One is that every being is created, and so displays its 'principle' or origin: the Father. A second is that each thing is a particular kind of thing, having a definite form and species. This reflects 'the Word, as the form of the thing made by art is from the conception [i.e., an inner word or an idea] of the artist' (ST 1.45.7). Third, each thing has its place within the ordered whole. Nothing is isolated;

everything is in relation to everything else within the order of creation. The relatedness among things displays the love of the Holy Spirit, which inclines us to something other than ourselves.

Clearly, Thomas does not mean to suggest that, without any knowledge of the Trinity, we could reason from this threefold trace to its Trinitarian origin. As he says, a 'trace shows that someone has passed by, but not who it is' (ibid.). We know where to look for the source of the trace only because we know by revelation who has passed by. This caveat applies also to Thomas's contention that in rational creatures there is more than a trace of the Trinity. We are made in the 'image' of the triune God so that the very form of the Trinity can be discerned in us. We may fittingly liken the processions of the Son and the Holy Spirit to their reflections in our intellect and will, our word and love (ST 1.93.6). The image gives us a 'natural aptitude' for imitating God's self-knowledge and love as we in turn know and love God. But the image gives us only the mere possibility, not the capability. We cannot actually know and love God unless grace operates in us, and even then only imperfectly in this life (ST 1.35.2 ad 3; 1.93.4). So the image does not endow us with any capacities that could bring us, of ourselves, cognitively or ontologically closer to God. Thomas is well aware that he uses these analogical concepts to make sense of what we can know only through revelation and by the grace of faith. We cannot move from what we know of the structure of the human mind to knowledge of the triune God.

The Word creates by organizing, defining and ranking things, thereby displaying God's wisdom. If God made only one thing or just a few different kinds of things, creation could not display God's perfection as well as it actually does. God is simply and infinitely perfect, while creatures are composite, finite and imperfect. No one kind of thing can match the creator, so God's richness and splendor of being must be displayed, albeit always inadequately, by creation's abundance and variety.[5] This notion helps Thomas make sense of the presence of evil in a world created by a perfectly good God. He denies the Manichean doctrine of two principles, one good, one evil. There is no evil principle or dark force in the universe; nor is there anything that is essentially or absolutely evil. Anything that exists is good at least to the extent that it is in relation to God for its being (ST 1.49.3). However, because creation is fittingly varied and complex, there are grades of goodness. Goodness, we recall, is convertible with being; hence those beings which are ontologically higher participate more in God's goodness. Humans are higher in rank than rocks, so they are superior in being and goodness. If evil is the relative absence of good, rocks are ontologically 'evil' by comparison to humans. And that, says Thomas, is a very good thing. God intends the good of the universe as a whole, which requires grades of being and the decay of some things in order to preserve others in being: lions need to eat (ST 1.48.2 ad 3). Evil is primarily an ontological concept, then, rather than a moral one, though what Thomas says here prepares for his later treatment of moral evil.

The Purpose of Creation

God creates what is not God out of nothing, and is thus the efficient cause of creation. God creates by knowing God and the divine ideas in the Word, and is thus the exemplary cause of creation. God creates with intent, with the purpose of bringing humanity into 'the full participation of the divinity', which is 'the true bliss of humanity and the goal of human life' (ST 3.1.2). God is also the 'final cause' of creation, by which Thomas means that God is the end for which creation is intended. These various meanings of 'cause' are taken from Aristotle, in whose terminology a woodworker makes a chair (efficient cause) according to an idea (exemplary cause) and with a view of the chair's purpose (final cause), namely as something to be sat upon. God's wisdom is active in all three kinds of cause: 'by the wisdom of God the secrets of the divine realities are revealed, the works of creatures are produced, and not only produced but also restored and brought to perfection, that perfection, indeed, by which every thing is called perfect insofar as it attains its proper end'.[6]

God intends creation to do more than perpetuate its existence, more even than continue indefinitely progressing towards ever greater knowledge and enlightenment. Creation's 'proper end' is a fulfillment that is beyond itself and its natural capacities. Our end as humans is 'supernatural' and we cannot attain it except by grace. The distinction between nature and grace is important for Thomas and, as I noted in Chapter 1, it has sometimes been misunderstood. One of its functions is to help unpack the way Scripture differentiates between God's creative and redemptive acts. 'Nature' is the rubric under which we talk about creation as it exists by its relation of dependence upon its creator. Thomas says that we can do some things by our natural capacities alone, with God's help indeed, but without the special action of sanctifying grace. We can propagate the species and build dwellings and plant vineyards even after our natures have been corrupted by sin (ST 1/2.109.2). But Scripture reveals another relation of creatures to God beyond this, one which is established by grace and which makes possible those activities that are involved in the *reditus* of creatures 'back' to God, who is our 'proper end'.

According to Thomas, then, nature is more a starting-point and a potentiality than, as the Neo-Scholastics sometimes had it, a sphere of activity that could at least hypothetically be a self-contained reality. The latter view is incorrect even as a hypothesis. We cannot prescind from the 'order of grace' because God's wisdom did not intend anything other than creation's final end, which is in God, not in ourselves and our 'natural' affairs and goals. Even before sin, Adam had a twofold knowledge, by nature and by grace. By nature he could know God only in creatures (DV 18.2, 3, 5), yet 'his intellect [had been] made for the purpose of seeing God' (DV 10.11 ad 7). Grace was necessary from the beginning for Adam to attain the purpose for which he had been created. A key text on this issue is Thomas's discussion of the traditional view that God's work was completed on the seventh day of creation. This might suggest that there was nothing more that remained to do or, to read into his text the Neo-Scholastic claim, that there *need be* nothing more to do. Hypothetically, God could have left it at that. In reply, Thomas notes that there are two kinds of perfection. The first is substantial, when the form of a thing is complete. The substantial integrity of creation as a whole was achieved on the seventh day; it was brought fully into existence as a non-divine reality. But there is also the 'perfection of operation' for a purpose and goal. This is 'the final perfection, which is the end of the whole universe', namely 'the perfect beatitude of the saints at the consummation of the world' (ST 1.73.1). That, needless to say, was not achieved on the seventh day. Yet 'by directing and moving creatures to the work proper to them … God made some beginning of the second perfection' (ST 1.73.1 ad 2).

A second important function of the nature–grace distinction is that it enables Thomas to acknowledge fully the ontological weight of created things. Something is what it is and acts in the way it acts by reason of its nature. If we are to be brought to our final end as ourselves, as human persons, rather than be turned into something other than ourselves, we must retain our human nature. Nature is the 'cause' of our proper end, in the sense of yet another kind of cause, a 'formal cause', because our form or nature is that which makes us what we are and enables us to act in our particular kind of way (ST 1.73.1).[7] If nature did not persist even as it is transformed by grace, the *reditus* would be too radical a change, involving loss of creation's integrity. Certainly, transformation is necessary. The path to the final end is not at all smooth, as the Cross and the difficulties we face in being obedient to Christ attest. But creatures retain their self-identity through the transformation and they operate as themselves even as they are brought to their final end.

To make sense of this we need to recall the radical transcendence of God discussed in Chapter 3. Suppose I help an old lady across the street. I cannot do this in a way that brings me towards my final end without the grace of God that transforms me and makes my action good and meritorious (more on this in the next chapter). Yet whether it is a grace-filled action or simply an ordinary, natural action, it is truly *my* action, an act fully informed by my human nature. It is not that God is the agent and I am simply a manipulated instrument. Against influential Arab philosophers and their supporters, Thomas insisted that creatures are true causes, albeit secondary ones. 'God so communicates God's goodness to created beings that one thing which receives it can transfer it to another' (ScG 3.69.16). I genuinely act and do indeed cause effects. But to forestall another mistake, it is not that I perform a part of the action while God does another part, or that we work together in harmony to produce the one effect. Both mistakes rely upon a univocal conception of 'action'. According to Thomas's understanding of the doctrine of the divine *concursus*, God acts immanently in my act. The two agents, divine and created, are so radically different and operate within such radically distinct spheres that there can be no competition between, or overlap or comparison of, their respective acts. Both may therefore be the cause of a single effect: God as the primary cause, the creature as the secondary. Were I a non-rational animal such as a mouse, I would act according to my nature and God would work providentially and immanently in me to bring me to my proper end as a mouse (DV 5.2). Whether I am human or mouse, God is responsible for the whole of my action, while I am also wholly responsible for my action.[8] God acts without undermining the freedom of the human agent or the natural integrity of non-rational creatures. Thus Thomas's concept of nature supports his contention that God respects and delights in the integrity of the beings God creates. The world is real and good, and it is truly active as such (Torrell, 1996b, pp. 317–22).

Christology

The Son proceeds from the Father within the immanent Trinity. The mission of the Word and the Holy Spirit establishes the relation of dependence that brings forth from God that which is other than God. Now I turn to Thomas's account of the Word incarnate, the Son of God who is the agent of our salvation and of creation's *reditus* 'back' to God. Through the Son's grace and wisdom, and the charity and gifts of the Holy Spirit, we who are other than God are transformed so that through our own actions we may participate in the life of God as fully as we can while still remaining ourselves.

Thomas divides his treatise on Jesus Christ into two parts, corresponding more or less to the person and the work of Christ respectively. In the first part (ST 3.1–26), where the influence of John's Gospel is particularly evident, he discusses how we should conceive of the union between the divine and human natures. In the second (ST 3.27–59), where he draws somewhat more upon the Synoptic Gospels, Thomas considers the theologically significant events of Jesus's life. Throughout, the form of argumentation is primarily that of *convenientia* or fittingness, by which Thomas seeks to display the reasonableness of what God has done in Jesus Christ rather than demonstrate its necessity. Throughout, too, Thomas displays his mastery of the Christian theological tradition, citing many passages and arguments from both the Greek and Latin Fathers.

The Union

Thomas begins his treatise on Christology by posing the question of the fittingness of God becoming human. Christians have lived for so many centuries with the notion of the Incarnation, of divinity assuming human nature, that they may no longer notice how strange their belief is. After all, it would seem preferable for God, who is spiritual and not at all material, to have made God known to us and have redeemed us in some immaterial way. Behind this objection is no doubt the ancient view that material things are lesser and possibly even evil by comparison to spiritual things. But the Old Testament (which cannot be said to subscribe to such a view) also strongly emphasizes the gulf separating God from creatures, a gulf too vast, one might think, for such a union to take place. Thomas replies that the Incarnation is both possible and most appropriate. We know this in the first place simply because it happened, and therefore it *must* be appropriate. It was not necessary in the sense that there was no alternative, since God's infinite wisdom could have redeemed us in other ways. Yet because God chose this particular way, the Incarnation is necessary in the sense that it is the best means to achieve the goal, as it is necessary to ride a horse if one goes on a long journey, even though one could conceivably make the journey on foot (ST 3.1.2).

Given the necessity of the Incarnation, it is the task of the theologian to discern the wisdom it displays and guard against misunderstandings by careful analysis of the language used to talk about it. We know that it 'belongs to the essence of goodness to communicate itself to others' (ST 3.1.1). God, the highest good, wills to communicate goodness in the highest and most complete manner, by personal union. This implies that the Incarnation might have occurred even if we had not sinned, an implication Thomas does not deny. However, we cannot meaningfully speculate on the question because Scripture gives us no knowledge of such an alternative. We do know that the Incarnation raises human nature to something greater than its original state prior to the first sin, because 'God allows evils to happen in order to bring a greater good therefrom' (ST 3.1.3 ad 3).

Thomas presents a collection of arguments for the fittingness of the Incarnation in ST 3.1.2. Among these is the traditional one to the effect that, for creation to be restored, justice requires a recompense that is greater than any human could make. The sin was committed against an infinite God and so is in some sense an infinite offence. Yet since Adam committed the sin, justice requires the recompense to be made by a human being. Hence it is necessary that the Redeemer be both God and man.[9] But Thomas gives a good number of more positive reasons for the Incarnation, too. In uniting with human nature in Jesus Christ, God delineated our way (*via*) to union with God in Christ. Jesus Christ is our way in a number of senses. It is through our union with him who unites humanity with divinity that our humanity is brought into union with God, enabling us to receive the 'full participation of divinity' (ST 3.1.2). Christ's redemptive work makes it possible for us to follow his way by the gift of his grace, by the infusion of the virtues of faith, hope and charity, and by the other spiritual gifts necessary for the Christian life. Through Christ we are brought into friendship with God and, since friendship should be between equals, this also shows the fittingness of God's becoming human like us (ScG 4.54.6).[10] Finally, and by no means of least significance for Thomas, the Incarnation has a kind of pedagogical function. We are shown how much God loves us and we are stirred to love in return. We are taught the virtues of obedience, humility, constancy and justice by his example. And since the Incarnation occurs at the middle of time, rather than at its end, we are given the opportunity to respond or to fail to respond. There is time for human history, during the course of which it may be, as Thomas remarks forebodingly, that 'the charity of many will grow cold at the end of the world' (ST 3.1.5).

Thomas's fittingness arguments clearly presume a thoroughly Chalcedonian conception of the union. Jesus Christ is both human and divine. *Who* he is, is the person, Jesus Christ. *What* he is, is both human and divine (McCabe, 1987, p. 59). He has a human nature and a divine nature without any confusion between them, yet without any separation either. The two natures are united completely yet distinctly in the one person. Thomas emphasizes the reality of Jesus's humanity somewhat more than other theologians of his time. The Son assumed real 'flesh', taking on a true human nature, with a body and soul that could truly suffer and decay and die (ST 3.5.2). But Thomas also never loses sight of the fact that, without Christ's divinity, his humanity could do nothing towards our redemption. Thomas's Christology is thus 'from above' in that he usually considers the humanity from the perspective of the divine rather than the divine from what we know of the human. In this he differs from most contemporary Christologies. Although he has sometimes been criticized for some of the things this approach leads him to assert, it has the distinct benefit of enabling him to treat the particularities of Christ's life with their full salvific significance. Because he is divine, what Christ is and does is unparalleled and effectively contributes to our redemption. Jesus Christ makes known and achieves in his particular life history what cannot be known or achieved more generally. He is not merely a symbol of things that could be represented in other ways.[11]

The Incarnation is the work of the Trinity as such (ST 3.3.4; 3.32.1 ad 1). Because the persons exist eternally and apart from any relation to creation, it is not unreasonable to think that any of the three could have assumed human nature. Again, though, it was most fittingly assumed by the Son because its consequence is that we, too, may become sons and daughters of God. We will not be just like him, to be sure, since he is Son by nature, not by adoption, as we are. Our own union with God is dependent upon his union, 'through a certain conformity of image to the natural Son' (ST 3.45.4). Christ was conceived in the power of the Holy Spirit, because love is appropriated to the Spirit, and the union of divine and human is a supremely loving act (ST 3.32.1; *Sup. Matt.* 1:18, n. 112). The Son comes from the Holy Spirit in his conception, as the Holy Spirit comes to us from Christ; the Son and the Holy Spirit 'are from one another' (ST 3.39.8). But the Holy Spirit cannot be the father of Christ, even in his humanity (*Sup. Matt.* 1:20, n. 132; ScG 4.47). Spiritual fathers produce their like. If Jesus is truly human, he cannot have a 'spiritual body'. So while Mary plays no active role in the Incarnation (an assertion which in part reflects Thomas's views about male and female roles in generation), she is its material cause (ST 3.31.5; 3.32.2 ad 3). She is truly his mother.

The question thus arises as to the most appropriate way of talking about the union between God and humanity (ST 3.2). Thomas goes through some of the possibilities considered in the course of the Christian tradition. A few of these tend to confuse or meld together the humanity and the divinity into one nature, while others tend to separate the two natures too much, making the union impermanent. Thomas sees the former tendency in the work of the Greek Father, St Cyril, who asserted that the union occurred in Christ's single nature. Thomas attempts to save Cyril's teaching by suggesting that what he means by 'nature' is really 'person', for that is where the union really occurs. He then defines the concept of nature along Aristotelian lines as 'the principle of motion in that in which it is essentially and not accidentally' (ST 3.2.1). This rules out union into a single nature. If Christ has only one nature, either the human or the divine would have had to change. Change is impossible for God, as Cyril well knew, and to suggest that Christ became essentially something other than human would be to say that the Son was never truly incarnate. Hence the union is in the person, within which both natures exist in their fullness. Against the Apollinarian error, Thomas insists that we cannot say that the Son took on a human body alone and not the human nature as such. The soul of Christ must be human if his body is to be truly human, for the soul is the form of the body and is that which makes it human (ST 3.5.3).

As I noted earlier, Thomas's definition of a person, following Boethius, is 'an individual substance of rational nature'. A person is thus a particular kind of individual substance; examples of other kinds of individual substances would be a flower or a star or a mouse. Each of these individual things can be called a hypostasis or suppositum, because each of them has something that underlies (the Latin is *supponitur*) all that the individual is and all that may be predicated of it (ST 3.2.3). In ordinary humans, the soul and body would together constitute the one person or hypostasis. Were that the case with Christ, we could reasonably assume, as some have, that the divine person united with a human person in Jesus Christ. But the union of two persons into one would permit the possibility of later division; it would be merely an accidental union. So Thomas says that in Christ the human soul and body do not make the person; they are united with an *already existing* person, the divine Son of God, to become that one person. As with us, Christ's soul is the form of his body, making him human. But Christ's humanity cannot exist in any way apart from the person who assumes it. His humanity is unique in that it is not, as such, a person (ST 3.4.2 ad 3, which corrects Pope Innocent III's language).[12]

Thomas's point may be easier to grasp if we use the terminology of later Christology. Christ's humanity is *an*hypostatic, meaning simply that it does *not* constitute his hypostasis or individual substance. He is not a person as a human; his humanity would not exist at all apart from the union with the

Word. Christ's humanity is thus *en*hypostatic, meaning that it exists truly and freely as human, but only because it is assumed *into* the person or hypostasis of the Son (ST 3.2.2 ad 2). The divine person *qua* person does not change; nor is there a new hypostasis formed by the union. Thus there is no process in the union. It cannot be that the man, Jesus, lived for a time before he was seen to be worthy or suitable to be 'adopted' as the Son (ST 3.2.11). Nor, against more subtle versions of adoptionism, could a kind of instantaneous adoption have occurred in which a human person was created who was immediately assumed. There is no person prior to the assumption of Christ's human nature (ST 3.2.6).

The enhypostatic conception of Christ's human nature also rules out errors associated with Nestorianism, in which the humanity and the divinity of Jesus Christ are too separate or impermanent. The union is not a matter of essential change, since both natures or essences persist. But neither is it accidental and separable, since there is only one person without which the human nature is non-existent. It cannot be that the divine person took over, as it were, the work of the human as his own, making Christ's human work divinely effective. The one person acted and suffered as both human and divine. It is thus not correct to say that 'a man was assumed' and any theological authority that uses such phrases should be 'loyally explained', i.e., reinterpreted (ST 3.4.3 ad 1).

The union is personal, then, not in that two persons are 'now' united into one person, but in that the one divine person assumed a human nature into himself.[13] As a personal union, it is not the product of grace. To be sure, grace was given Christ with the union and grace flows from him thenceforth as its consequence. But grace is by definition accidental since it is not part of our essential being or nature; it is bestowed by God entirely gratuitously. So the union is more like a natural union, in the sense not of an essential principle, but as something had from birth without any additional movement of grace (ST 3.2.12; 3.6.6). Furthermore, the uncreated suppositum – the divine person – assumed human nature *in atomo*, in individual form. The Son took on human nature as such, but did so by taking on *this* human nature. If the divine person took on human nature *only* as such it would follow, says Thomas, that all humanity would thenceforth be united with divinity personally; we would all be christs.

Thomas distinguishes his Christology from those which assert or imply that the Incarnation alone is sufficient to transform and save our humanity.[14] On Thomas's view, the conception of Jesus Christ is but the beginning of his salvific actions, which are completed only with the Ascension. Consequently, the humanity of Christ is far more than a mere passive medium through which the divine power works for our salvation; it takes on an active role. As Thomas explains it, 'the humanity of Christ is an instrument of the Godhead – not indeed, an inanimate instrument, which nowise acts, but is merely acted upon [as a hammer, for example]; but an instrument animated by a rational soul, which is so acted upon as to act' (ST 3.7.1 ad 3). Christ's humanity has a positive, instrumental yet freely willed role, a role that increased in significance for Thomas as his thought developed (Torrell, 1999, pp. 645, 270). The whole Trinity works through the humanity (ST 3.34.1 ad 3). Everything Christ does in the flesh is salvific by the power of the divinity operating within him. But instrumental causes leave their imprint upon that which they are used to cause, as the chisel leaves its mark on the sculpture or, better, as a musical instrument informs a composer's ideas. When the instrument is human and united with the person who is the primary agent, the imprint is all the greater. The most significant of all such imprints is the time between Christ's conception and his Ascension, during which he worked to redeem us. His time on earth opens up for us a corresponding time during which we may appropriate his work by our own obedient activity and thereby merit our salvation.

Christ is truly human, 'called a man univocally with other men and women' (ST 3.2.5). His humanity is exemplary because it is perfect, joined ontologically and naturally *in* the Son so that it *is* the Son. In the union, then, the human flesh of Christ is not changed. It is deified in that it is assumed by the divine person so that it becomes an aspect of that person, but it remains human none the less. It is not that his humanity is somehow 'divine humanity': 'flesh is said to be deified, … not by change, but by union with the Word, its natural properties still remaining, and hence it may be considered as deified, inasmuch as it becomes the flesh of the Word of God, but not that it becomes God' (ST 3.2.1 ad 3). Thomas thus preserves the Old Testament stress upon the vastness of the gulf that separates God from creation. Like the humanity of Christ, our humanity will be transformed so that it may participate in divinity. But we will retain our bodies, as Christ retains his body, scars and all, in heaven after his Ascension (ST 3.54.4).

Christ's Unique Humanity

Though Christ is fully human, the closeness of the union has considerable bearing upon his humanity. He has all the gifts of the Holy Spirit he needs to fulfill his work. Because of the union, he has the fullness of grace, so we cannot say that grace increased in him as his life unfolded. From the very first, Christ had the kind of human perfection – and in a pre-eminent way – that we will have only when we attain the state of glory (ST 3.7.12). Yet Christ was born, lived, suffered and died, so his life had a trajectory rather than being just static in its perfection. As Thomas puts it, in his earthly life Christ was both a *viator*, one who is on the way to the Father in the flesh, as we are before our deaths, as well as a *comprehensor*, one who is already blessed with the beatific vision (ST 3.15.10). Like the blessed in heaven, he had no need of faith in God since faith is belief in that which cannot be seen. Christ's divinity enabled him to 'comprehend' God's essence from the very instant of his conception (ST 3.7.3). Yet as a *viator*, his soul was passible, still subject to suffering, and his body remained both passible and mortal.

In this area there is some evidence of development in Thomas's thinking. He himself points out (in ST 3.12.2) that in his early *Commentary on the Sentences* he had argued that Christ could not acquire knowledge because total *comprehensor* knowledge was infused in him from the very beginning. Like those in the state of glory, Christ did not acquire knowledge in the way we do as *viatores*, by reasoning upon the data given us by our senses. *Comprehensores* have no real need of their bodies because they know by direct illumination from God. By the time he came to the Christology of the ST, however, Thomas realized that if Christ is truly human he must be able to do all that ordinary humans can do as part of their natural goodness. So he argues that Christ reasoned discursively, using the principles infused in him by the union, to gain new knowledge from his empirical experience of the created realities around him. Christ's human soul did not have the knowledge of God which the Son has, nor did his body have the glory and impassibility of the *comprehensor* until after the Passion. Thomas does not take this very much further, however. Christ did not learn anything from any human or any angel. The Word is the concept of God's wisdom, from whom all our wisdom is derived (ST 3.3.8), and because Christ's humanity is unified with the Word, there would be no need to learn from others; indeed, it would be unfitting. There was never any real ignorance in Christ in the sense that he did not know what he needed to know to accomplish his task.

Jesus Christ has two wills because every nature has a will, and he has two natures without diminution of either of them (ST 3.18). To will is to incline towards something perceived as a good or to reject something perceived as evil. Clearly, Christ's divine will is inclined to God alone and entirely. But his human will is embodied and thus subject to bodily emotions. Humans may will something rationally by desiring something which they have reason to know is good. Or, more simply, they may have an emotional reaction to something, a reaction that Thomas terms a movement of the sensitive appetite or a passion. Thomas rejects the Stoic view that emotions are wrong. There is nothing sinful about experiencing feelings such as fear or sorrow, pleasure or pain. Passions become sinful only when they control or deflect our reason away from the good (more on this in Chapter 6). Christ could feel sorrow, but not to the extent that he sinned by giving way to despair. He felt anger, but never of an uncontrollable or irrational kind, only the righteous anger which conforms to and is prompted by reason. There was no possibility of sin in Christ because his will always conformed to his reason and his reason was never misguided. So his passions are what Thomas calls, following Jerome, only 'propassions' (ST 3.15.4). Such emotions were assumed by Christ voluntarily when he assumed human nature. In the suffering at Gethsemane, Christ experienced real fear and sorrow, but not to the extent that he at any time willed something contrary to his divine will. 'Both' wills obeyed the command of the Father freely and fully. Christ's human soul feared the means to the end he willed, the extreme suffering he knew he was about to undergo, but never to the extent of turning away from that end (ST 3.18.6 ad 3; 3.47.2 ad 1).

That Christ has a divine will bears upon the manner in which he accomplished his work on earth. As a human, Christ was not omnipotent (ST 3.21.1 ad 1), nor was his body free from our usual 'defects and infirmities'. He chose to take on the feebleness of humanity in order to take on our punishment, to demonstrate the reality of his flesh and to give us an example of patience (ST 3.14.1). However, Christ remained sufficiently in control of things so that he was never entirely at the mercy of those who killed him. Although the violence done to his body killed him, it was Christ who decided at the appropriate time to withdraw his spirit from his body. Conceivably he could have prevented his death by maintaining his body alive indefinitely through the power of his divinity (ST 3.47.1 ad 2). In making these claims, Thomas seems to be concerned to preserve the freedom and sovereignty of God's salvific actions in Christ. Recently it has sometimes been asserted that Christ died because anyone in our sinful world would be killed who loved as absolutely as he did. Such a view might suggest that it was necessary for our salvation that our sinful will should prevail over Christ's will. As our scapegoat, he would then be *our* sacrifice and the Cross would be *our* act, out of which God then made something good. Against this, Thomas insists that Christ is the primary agent even as he is acted upon by sinful people. *He* offered the sacrifice, not we; all we did was commit 'a most grievous sin' (ST 3.47.4 ad 2).

Preaching the Incarnate Son

It may be that this account of Thomas's Christology has given the impression that he examines the complexities of the incarnate Word a little too closely. His inquiries seem almost to be trying to picture what it must have felt like to be Jesus Christ. In this Thomas shared the company of many of his contemporaries and, though they have quite different concerns, not a few modern theologians. As Herbert McCabe points out, the details of Jesus Christ's psychology and how he experienced reality are largely irrelevant for Christology (see McCabe, 1987, pp. 58f.; also Torrell, 1999, pp. 337ff.). In Thomas's defense, we should recall that his effort is directed towards showing the reasonableness, coherence and wisdom of what Scripture says about Jesus Christ. His goal is to help his readers preach the Gospel fruitfully and without misleading the faithful. Because the church has found it best to use certain concepts in its defined doctrines, Thomas's inquiries are structured by the need to clarify what it means for Christ to have two natures in one person. If he appears to go too far at times, his concern for fitting language is reasonable.

Having learned and become sufficiently skilled in Christological grammar, one may preach the person and work of Jesus Christ without falling into heretical errors. The way we should talk about who Christ is and what he did for us and our salvation must be quite different from the way we talk about the divine *concursus*. When we act, whether naturally or by grace, there are two agents involved, two persons: God, the divine agent, and us, the human agent. My act of helping the old lady across the street may be fully describable from two radically different perspectives since two radically different agents are both wholly responsible for the act. Christ, however, is one person and one agent. He brings together in his one person the radical difference between divinity and humanity. He is one person, so each of his acts has only one agent and only one description. But because Christ has two natures, the actions that occur by means of one nature may be attributed to the other, since their respective actions are effected in the one person.

In this Thomas follows the traditional Christological doctrine of the *communicatio idiomatum* whereby the predicates from what belongs properly to one nature may be applied to the other nature within the one person. It is appropriate to do this provided we do not confuse matters by predicating of the divine *nature* what should be predicated only of the human, or vice versa, and provided we rule out any possible separation of the two natures. If we refer to the *person*, we may apply both sets of predicates without distinction. We need only 'distinguish that by reason of which they are predicated' (ST 3.16.4). This is the doctrinal basis for traditional Christian language about Jesus Christ. His suffering and death, made possible by the assumption of human nature, may be fittingly attributed to his divine nature, not because the divine nature suffers (it cannot), but because *he*, his person, suffers in the human nature (ST 3.46.12; ScG 4.55.17). Similarly, it is fitting for us to worship Jesus Christ even though his human nature is created. Were we to worship the human nature as such, we would commit idolatry. The most we may offer Christ's humanity is what Thomas calls 'hyperdulia', the highest form of veneration (ST 3.25.2). When the Creed articulates the salvific work of Jesus Christ, it does so in terms of his person. And it is the person whom we worship, who cannot be said to be created without considerable qualification (ScG 4.48).

Acta et passa Christi

I now turn to the second part of Thomas's Christology, to the work of Jesus Christ. A little of 'what Christ did and what was done to him' has already been presented in the discussion of Jesus's 'manner of life' in Chapter 2 and in the previous section of this chapter. Thomas's treatise examines the gospel accounts of Christ's work in four stages: how he came into the world; his life in the world; his departure from the world; and his exaltation after this life (ST 3.27 prol.).[15] Among French Roman Catholics, this section has been called Thomas's 'Life of Jesus', but it is clearly not that (Torrell, 1999, pp. 20f.). Here Thomas seeks to display the mutual conformity of doctrine and gospel text. The treatise is neither a commentary nor a biography. It is an examination of some of the details of Jesus's life in light of the earlier Christology in order to show their fittingness and to demonstrate the reasonableness of what, *prima facie*, might seem to be problematic texts.

Entry into the World: Mary

Thomas begins with the Blessed Virgin Mary. Mary is often understood today in the Roman Catholic church as unique in her saintliness. It was she, it is said, whose 'Yes' to God was the human condition of the possibility for our salvation, so her humility and obedience are paradigmatic for the Christian and the church.[16] Thomas is somewhat more restrained in his account of Mary, even by comparison to some of his contemporaries. For the most part, he attends to her only as she bears upon our understanding of Christ or the Christian life. He certainly gives her her due. Mary was given and accepted the opportunity to offer to God 'the free gift of her obedience' (ST 3.30.1). Her questioning of the archangel Gabriel's announcement to her was not, like Zechariah's, the product of doubt but of wonder (ST 3.30.4 ad 2). She is truly the mother of God (ST 3.35.4), since the word 'God' may be truly applied to the humanity that was assumed into the one person, Jesus Christ. Her uterus remained a 'shrine' to the Holy Spirit by her perpetual virginity (ST 3.28.3).

At the same time, Thomas is very careful to distinguish between Mary and Jesus. While her son must be offered worship or 'latria', she should not. She is offered 'dulia', the veneration due to any saint, though because she is truly and by nature the mother of God, she is to be offered 'hyperdulia'. That, we recall, is the very highest form of reverence, given only to her and to Jesus's humanity (ST 3.25.5). Thomas's concern to note the distinctions between son and mother is evident, too, in his account of how she was made worthy to bear the incarnate Word. Like the rest of us, Mary was of the stock of Adam, born through 'fleshy concupiscence and the intercourse of man and woman'. All flesh born in this way is sinful, not because the act of sexual intercourse is sinful; it is not, according to Thomas. Rather, intercourse is the means by which the guilt and consequences of original sin are transmitted from one generation to the next (ST 3.27.2 ad 4). Were she born in the usual way, Mary's human nature would have been infected with original sin and she would have committed actual sins. Jesus Christ could not fittingly be borne by a sinner. So Mary had to be sanctified at some point prior to her birth.

Thomas notes that Scripture is silent on when exactly Mary was sanctified, as it is silent on the whole matter of her birth (ST 3.27.1). He suggests that Mary was first conceived in the flesh, in the usual way, and then sanctified while still in her mother's uterus. Thomas gives two reasons for this view. One relies upon beliefs about human gestation that prevailed at the time. For Thomas, conception produces a mere body, animal material, so to speak, which is not yet properly human. It becomes a human body at its 'animation', when it is infused with a human, rational soul. This event occurs towards the end of the first trimester. Before it, the matter in the uterus has no human nature since it is the soul, the form of the body, which determines the nature.[17] Thus it would be impossible for Mary to be sanctified at her conception or at any time before animation since she did not yet have the human nature to be sanctified.

The second reason is the more significant. If Mary were somehow sanctified *before* her animation she would never have incurred the stain of original sin. Consequently, she would not have needed redemption by her son. But that is unfitting, since it would place Mary outside the scope of salvation in Jesus Christ, whom Scripture says is the savior of all (1 Tim. 4:10). If Christ is indeed the *universal* savior, Mary must have incurred original sin and then been sanctified through him before her birth. After her birth she was kept from the consequences of original sin, which remain even after sanctifying grace, by a special act of the Holy Spirit, who prevented the 'fomes' from working in her to sin. The fomes is one of the consequences of original sin that remains with us even after we have been sanctified by grace. It is 'a certain inordinate, but habitual, concupiscence of the sensitive appetite' (ST 3.27.3). In other words, it is the ever-present tendency to slip into sin, to be drawn away by our emotions and desires from what is truly good. And one may slip suddenly, perhaps by being surprised by an emotion and, without thinking, give way to it. The fomes is not of itself sinful, but it leads to sin. Mary was not actually purified of the fomes until after the birth of Christ, again in deference to Christ's 'dignity' as the Redeemer. Because Mary was free of the effects of the fomes, she remained of the highest purity and never committed any sin (ST 3.27.4). So Thomas rebukes John Chrysostom for accusing Mary of acting out of sinful vainglory when she asked Jesus to do something about the lack of wine at the marriage feast at Cana (ST 3.27.4 ad 3). Because Mary was sinless and full of grace she merited direct assumption into heaven.

Clearly, Thomas does not anticipate the Roman Catholic church's more recent teaching on this matter. According to the dogma defined many centuries later (in 1854 by Pope Pius IX), Mary was conceived immaculately, without the stain of original sin. Thomas seems to have heard something of the initial movement in support of this doctrine. He mentions the celebration of Mary's conception in certain churches (ST 3.27.2 ad 3), a relatively popular feast in Britain which was supported by theologians influenced by St Anselm. But many others rejected the doctrine, including Peter Lombard, Bernard of Clairvaux, Bonaventure and his teacher, Albert the Great. Thomas argued that it was better to celebrate Mary's sanctification rather than her conception (ibid.).

Mary bore Jesus even though she was a virgin, in accordance with the prophecy, as Thomas reads it, of Isaiah 7:14. The conception and birth are entirely miraculous from the viewpoint of the action of the Holy Spirit, though natural from the viewpoint of Mary. Thomas denies that Jesus's body had something 'subtle' or spiritual about it such that it could be born without affecting Mary's body. Only the action of the Holy Spirit could preserve Mary's virginal integrity throughout the birth. To suggest otherwise would be to undermine the reality of Christ's human flesh (ST 3.28.2 ad 3). Mary's perfection enabled her to avoid the pangs of childbirth, since they are the result of sin. After the birth, she took a vow of perpetual virginity with her husband, reflecting Thomas's belief that good works are even better when performed in fulfillment of a vow (ST 3.28.4; 2/2.88.6). She remained a virgin after the birth of Jesus and had no more children.

Nativity and Baptism

Thomas devotes a number of questions to the key events of Jesus's nativity. Christ's conception was, of course, quite different from Mary's. With the matter provided by Mary according to nature (the material cause), the Holy Spirit (the efficient cause) miraculously and instantaneously infused his soul to form the assumed and sanctified human nature. Conceived without intercourse, Christ had no taint of original sin. While he suffered the usual 'defects of infancy' (ST 3.39.8 ad 3), his humanity was perfectly formed and complete from its very beginning. Because he was spiritually perfect, he must have had free will from the very beginning, too, since that would be necessary for him to move willingly and meritoriously toward God (ST 3.34.2).

Thomas interprets the events of Jesus's life by the principle that 'all that Christ does is for our instruction' in the Christian life. The birth itself is to be made known, not to all, but to fitting examples of certain types among all those who are to be saved. The shepherds are privileged with the sight of the newborn because they represent the 'simple and lowly' and ordinary Jews. The Magi represent the 'wise and powerful' and sinful Gentiles, in contrast to the righteous Jews, Simeon and Anna (ST 3.36.3). Jesus affirms the Law in his circumcision to show us that he is really human, a Jew who is obedient to the Law given to his ancestor, Abraham. Throughout these questions, Thomas draws out the 'instruction' of the events for us by many spiritual interpretations. An appealing instance can be found in his treatment of the sacrifice of two birds offered at Christ's Presentation at the Temple:

> the turtle dove, being a loquacious bird, represents the preaching and confession of faith; and because it is a chaste animal, it signifies chastity; and being a solitary animal, it signifies contemplation. The pigeon is a gentle and simple animal, and therefore signifies gentleness and simplicity. It is also a gregarious bird; wherefore it signifies the active life. Consequently this sacrifice signified the perfection of Christ and his members. (ST 3.37.3 ad 4)

Christ's baptism at the hands of John is similarly related to the Christian life. John the Baptist was the end of the Law of Moses and the beginning of the Gospel. His baptism was not a sacrament, yet because it was 'preparatory' to the 'law of Christ', it belonged to the Gospel and should therefore be called a 'sacramental' (ST 3.38.1 ad 1). While the ceremonies of the Law of Moses are figures of Christ's sacraments and do not confer grace, John's baptism is more than figurative, since it prepares for the gift of grace in Christ. Yet his baptism would not have been enough for Christians, who would have had to have been baptized again with Christ's baptism (ST 3.38.6, against Peter Lombard). Christ, of course, needed neither John's baptism of penance nor the baptism of the Holy Spirit. Yet his baptism at the hands of John was fitting for it showed Christ's approval of the practice and, more generally, the completion of the Law in him. It occurred at the Jordan, which the Israelites crossed to enter the Promised Land, indicating that Jesus is the way to the kingdom. The heavens opened so that the voice could tell the onlookers who Christ is, and to show that it is in baptism in Christ that the heavens are opened for us (ST 3.39.5 ad 3). The dove shows that, while Christ's Passion opens heaven for all, it is the Holy Spirit who applies the benefits of the Passion to each one of us through baptism. Here, again, Thomas offers a spiritual interpretation of the dove to show its fittingness as the form of the Holy Spirit (ST 3.39.6 ad 4).

Christ's Ministry

I discussed Thomas's understanding of Christ's ministry in Chapter 2 in relation to the thirteenth-century Dominican conception of the Christian life. There are only a couple of additional points that need to be made here. Christ's temptation by the devil (Matt. 4:1–11 and par.) requires explanation in light of Thomas's contention that Jesus was not subject to passions and irrational desires. He explains that there are two kinds of temptation. The kind that come from within ourselves are sinful because they are caused by emotions, by movements of the sensitive appetite which disorder the will, prompting us to desire something irrational or wrong. Jesus was not subject to these temptations because he was free from the consequences of original sin. He did experience the other kind of temptation, however. These come from outside ourselves in the form of suggestions made by the devil and those in thrall to him. Those who are tempted in this way do not initiate the temptation, so they remain sinless, provided that they do not give way to it, as Christ, of course, did not. Christ's struggle with the devil in the desert shows us that it is necessary that we gain control over ourselves before we take on the task of preaching the Gospel. It also teaches us that the way to fight the devil is 'not by powerful deeds, but rather by suffering from him and his members, so as to conquer the devil by righteousness, not by power' (ST 3.41.1 ad 2). The Temptation thus anticipates the Cross.

Christ performed various kinds of miracles which, taken together, display his power over every aspect of creation. A miracle, according to Thomas, is not an event that breaks the natural order but rather one which temporarily changes it, enabling nature to do or become what otherwise it could not. The miracles of Christ were signs meant to teach those around him. Because they are in effect empirical proofs of his divinity, they lessen the merit of faith, and Thomas points out that the disciples followed Christ before they saw any miraculous signs (ST 3.43.3 ad 3). The greatest miracle is the Transfiguration. Christ's body, we recall, was prevented from displaying the glory of his soul that was a consequence of the union. During the time he was transfigured, Christ chose to display that bodily glory in order to give the chosen disciples some idea of the 'clarity' or brightness and splendor that our bodies will have when we are glorified. The Transfiguration therefore complements the Baptism. The latter shows us that the way to heaven is through Christ, while the former shows us the perfection of life in heaven (ST 3.45.4; ScG 4.86).

The Passion

Thomas moves away from juridical explanations of the Atonement to favor those that reflect God's mercy and love. The suffering and death of Christ were not necessary for our salvation in the sense that Christ had to suffer on our behalf to appease an angry God. Nor was there a question of paying some kind of ransom to the devil, as if the devil had control over God's will for us (ST 3.48.4 ad 3). Nor do Christ's suffering and death simply substitute for ours without any complementary action on our part. On the contrary, we have to become like Christ for us to receive the effects of the Passion; we must be 'made one with the crucified Christ' through the sacraments (ST 3.49.3, 4). Thomas retains the traditional language of debt, ransom and sacrifice, but stresses that it is the person of Christ who is the efficient cause of our redemption as both the one who sacrifices and the sacrifice itself, both the ransomer and the ransom. While the Son obeyed the command of the Father, the Father did not simply deliver his Son up to suffering; 'he inspired him with the will to suffer for us' (ST 3.47.3). So Christ's person is the free agent of our redemption; his humanity its instrumental cause. To repeat a point made earlier: it was not Christ's suffering or passivity as such which saves us but his voluntary self-sacrifice as the incarnate Son of the Father. The death on the Cross was freely willed and chosen by Christ.

Christ teaches us in his Passion by his supreme example of humble and loving obedience even unto death. His suffering for us excites our love for God in return and prompts us to act likewise in gratitude and by the grace that flows from him. None the less, his suffering was unique in its severity, exacerbated by the perfection of his body, which felt pain more than usual, and by his soul, which took on the sins of all (ST 3.46.6). Yet Christ remained a *comprehensor* throughout the Passion, so he continued to experience the joy of the blessed. Thomas explains this by making a distinction between the soul's essence and its faculties. In its essence, the whole of Christ's soul suffered while it also enjoyed its union with God. But in terms of its faculties, it may be said that the lower part of the soul bore the suffering while the highest retained the joy.[18]

The Creed says that Christ died, was buried and descended into hell before rising again. Christ truly died, and fittingly so. His death convinces us of the reality of Christ's body; since he rose again, our fear of death is mitigated and we more readily hope in our own resurrection. According to Thomas's anthropology, death is the consequence of the separation of the body from its form, the soul. Christ's humanity was entirely natural, so at death his soul and body must have separated. Yet both remained united with the divine person of Christ since only sin can separate us from God. Thus Christ was truly buried because his body remained united with his person. As one might expect, the union prevented the body from decaying. At the same time, Christ could descend into hell because he remained united with his assumed human soul. In hell he freed the just, thereby displaying his complete power over the devil even in the latter's own territory. In both the burial and the descent the 'whole Christ' was present, though not the whole human nature (ST 3.52.3 ad 2). After the three days, Christ's body and soul were rejoined and he then allowed the glory of his soul to flow into his body and glorify it (ST 3.54.2 ad 2). Christ rose in the same body he had before because *all* his humanity had to be raised in order that all that pertains to our humanity might likewise be raised up in him.

Exaltation

Thomas's treatment of the Resurrection and the Ascension differs both from his predecessors of several centuries as well as from many of his later followers. He was the first for some time to recover the tradition that Christ's Resurrection and Ascension are as much causes of our salvation as his suffering and death. From his conception until he sits at the right hand of the Father, Christ's acts are all salvifically significant. Each one causes our salvation in its particular way; together they make up the one complete work of redemption (ST 3.53.1; 3.57.6). Later Thomists, unlike Thomas himself, sometimes considered the Passion as the 'objective cause' of salvation in contrast to the Resurrection, which is the 'subjective cause', that by which the effects of the Passion are applied to each of us (see Torrell, 1999, pp. 545–7, 647f.). Thomas is evidently more Pauline than Thomistic in his own teaching, citing Romans 4:25, 6:4 and the like (ST 3.53.1). Even in the ScG, where Thomas obscures the issue somewhat by placing his discussion of the sacraments immediately after his treatment of the Passion and before the Resurrection, he clearly views the Resurrection as more than the event which makes possible our appropriation of what has already been accomplished: 'He chose both to die and to rise. He chose to die, indeed, to cleanse us from sin ... But he chose to rise to free us from death' (ScG 4.79.2). In the ST, the two acts are related in a comparable way. The Passion removes evils, while the Resurrection is 'the beginning and exemplar of all good things' (ST 3.53.1 ad 3). Thus, against some later commentators, Christ does not save us by becoming the Risen One. It is his act of rising from the dead which contributes to the complete work of salvation (Torrell, 1999, pp. 637f.).

The Resurrection should not be confused with resuscitation. Christ brought Lazarus back to life and he raised the dead at his Resurrection. While there was some development in Thomas's thinking, by his later years he seems to have decided that in neither case was the resurrection a true one. Those who rose must eventually have died again, for Christ must be acknowledged as the first to rise from the dead to die no more (ST 3.53.3 ad 2). Christ's Resurrection not only restored him to life, but to a new kind of life within a new order in which death is no longer a possibility. The new life of the Resurrection informs our lives as Christians, setting 'in order the lives of the faithful' so that we 'also may walk in newness of life' (ST 3.53.1, citing Rom. 6:4).

The Ascension also causes our salvation. It is not merely a manifestation of what has already come about, nor is it simply the move to heaven as a more suitable place for the Risen Christ. The movement is certainly fitting, but following John's Gospel, Thomas argues that it was necessary for Christ to ascend as he had descended. There was a twofold descent as the Son humbled himself by taking on humanity and again as he descended into hell. Similarly, there was a twofold ascent as he rose from the dead and ascended into heaven (ST 3.57.2 ad 2). Christ's whole person, including his humanity, ascended to the living God in order that he may send us his gifts (ST 3.57.6). His Ascension was necessary because it was not fitting for Christ to send the Holy Spirit upon his disciples until after he had left them (*Sup. Ioan.* 16:5, n. 2088). The Ascension prepares heaven for us by having Christ's humanity go there first, and it prepares us for heaven, which is not naturally our home. 'Heaven', though, is better understood not as a place but as a metaphor for life in 'the Blessed Trinity, who is the light and the most high Spirit' (ST 1.68.4). Our own ascent will follow Christ's by the power of the Holy Spirit, who is 'love drawing us up to heavenly things' (ST 3.57.1 ad 3).

Christ has now taken his seat at the right hand of the Father to judge the living and the dead. Thomas insists that it is the Son of Man who judges, against John Chrysostom who argued that John 5:27 should be interpreted as if it said 'Son of God'. As Christ's body is exalted in his person, so, too, is it instrumental in his judgment (ST 3.59.2). Christ's judicial authority means that his humanity is the head of the church. And, to complete the Christological dialectic, Christ's humanity even 'surpasses all spiritual substances in dignity' by its union with his person (ST 3.57.5), thus upsetting the philosophers' hierarchy of being. It is as the 'Son of Man' that Christ is given the power to judge all things (ST 3.59.4), the Son whose person 'is Wisdom begotten, and truth proceeding from the Father, and his perfect image' (ST 3.59.1).

Conclusion

This chapter has focused primarily upon the mission of the second person of the Trinity, the Word and wisdom of God. The Word plays the central role both in creation, the *exitus* from God of that which is not God, and in the redemption, the *reditus* of all things back to God. In his treatment of the Incarnation, Thomas stresses the genuineness of Christ's humanity, yet also its distinctiveness as assumed into the person of the Word sent by the Father. The work of the Son is truly a work; as Scripture describes it, Christ saves us, not just by taking on our humanity, but by his action, and at considerable cost. Because the *exitus* and *reditus* are both under the aegis of the one Word, what is created in its image may become the instrument of redemption. So, in turn, created persons may work to be perfected by grace.

On our part, too, redemption involves cost: struggle and hardship as well as comfort and joy. Our efforts to follow Christ in obedience and humility are aided and enabled by the application of Christ's salvific work to us through the work of the Holy Spirit, which is the topic of the next chapter.

Notes

1 As in the phrase '*status perfectionis*', 'state' here refers to a way of being that is distinguished by the possibility and/or necessity of certain kinds of acts and the impossibility of others. Thus, for example, in the state of sin, one cannot help but sin.

2 Torrell stays with Thomas's order because he is concerned to show how what he calls Thomas's 'absolute theocentricism' bears upon his work as a spiritual master. This is quite reasonable. I depart from Thomas's order here because I have been taught by commentators like Torrell to see how thoroughly Christoform Thomas's theocentricism is and it is my concern to show this. See Torrell (1996b), pp. 135, 137, 498.

3 Especially significant is the work of Gilles Emery (1995), to which this section is especially indebted.

4 Emery (1995, p. 480) notes the presence of the *exitus–reditus* motif in Thomas's teacher, Albert the Great, and his colleague, Bonaventure, but in both it is not emphasized as much.

5 Echoes here of the 'principle of plenitude' may remind readers of the traditional notion of the Great Chain of Being, classically described by Arthur O. Lovejoy (1964). However, this passage is more appropriately seen as an explication of scriptural texts such as Psalm 104:24, read Christologically and explicated by the use of traditional philosophical notions. Lovejoy is another modern who reads Thomas from the perspective of his (Lovejoy's) interest in the history of ideas. He has no sense of Thomas's dialectic, either; see e.g. Lovejoy (1964), pp. 73–9.

6   The quotation is from Thomas's *Commentary on the Sentences*, cited by Emery (1995), pp. 531ff.

7   To be sure, nature must also be informed by the charity of the Holy Spirit for it to achieve that end. See Chapter 5 below.

8   One of the best accounts of the divine *concursus* can be found in Tanner (1988), ch. 3.

9   As I noted earlier, Thomas's argument is not quite the same as Anselm's. Thomas is concerned that God's actions be allowed to determine the meaning of justice, rather than our conception of justice determine the identity of God.

10   The friendship argument is not found in the ST collection, though it is implicit there. It is explicit elsewhere in the ST (e.g., ST 1/2.65.5) in the context of the theological virtues, which I discuss in the next chapter.

11   The 'from above' Christology is evident in Thomas's habit, throughout ST 3, of writing about 'Christ' rather than 'Jesus' or 'Jesus Christ'. I make these last few remarks in reference to Bruce Marshall's excellent analysis of the particularity issues in modern Christology and his discussion of Thomas (Marshall, 1987, ch. 5).

12   It may not be out of place to make a couple of remarks here on an issue that exercised Karl Barth and some of those influenced by his theology, namely the theologoumenon of the *logos asarkos*, the 'unfleshed' Word existing 'prior' to the Incarnation. Barth discussed this doctrine early in his *Church Dogmatics* (Edinburgh: T. and T. Clark, 1975), noting that Christ is 'antecedently in Himself' prior to his revelation (CD 1/1 pp. 414–20), and affirming the doctrine in terms of the Extra Calvinisticum (CD 1/2 pp. 168–70). He reaffirmed the latter doctrine in CD 4/1 pp. 180f., but with two major reservations about the *logos asarkos*. First, he argued against any notion that one could use the doctrine speculatively as the ground for claims that it is possible to know God apart from the revelation of the incarnate Word. Thomas would agree in ruling out such speculation within theology. While the philosopher might argue for the existence of God from God's effects, one does not thereby arrive at any saving knowledge, only the knowledge that condemns. Second, Barth believed the doctrine abstracted from the concrete revelation of God in Jesus Christ. The latter should be 'materially decisive' for theology, in Marshall's phrase (see the previous note). For Thomas, the doctrine of the Trinity is an inference, made by the church, from the scriptural witness to the materially decisive descriptions of God's salvific actions in Jesus Christ. The doctrine of the immanent Trinity comes before the Christology in the ST for the same reason that it does in the CD: both Thomas and Barth were *church* theologians. Moreover, in Thomas's theology, Christ is never apart from his humanity from the viewpoint of eternity. The purpose of God achieved in the Incarnation is intended eternally, so the Incarnation, though occurring in time, is, from God's perspective, eternal (ST 3.6.3 ad 3; 3.24.2).

13   My use of male pronouns to refer to the second person is justifiable on theological grounds. According to the doctrine of the Trinity, the second person is to be spoken of as the Son of the Father. Both the Father and the Son are 'male', though only in the sense that their relation is more fittingly understood, according to the tradition, as father and son rather than mother and daughter. To avoid such pronouns could be construed as denying the truth of the doctrine, not an option for orthodox Christians like Thomas.

14   I do not mean to imply that any Christologies which stress the salvific significance of the Incarnation as such must also assert that we are all christs. Thomas would agree that they do not, but he would argue that where those Christologies assume a Platonic understanding of human nature as something separable from human individuals, they are not only incorrect in their anthropology; they also imply such an assertion (see ST 3.4.4 and 5).

15   For an excellent and very thorough analysis of this section, taking up two good-sized volumes, see Torrell (1999), to which I am frequently indebted for this section.

16   Some idea of the recent official position on Mary can be gained from the *Catechism of*

the Catholic Church (Liguori, MO: Liguori, 1994), pp. 251–4. It is arguable that Thomas would have applied much of what is said there about Mary to Jesus Christ instead.

17 From this one should not infer that Thomas would have supported induced abortions up to, say, the fortieth day, on the grounds that the 'matter' in the uterus is not human. Thomas here makes an argument for a piece of speculative theology that supports a way of talking about Jesus Christ sanctioned by Scripture. He is not addressing the issue of abortion at all. More significant is the second argument.

18 As I noted earlier, it is sometimes best not to try to imagine what this would feel like. Torrell is critical of Thomas here (1999, p. 337), but Thomas's way of putting the point does not seem too unreasonable to me, given his linguistic resources.

Chapter 5

The Christian Life:
Christ and the Holy Spirit

Having discussed Thomas's doctrine of God and his Christology, we can now return to consider in rather more detail and depth his understanding of what it means to be a Christian. The focus of this chapter is on how God works within us to make it possible for us to live the Christian life, while the next chapter looks at our response to God's work. Here, then, I discuss the work of the Holy Spirit: grace, the theological virtues and the gifts. In the next chapter I consider the sacraments and what might be called, albeit anachronistically, Thomas's moral theology, his theological anthropology and his ecclesiology.

Grace and Merit

Thomas maintains that the Christian life is not one for which we have a natural capacity. It is not possible for us simply to decide one day to be a Christian, as we might decide upon a career in the law, and then devote our days to the spiritual labor of following Christ obediently with the intention of achieving union with God in the next life. Membership in the legal profession is open to virtually anyone with the requisite natural abilities and financial resources. Obedient following of Christ – the Christian life – is simply beyond us, however intelligent or well intentioned we might be. All our efforts to live as Christians are quite useless unless God acts within us to enable us to do what we otherwise cannot do (ST 1/2.106.2). Thomas calls that action on God's part 'grace'. None the less, effort on our part is certainly appropriate. Even though everything finally depends upon grace, we, too, must act. Indeed, if we think we can obtain glory without grace-enabled activity, we sin against the Holy Spirit by 'presumption' (ST 2/2.14.2). God works to achieve what has been divinely ordained as the goal of creation by means of secondary, created causes, so that 'each thing attains its ultimate end by its own operation' (ScG 3.147.5). As rational animals, humans are called to perfect themselves through their own voluntary activity. So we must earn our salvation or, as Thomas terms it, we must 'merit' eternal life with God. Christ acted in his human nature to merit the salvation of all humanity. Similarly, we must act meritoriously in order that we achieve – really achieve, not merely have done for us – what is beyond our nature.

Merit cannot be conceptually separated from grace without greatly distorting our understanding of the Christian life. Talking of merit apart from grace would suggest that we could earn our salvation without God's action, a heretical position usually (though perhaps unfairly) associated with a fourth-century British monk called Pelagius, which was condemned by Augustine. Simply put, grace is that action on the part of God that enables our actions to be meritorious, to become deserving of eternal life with God. A meritorious act can be performed only by those who have been infused with grace so that their human nature is raised up beyond its natural capacity. Merit is thus a function of grace. However, grace depends upon Jesus Christ, who is its sole source. Hence grace and merit cannot be understood apart from Christ. To make theological sense of the Christian life, then, we must return once again to Thomas's Christology.

The Grace of Christ

It is through the person and work of Jesus Christ and by the operation of the Holy Spirit that we are brought to our proper end, which is to participate in the life of the triune God. Grace is that movement on God's part which brings about our participation in the divine life. The word is used, then, to talk about the ways by which God conveys to us what Christ did for us. In addition, Thomas uses the concept of grace to make the connection between Christ's humanity and our own. In his person, Christ did not need grace since he was from his conception already a *comprehensor*. His humanity was in the state of glory through its assumption into personal union with the Son, so in one sense his human nature did not need grace either. Yet because his humanity was not naturally or essentially divine, it was brought to participate in the divine life by being united with the Son, and thus was acted upon by grace (ST 3.7.1 ad 1). By its own powers, his soul could not achieve the uncreated knowledge and love of God which he had as a person. And since Christ was also a *viator*, one who is on the way, he could be transformed by grace. We recall that the glory of his soul was prevented from flowing into his body (except, miraculously, at the Transfiguration) until after the Passion. Grace could therefore be operative in Christ's human nature, transforming it so that in it he could merit his salvation. What Thomas calls Christ's 'personal grace' enabled him to act meritoriously, to earn in his human activity eternal life with God.

Jesus Christ had grace perfectly and completely because his humanity was fully joined to the divine cause of grace; he had the highest kind of grace, the 'grace of union' (ST 3.7.11). But Christ's grace is not only the most perfect; it is the source of all grace. Grace was bestowed upon him 'as upon a universal principle in the genus of such as have grace' (ST 3.7.9). Through his humanity he is the cause of grace in all others who are human like him. Anyone who has grace has it to the extent that they participate in the fullness of Christ's grace. In accordance with the divine plan for creation, Christ's merits not only brought his own humanity to glory; they overflowed into every other human being, because his divinely empowered actions merited the glory of all humanity (ST 1/2.114.6). Thus for Thomas, it is Christ's *humanity* that is gifted with grace and, through the power of his divinity, is the source of our grace. Our acts are meritorious in so far as they are informed by Christ's grace or, to say almost the same thing, in so far as our humanity conforms to his. That conformity is necessarily more than merely moral. I noted earlier that Thomas considers Christ to be our onto-logical exemplar as well as our moral exemplar. The Christian does not seek to follow Christ obediently just because Jesus was a good man. Such efforts would have no bearing upon our salvation. Christ's humanity is unique in that it enables our humanity to follow him meritoriously. Christ's humanity was so imbued with the fullness of grace that grace is essentially *his* grace, the grace of the man, Jesus Christ. The ontological transformation of grace is therefore Christoform; it is informed by the particularities of the life of the incarnate Word, which have ontological as well as moral weight.

Christ's Headship

From Christ's merits flow the grace which makes it possible for us to conform to him ontologically as well as morally in our actions and thereby to become in him adopted sons and daughters of God. Although Thomas frequently describes this conformity in reference to the lives of individual Christians, the flow of grace from Christ to us is fundamentally communal in form.[1] 'Grace was bestowed upon him not only as an individual, but inasmuch as he is the head of the church, so that it might overflow into his members' (ST 3.48.1). Grace comes to us as we become one in the mystical person of Christ (ST 3.48.2). Thomas makes the connection between Christ's grace and its gift to others in ST 3.8, where he makes use of Paul's metaphor of the head and the body or members of Christ (e.g., Ephesians 4:15f.). All grace comes from Christ on account of his meritorious actions in his hu-manity. Accordingly, it is through the instrumentality of his humanity and its corporeal visibility that Christ is the head of his body, the church. We derive from his human body and soul the possibility of eternal life in our human bodies and souls (ST 3.8.2). Our created and redeemed bodies and souls are thus brought to participate in the life of their head.

Thomas calls this aspect of Christ's grace his 'capital grace', the grace of his headship (Lat. *caput*) which, flowing to others, constitutes them as a body, *his* body. Usually the Pauline metaphor, 'body of Christ', refers to the church, as it does for Thomas for the most part. But in this question (ST 3.8) he includes all rational creatures within the body of Christ, so that the referent of the word 'church' is more extensive than in many later ecclesiologies. Thomas argues that there is a difference between the 'natural body of humanity' and the 'mystical body' that is the church, the body of Christ. One might expect that the difference would reflect the faith or the baptism of the church's members, or even an implicit faith in God, but this is not the case. Rather, what makes the church a mystical rather than a natural body is simply that it cannot come together in a natural and visible way, because it consists of all people throughout all times and places. Everyone is a member of the body of Christ, whether or not they are aware of it, because – and this is Thomas's main point – the 'power of Christ' is 'sufficient for the salvation of the whole human race' (ST 3.8.3 ad 1). In terms of its proper end, humanity is constituted as a group or 'body', not by something that pertains to itself so much as by its relation to Jesus Christ.

Thomas explicates this relation as a hierarchy. The first and highest form of relation is, as we might expect, that enjoyed by those in the state of glory. Second come those who not only have faith in Christ but act in the Holy Spirit, uniting themselves to him in the love and friendship of charity. Then, third, are those who are united to Christ by their belief in him, but are not united with him in charity. They may be baptized Christians, possibly even active members of the empirical church, but they are presently in mortal sin. Finally, the fourth group consists of those who are only potentially united with Christ. They may be predestined either to become actually united with him one day or else to die without becoming united, thereby ceasing to be members of Christ's body even potentially (ST 3.8.3). Significantly, Thomas makes the third and fourth group overlap somewhat, placing among those who are only potentially united to Christ some of those in the third group, because their loveless faith does not 'actually' unite them to Christ. Thomas does add, however, that their 'formless' faith, faith that is not enlivened by charity, unites them to Christ relatively, albeit lifelessly (ST 3.8.3 ad 2).

Thomas introduces some other significant distinctions in his fundamentally Christological understanding of the church. Christ is the head of *all* rational creatures, so his body, the church, includes the angels as well as humans. The church on earth, at least that part of it sufficiently actualized by grace to be what he calls elsewhere the 'congregation of the faithful' or, as here, the church of the *viatores*, is different from the heavenly church, which consists of the *comprehensores*. Only the heavenly church is without sin; the earthly church, which is not yet in the state of glory, remains sinful (ST 3.8.3 ad 2). It is usually through the earthly church that we receive the theological virtues of faith, hope and charity and the gifts of the Holy Spirit. But Thomas does not rule out the possibility of acquiring grace sufficient for salvation outside the empirical church (but, of course, always within the body of Christ). Thomas follows the tradition in holding that there have always been members of Christ's church who have not been members of the empirical church. Ever since Abel, the brother of Cain, there have been just people, obedient and pleasing to God because they were 'instructed by an inward instinct as to the way of worshipping God' (ST 2/2.93.1 ad 2). Clearly, for Thomas, Christ's salvific power is not limited by natural or institutional boundaries; it is universal in scope.

The Holy Spirit

Thus far I have talked of grace in relation to Jesus Christ, but Thomas by no means forgets the mission of the third person. Salvation is brought about by faith in Christ, but we have seen that faith as such is insufficient unless it is quickened by love, the charity (Lat. *caritas*) which comes to us through the Holy Spirit. The work of both divine persons is necessary, then, for grace and merit. It is the Holy Spirit who transforms us and heals us of our sins through Christ's merits: 'The Holy Spirit comes only to those who are joined to Jesus Christ as their head, and it is only through the Holy Spirit that our sins are remitted' (*Sup. Rom.* 8:2, n. 605). The Spirit operates by moving us towards God, making us God's 'lovers' or 'friends' (ScG 4.22.2). We want to do the will of our friends, so it is the Holy Spirit who moves us to obey God's will freely and willingly (ScG 4.22.4–6, citing Rom. 8:14f.). The Holy Spirit, then, works in a distinctive way in the economy of salvation, primarily as an interior movement that inclines us to the good and prompts us to move towards it. The 'fruits' of the Holy Spirit are our meritorious acts which, in the same way that fruits are pleasurable, give us delight simply in doing them (ST 1/2.70.1 ad 2).

The Holy Spirit, we recall, is properly named 'love' and 'gift'. Thomas tends to discuss the work of the Spirit using abstract terms like 'grace' and 'merit'. As I continue my account of his treatise on grace, it is important to remember that we are really considering a treatise on the work of the Holy Spirit, for grace is the Spirit's loving and self-giving mission which, though often working incognito, is ever present in the Christian life.

Grace

Grace is the action of the triune God that brings us into a relation with God that so transforms and perfects the created relation that we may live a new life in the Risen Christ. Grace originates with, and remains entirely dependent upon, the person and work of Christ, but it is appropriated by us and works in us through the power of the Holy Spirit, who draws us to the Father in the Son.

All grace comes solely through 'the personal action of Jesus Christ himself', never through our created relation to God or through our nature (ST 3.8.5 ad 1). The grace of Christ is therefore necessary for us to achieve our proper end. Its necessity does not undermine its gratuity, however. Grace is given 'graciously', i.e., without necessity, as a genuine gift that God is under no obligation to give. God loves with 'a special love' – that is, with the love of the Holy Spirit – those creatures who are most like God in that they have free will. So it is through God's love that God draws the rational creature to participate in the divine good (ST 1/2.110.1). The necessity of grace for us, then, is a consequence of God's loving and free eternal decision to bring us to our proper end in this way in accordance with the divine plan.

The two main reasons why grace is necessary reflect what might loosely be termed the negative and the positive effects of Christ's redemptive activity. Christ suffered and died in order to free us from sin; he rose and ascended in order to bring us the gifts that make possible our journey into God. Likewise, Christ's grace overcomes sin and works to heal us of its effects; it also enables us to work towards our proper end, to rise beyond our capacities. The second, 'positive' effect of grace indicates that even if the first humans had remained innocent and without sin, they would still have needed grace to achieve their proper end. (Angels need Christ's grace, too (ST 1.62.3).) In the state of innocence before the Fall, Adam had a natural love for God, whom he desired above all things without any help beyond his nature. But he could not have moved towards God, nor could he have acted in any way to merit everlasting life, unless he had additional help, the gift of grace, because grace is required 'to do any good whatsoever' that is directed to our supernatural end. No action of ours can be proportionate to our end, which is our 'enjoyment of God'; 'for this a higher force is needed, viz., the force of grace' (ST 1/2.109.5). Moreover, though in the state of innocence it would have been possible for Adam to avoid sin, this, too, would have been possible only with God's help. And once our natures became corrupt and we were in a state of sin without the help of grace, we could avoid some sins but not all of them; we could not remain for long without mortal sin (ST 1/2.109.8). Grace has been and always will be necessary for us until we attain the glory of full participation in the life of God.

Thomas spends about six questions carefully going through the various things that need to be said about grace, building on the influential work of Augustine in this area. He makes a few distinctions between the different ways in which grace operates. These were developed later by Neo-Scholastic theologians in terms of different 'kinds' of grace – elevating, sanctifying, created, actual, habitual and the like – a process which tidied up what Thomas often leaves comparatively vague. Almost all that Thomas says in these questions is concerned in one way or another to forestall two frequent misunderstandings, the first of which he may well have fallen into himself in his commentary on Peter Lombard's *Sentences*.[2] First, he rules out any notion that we can do anything whatsoever towards our salvation by ourselves without grace. Second, he rules out the idea that we are merely manipulated by grace, as if it programs us to act without our free consent or active involvement. Again, throughout the discussion, it is important to remember that Thomas uses the word 'grace' as a useful abstract term for the work of the Holy Spirit within us. Especially in light of later Roman Catholic theology, it is all too easy to think of grace as an 'it', as a 'thing' that exists or acts in a way somehow separate from God. It is not unreasonable to talk about God being 'in' us, especially with regard to grace. In fact, however, God is and works in things 'as containing them' rather than as contained by them, on the analogy of the soul, which is not contained by the body, but contains it (ST 1.8.1 ad 2).

As he often does, Thomas draws a parallel between natural and super-natural matters. All creatures are naturally (i.e., apart from grace) dependent upon God's work within them in two ways, for their existence and for their operation. God brings creatures into existence by infusing into them their form or soul which enables them to be what or who they are. That move-ment enables creatures to perform their 'first act', the act of existence as such (*actus essendi*) (ST 1.48.5; 1.75.5 ad 1). But the soul provides only the basic equipment for a creature's operation; having a soul does not of itself lead the creature to perform any particular action. So God acts in a second way to move creatures so that they act in accordance with their natures. How we act is therefore determined by our natures and by God's providen-tial oversight (ST 1.103.1). Rational creatures like humans are different from other creatures in that they are moved through their free will. Earlier I noted Thomas's doctrine of the divine *concursus*, according to which both God and I are the efficient causes of my one action, but at such radically different levels that each of us is wholly and freely responsible for it. The transcendent God is the primary cause of my action, working immanently within me so that I can be the secondary though genuine cause of, say, driving my car to work.

For Thomas it is quite conceivable that what appears to be an obviously 'good' act, such as helping an old lady across the street, could be merely a 'natural' act, one, that is, which could be performed without the gift of grace and thus without any merit attached. It would then be merely 'generically good' at best. Without grace, all actions, including acts of 'patience and fortitude' and even the act of faith itself, lack merit (ST 1/2.114.4 ad 3). If I am infused with grace, two changes take place in me that parallel the two acts of God in the natural sphere. First, on the analogy with my 'first act' of existence, God re-creates my nature so that it becomes capable of doing more than it could by its natural power. I now have been given the basic equipment to act 'supernaturally' and thereby meritoriously. My soul has been qualitatively transformed so that I could help the old lady in a way that would draw me closer to God. But this transformation is only the formal cause of meritorious action, as the human soul is only the formal cause of natural actions. Formal causes are not enough to move me to act (as Thomas realized by the time he wrote the ST). So by a second movement, God, who is the efficient cause of my meritorious action, moves me and prompts me, the secondary cause, to perform the meritorious action of helping someone.

Both of these movements on God's part are called 'grace'. The first movement 'elevates' me, lifting me up beyond my nature so that I now have the basic equipment to do more than I would otherwise be able to do. It gives me a 'habit' (*habitus*), a technical term for Thomas which refers to a particular quality I now have (Lat. *habeo*) that gives me the potentiality or capacity for doing particular actions. The term shares something with our more ordinary usage in that a habit is hard to get rid of. Thomas quotes Aristotle as saying it is 'a quality which it is difficult to change' (ST 1/

2.49.1 *sed contra*). One may have an 'acquired habit' by repetition of an action, as one might gain the habit of getting up at a particular time in the morning. Or a habit may be 'infused' in us without any activity on our part, as our ability to understand the first principles of reason is infused in our intellects (ST 1/2.51.4). Some habits dispose one to do good acts, in which case they are virtues. Other habits dispose one to evil acts and are called vices (ST 1/2.54.3).

It is as an infused habit that grace inclines the soul towards meritorious actions. As a quality infused into the soul's very essence, habitual grace becomes something I 'have', part of my equipment, almost – but not – as if it were part of my nature; it is a kind of 'second nature' for me which Thomas calls 'connatural'. Thomas distinguishes habitual grace from the infused theological virtues, with which one might have expected them to be identical, as Peter Lombard thought they were. Thomas draws the parallel with nature again. My nature provides the basis for actions which are made possible by my natural virtues; only because I am human can I acquire or have infused in me the virtues that enable me to help someone across the street. But my nature is only potentially active; to act, the virtues must come into play. Similarly, habitual grace is that basic quality in me which makes it possible for the theological virtues to bring me to act meritoriously (ST 1/2.110.3; 1/2.49.3 ad 1). 'Grace is the principle of meritorious works through the medium of the virtues, as the essence of the soul is the principle of vital deeds through the medium of the powers' (ST 1/2.110.4 ad 2). Habitual grace, to be sure, is not a natural quality or habit, like being healthy is. It is gratuitous and therefore accidental and additional to our nature, though it is one which remains in us permanently unless we sin mortally.

The effect of the first movement of grace is to justify those who receive it. This happens instantaneously, with the infusion of grace, rather than as a process over time, because we must first be justified in order to enter as *viatores* upon the Christian life. For Thomas, justice is achieved when those involved are given what is due to them so that they are in a right relation to one another (ST 2/2.58.1). Sin offended God; by grace, God is at peace with us, a peace which consists simply 'in the love whereby God loves us'. Our sin is remitted and we are 'turned' by a 'movement of the mind' to desire God and hate sin. There is now 'a certain rectitude of order in our interior disposition', making it possible for us to overcome our servitude to sin. Our emotions and appetites are now subject to our reason and our reason obedient to God (ST 1/2.113.1). Following Romans 5:1, Thomas argues that there is no other way to be justified before God except through faith. We cannot turn to God by our natural powers because our unaided reason is unable to know God as the cause of our justification (ST 1/2.113.4 ad 2). Only faith moves the mind beyond its natural powers so as to turn us to God.

To repeat, the gift of habitual grace does not yet enable me to act; it only turns me in the appropriate direction, so to speak, so that I am disposed to act 'sweetly and promptly to acquire eternal good' (ST 1/2.110.2). For me actually to perform a good work I need the second movement of grace 'beyond' the 'first effect' of grace. In this movement, the Holy Spirit, 'together with the Father and the Son, moves and protects us' (ST 1/2.109.9 ad 2), prompting me to act with free will to do the good.

Thomas makes a distinction between what he calls *gratia gratum faciens* and *gratia gratis data*, between the grace that 'makes one gracious' or pleasing to God, and the grace that is 'given freely'. The first kind of grace is often and quite reasonably translated as 'sanctifying grace' because it makes us holy.[3] However, later Roman Catholic theology tended to restrict *gratia gratum faciens* to habitual grace, as if it involved only the first movement of grace, the transformation of the soul, without the second movement, which prompts meritorious action on our part. Thomas is not very clear on the matter but it would seem at least as reasonable to think that he considers grace *gratum faciens* to be the movement of grace *as a whole*, encompassing both operations of the Spirit, which together bring us beyond mere inclination to act in conformity to Jesus Christ and thereby to 'a participated likeness in the divine nature' (ST 3.62.1). If this is a reasonable interpretation, then the phrase 'justifying grace' refers only to the infusion of habitual grace (as in ST 1/2.113.3 ad 3, where it is explicitly so in the Latin) and not used to translate *gratia gratum faciens*, which requires action 'in charity', i.e., done with the help of the Holy Spirit (ST 1/2.114.4 ad 3, where Thomas cites 1 Cor. 13:3).

The movement of grace in us may thus be compared to the work of the divine person in the humanity of Christ. It is by grace that we are brought into conformity with Christ, and our conformity is in significant ways analogous to his way of being. Like Christ, though in a dependent and appropriately limited fashion, our grace-enabled action may well include work that contributes to the salvation of other people. Hence Thomas's second kind of grace, *gratia gratis data*, grace which is 'freely given' in the sense that it does not contribute to one's own sanctification but instead enables us to help others so as to lead them to God. Thomas has in view 1 Cor. 12:8–10, where Paul lists the charisms of the church's leaders given by the Holy Spirit, such as the wisdom to preach and to teach, the ability to prophesy, work miracles, speak in tongues and the like. Though Thomas himself does not use the phrase, this kind of grace could perhaps be termed 'ecclesiastical grace' because, as he says, it is 'ordained to the common good of the church, which is ecclesiastical order' (ST 1/2.111.5 ad 1) and 'ordained for the manifestation of faith and spiritual doctrine' (ST 3.7.7). As one would expect, Christ is the source of this grace and had it to an unparalleled degree as head of the church and as its first and chief teacher.

Thomas further addresses the issue of dual causality in human meritorious action by making another distinction, namely between operating and cooperating grace. Operating grace is reserved to those occasions when only God works in us without any movement on our part. God works alone in moving us to will the good rather than evil; for example, by prompting me to consider helping someone, prior to any decision or action on my part. More fundamentally, operating grace works as such to justify me and transform my soul, elevating it without any movement on my part. Cooperating grace, on the other hand, comes into play when God helps me make the decision to help someone, and then again when I act meritoriously (ST 1/ 2.111.2).

Merit and Predestination

With these clarifications of our language regarding the work of the Holy Spirit within us, Thomas has made it clear that we can do nothing that effects our salvation without grace. Having been given grace, though, we must act so as to cooperate in God's work for our salvation. Cooperating grace enables and prompts us to achieve our salvation by our meritorious action. The final question of the treatise on grace addresses the notion of merit. Here Thomas is concerned to forestall misunderstandings, common throughout the church's history, regarding the relation between merit and grace.

We have seen that the Pelagian view of merit – the notion that, if we do our best, God will give us the grace of our heavenly reward – is far too simple-minded. We may indeed do the best we can, but without grace, not one of our actions has any bearing whatsoever upon our relation to God. A more subtle form of the Pelagian view, sometimes called 'semi-Pelagianism', contends that we, while yet unaided by grace, must make the initial move. We must merit grace by showing our worthiness for it and its effects before we are given it. Once it has been given to us, we can then go on to merit salvation more or less in the way Thomas describes. A common formulation during the Middle Ages was to say that we must 'do the best we can' (Lat. *facere quod in se est* – to do what is in one), so that God has *reason* to reward us with the grace that we *then* cooperate with to act meritoriously. Indeed, if we do our best, then God may be understood to *owe* us grace. Augustine suggested something like this when he said that 'faith merits justification', where 'faith', at least in its inception, is something we do by our natural powers alone. On this view of merit, we would earn our subsequent justification without the aid of grace. Augustine himself later retracted this view, as Thomas notes, acknowledging that faith itself is from its very beginning an effect of grace; 'we believe, whilst we are being justified' (ST 1/2.114.5 ad 1). Any notion that God becomes indebted to us because of our natural efforts is thus ruled out.

Thomas prepares for his discussion of merit by making a distinction between prevenient and subsequent grace. Prevenient grace is the movement of grace that is prior to our response; subsequent grace is the effect of prevenient grace, which involves our response. Thomas notes that there are 'five effects of grace in us: of these, the first is, to heal the soul; the second, to desire good: the third, to carry into effect the good proposed; the fourth, to persevere in good; the fifth, to reach glory' (ST 1/2.111.3). Each effect is by grace, but after the first each can be looked at in two ways. The third effect, for example, is from one perspective a grace subsequent to the second effect, while it is a grace prevenient to the fourth effect. For example, when I carry into effect the proposed action of, say, fasting or making a vow, I do so subsequently to the grace which enables me to desire the good. But my fasting or vowing is prevenient to the subsequent grace which effects my persevering in the good. The Holy Spirit is always prevenient, always there prior to our response, making the first move. There can be no initial movement of grace that we could merit without the presence of the Holy Spirit. The first grace which is prevenient to all others is merited by no one. It comes to us through our incorporation into the body of Jesus Christ, whose actions alone were sufficient to merit grace for others (ST 1/2.114.5).

Once the necessity of prevenient grace is acknowledged we can retrieve the notion – fundamentally a pastoral counsel rather than a moral principle – of 'doing the best we can'. Here, once again, Thomas makes a distinction that reflects two perspectives on the one action. Willingly doing whatever we can to follow Christ obediently by grace is sufficient for us to merit eternal life 'congruently' or proportionately. It is proportionate in the sense of 'fitting' because our merits are achieved in free will, and free will is the distinctive attribute of the rational creature by which it operates for its proper end. It is proportionate, too, in the sense of 'relative', because our action can be only relatively meritorious, since there is 'very great inequality' between the act and the reward. No human action is sufficient to earn heaven by right, as if we could possibly give God something of equal value to eternal life. From another perspective, though, our meritorious works proceed 'from the grace of the Holy Spirit'. Consequently, and only as such, can they be considered 'condign', truly worthy of eternal reward (ST 1/2.114.3).

If we can do nothing to affect God's decision to give us grace, the question arises as to why grace is given and why we have to merit our proper end. Certainly, there is nothing for God to gain by what we do, meritoriously or otherwise, since God has no real relation with us. Grace and merit only bring us into a salvific relation with God; God remains unchanged. Thomas suggests that 'God seeks from our goods not profit, but glory, i.e., the manifestation of God's goodness' (ST 1/2.114.1 ad 2).[4] But God's glory could conceivably be manifest in other ways, perhaps, for example, by simply bringing us into eternal life without our having to do anything. This would not be fitting, however, because God created us so that our proper end is to be achieved by the exercise of our free will. And if we ask why God created us in this way, we must fall back upon the most basic reason for everything. Humanity is to merit eternal life with God by grace 'chiefly' because God ordained it to be that way (ST 1/2.114.4).

Thus the larger context for Thomas's teaching on grace and merit is his understanding of God's eternal plan for us, his doctrine of providence, of which predestination through grace and merit is a part. God has complete and absolute power over everything, but God uses that power to fulfill a plan conceived eternally and freely in God's wisdom (ST 1.25.5 ad 1). God's creation and ordering of things is done according to God's foreknowledge, wisdom and prudence, i.e., by divine providence (ScG 3.97.10). According to God's providential design, creation is good in two ways, reflecting the overarching pattern of *exitus* and *reditus*, creation's movement forth from God and its return to God. Creatures are good because they exist; they also have the good that is their last end, which is God. God directs all creatures to their last end by providence, both directly, through their natures and operations, and indirectly, through other creatures, because 'the dignity of causality is imparted even to creatures' (ST 1.22.3; 1.73.1). God thus has complete and direct power over all things because they exist and they operate as they are known by God in the Word. Divine providence is thus the primary cause of why things happen, including things that happen contingently or by chance. It is by the will of God that they happen just so (ScG 3.94.10), for the 'idea' (Lat. *ratio*) of what occurs determinately or contingently pre-exists in God's intellect (ST 1.23.1).

Rational creatures like angels and humans are different from all other creatures in that God permits them to operate according to their own 'providence'. That is, we are to use our reason and free will to order ourselves with foresight, or 'providentially', to our last end, rather than being directed to it involuntarily and by nature, as are creatures that lack reason. However, our 'providence', our willing and reasoning, is still governed by God, 'as a particular under a universal cause' (ST 1.22.2 ad 4). And God's providence has predestined some rational creatures, both human and angelic, to order themselves to their final end, while others are to fail to do so. For those elected to eternal life, God prevents anything happening that would impede their final salvation. For those not elected, the will of God is to 'permit a person to fall into sin, and to impose the punishment of damnation on account of that sin' (ST 1.23.3). Thus rational creatures are either predestined to eternal life or they are 'reprobated'.

There is nothing whatsoever that we could do which would affect this decision since it is made prior to our coming into being. In grace, we may hope that our efforts to follow Christ obediently are indeed meritorious. We may hope, that is, that we have been predestined to salvation, but the success of our efforts is entirely determined by God's universal providence. Predestination is not something that is 'in' us in any way; it is God's eternal decision quite apart from what and who we are. Thus it cannot be that God looks on to see how we are doing, and then decides our fate. Nor is it the case that God knows beforehand what we will do when we are given grace, and so decides prior to our creation what will happen to us in light of foreknowing our efforts. God gives grace to some such that they merit glory. Grace is given to others, yet they fail through sin to merit glory. And saving grace is not given to others at all. Although he argues that the number of the

elect is known only to God, Thomas does not seem to think that the repro-
bate are only a few. On the contrary, he insists that 'those who are saved are
in the minority' (ST 1.23.7 ad 3). He suggests that this is fitting because it
better displays God's goodness. As the diversity of creatures is better than
uniformity for manifesting the beauty of creation and the dignity of its
creator, so the diversity of election and reprobation better manifest God's
mercy and justice (ST 1.23.5 ad 3).

Clearly, then, we are entirely at the mercy of God. God displays mercy by
offering grace to all who do not prevent it from entering into them (ScG
3.159.2). To be sure, unless prevenient grace works in us, our sinfulness will
make us obstruct any movement of grace (ScG 3.160). And however saintly
we are reckoned to be by others or by ourselves, we cannot be sure that we
have received grace. The best we can do is infer our predestination by signs
such as our joy in worshipping God and our lack of concern over worldly
things (ST 1/2.112.5). And even though we may have been given grace, it is
very possible that we will not be given the grace to persevere in grace (the
fourth effect of grace needed to attain the fifth, which is glory). The grace of
perseverance in the Christian life until the last act is given only to those who
are predestined to achieve their proper end (ST 1/2.114.9).

The Theological Virtues

Habitual grace elevates us beyond our natural capacities, disposing us to act
meritoriously. The second movement of grace causes us to perform the act.
The means in us by which we act are the virtues, both infused and acquired,
theological and natural. They are in effect the bridge between our intention
to act and our actual performance. In his account of the virtues, Thomas
makes considerable use of Aristotle's moral theory, especially when he
discusses the natural virtues. However, he makes it very clear that what may
be ours by nature, or acquired naturally, is entirely inadequate by itself for
achieving eternal life. The natural virtues are virtues only 'in a restricted
sense', since they are not oriented towards our final end (ST 1/2.65.2).
They must be transformed by the infusion of the theological virtues. Failure
to acknowledge this makes it all too easy to interpret Thomas's moral
theology (as some have done) as simply Aristotelianism with a veneer of
Christianity.

A virtue is 'an operational habit', a disposition towards a particular kind
of action. A theological virtue is an operational habit informed by grace. As
Augustine defines it, it is 'a good habit of the mind by which we live
righteously, of which no one can make bad use, which God works in us,
without us' (ST 1/2.55.4). God works in us as the efficient cause of infused
virtue, and works 'without us' in that we cannot contribute to the effect by
our natural powers, as we could contribute to God's work within us through
our natural virtues. Yet God works in us with our consent and in a way that
fits our nature, and thus works through our voluntary action. Our true

happiness is God, our last end, whom we attain by our action (ST 1/2.3.2). Thus because it is the virtues that move us to act, they are the means by which we move towards happiness. Virtues are settled dispositions; they are part of who we are concretely. So happiness is contingent upon becoming a certain kind of person, one whose actions have been perfected and completed by participation in God's nature. And because that completion will occur only after our death, when we are glorified by participation in the divine life, the virtues are oriented beyond this life to the next.

Christ achieved our salvation by means of his humanity, not by overriding or ignoring it. Similarly, our last end is attained through our nature, provided that it becomes elevated by our participation in Christ's grace through the Holy Spirit. Our natural capacities need to be formed and strengthened by the natural virtues, of which there are two kinds. The intellectual virtues empower the speculative reason, i.e., thought without direct concern for action, and include wisdom, science and understanding (ST 1/2.57.2). The moral virtues – the chief of which are temperance, courage or fortitude, justice and prudence – pertain to practical reason, i.e., thought which leads to, and is completed by, action. The moral virtues bring our appetites under the control of reason. Again, though, because

> our happiness surpasses the capacity of human nature, our natural principles [= the virtues], which enable us to act well according to our capacities, do not suffice to direct us to this same happiness. Hence it is necessary for us to receive from God some additional principles, whereby we may be directed to supernatural happiness, even as we are directed to our connatural end, by means of our natural principles, albeit not without the divine assistance. (ST 1/2.62.1)

These 'additional principles' are called 'theological' virtues because they direct us to God as our final end; they are infused by God rather than acquired in the usual way by practice; they are made known to us through revelation; and they unite our minds to God. Thomas sums up the relation between the two kinds of virtues:

> wherever we find a good human act, it must correspond to some human virtue. Now in all things measured and ruled, the good is that which attains its proper rule: thus we say that a coat is good if it neither exceeds nor falls short of its proper measurement. But ... human acts have a twofold measure; one is proximate and homogeneous, viz., the reason, while the other is remote and excelling, viz., God: wherefore every human act is good which attains reason through God. (ST 2/2.17.1)

To be rational is to be free; and to be rational is to think and freely act in accordance with God's reason and will. The theological virtues enable us to act rationally for our last end, and thereby enable us to follow Christ and his way obediently, since for us to be obedient, we must be able to have free choice and follow our own counsel (ST 2/2.104.1 ad 1). It is through Jesus's

humanity, his meritorious obedience and his capital grace that our humanity
is linked to God. The purpose of our existence, our *raison d'être*, is to
become like Jesus, as far as the radical differences between us and him will
allow, for it is in becoming like him that we will become fully human and
fully ourselves. Our humanity is complete and perfect only when we are
drawn through our obedience into the person of Christ, something which is
possible only because of the obedience of Christ himself to the Father. But
the theological virtues, like habitual grace, are not sufficient of themselves
for us to follow Christ obediently; we still need the second movement of
grace. 'By the theological and moral virtues people are not so perfected in
respect of their last end as not to stand in continual need of being moved by
the yet higher promptings of the Holy Spirit' (ST 1/2.68.2 ad 2). The
virtues, though, both natural and theological, are the essential equipment.
They are discussed in detail in ST 2/2, beginning with the theological and
then the acquired. I will follow Thomas's order.[5]

Faith

Faith is the potentially salvific orientation towards God made possible in us
by grace alone. It is the only entryway we have into the Christian life and is
necessary for anyone's salvation. According to Thomas's definition, 'faith is
a habit of the mind, whereby eternal life is begun in us, making the intellect
assent to what is non-apparent' (ST 2/2.4.1). Because the object of faith –
that which is believed – is God as the first truth, faith is primarily a matter of
the intellect. But faith should not be confused with simple intellectual
assent; it involves a free decision on our part. God does not move our minds
in the same way empirical objects or necessary truths do. I am compelled to
assent to the existence of the person who stands visibly before me; denying
what is patently obvious would be irrational. Likewise, it would be irrational for me to deny the truth of a Euclidean theorem. In contrast, God is
never present before us in a way that would compel us to assent to God's
existence, so we have to decide whether to believe or not. Faith is the act of
will by which we decide – aided by the gift of grace which moves us to our
decision – to believe in what is 'invisible' to us, in the broad sense of what it
is logically possible *not* to believe in.

Thomas illustrates his point by referring to the story of 'doubting Thomas' (John 20:24–9). The apostle saw and acknowledged the existence of
Jesus, but so could anyone else who saw him risen and had known him
before his death; they had no choice in the matter. Thomas the apostle had
faith, not in what he saw, though that certainly contributed to his act of faith.
He had to decide, like anyone else who saw Jesus face to face, whether or
not the man standing before him was indeed his Lord and God (ST 2/2.1.4
ad 1). Because faith is fundamentally an act of will, it is useless and beside
the point, as we saw earlier, for Christians to try to make water-tight demonstrative arguments for what they believe. All we can do is argue against

erroneous beliefs and show the flaws in false arguments so as to keep the decision to believe a subjective possibility. Only in heaven, as *comprehensores*, will we see God face to face and have, so to speak, the empirical evidence that will render faith unnecessary, indeed, impossible.

Christian faith is quite specific: it is freely willed intellectual assent to what is revealed by God. One believes in God because one believes God, one trusts what God teaches. Concretely, this means that the Christian believes God by believing what the Word reveals about God through Scripture and the church. Faith is therefore belief in the God revealed in Jesus Christ, the three-personed God described in the articles of the church's Creed. The triune God is the 'formal object' of faith, by which Thomas means that faith is an orientation to all things in so far as they have some relation to God. Faith thus encompasses absolutely all things 'insofar as by them we are directed to God, and in as much as we assent to them on account of the divine Truth' (ST 2/2.1.1 ad 1). Thus Christians are required to believe in creation, for example, in that they assent to the claim that creation is in a relation of dependence upon God both for its existence and for its operation. But Christians are not required to believe in those things which we may know or discover about creatures apart from their relation to God. One reason for this is that such knowledge is likely to be empirical or demonstrative and thus, by definition, cannot be faith knowledge. Moreover, it is likely that Thomas would consider that modern scientific theories, such as the theory of evolution, the 'Big Bang' theory and even the 'Grand Theory of Everything' sought by some scientists, have little or no direct bearing upon faith, since they all view created reality *apart* from any relation to God. To the extent that they could clarify that relation, they are useful to the theologian; to the extent that they raise difficulties for the act of faith, the theologian may need to engage them in argument.

Thomas's concept of faith cannot be reduced to a kind of generic belief in God as, say, the designer of the universe, or as the divine power which will make everything turn out well in the end, though faith may include such beliefs. As a habit, faith is a disposition to assent willingly to what Christ taught through the apostles and the church (ST 2/2.11.1). Though it is a matter of will or even, as one might say today, of personal choice, it evidently involves a will to *obey*, because the infusion of faith moves the will interiorly by the Holy Spirit to assent to the church's teachings. Thomas's notion of faith might be difficult to accept by some contemporaries because faith in God is now sometimes thought of as such a personal matter that the notion of obedience seems foreign to it. Thomas explicitly rules out the notion that one can pick and choose among the various beliefs of the church so as to construct a personal form of Christianity. To reject one of the articles of faith is to follow merely a personal choice, and thus to hold what Thomas calls a mere 'opinion'. If I persist in my erroneous belief even after I have been informed that it is wrong, I fall into heresy. For example, I might accept most Christian beliefs but I have some difficulty accepting the teaching on grace and merit, perhaps choosing a form of Pelagianism. It may be that I do not understand the incoherence of Pelagianism and am unaware of its condemnation by the church. Once informed, though, I must reject my error if I am to avoid heresy.

However, this applies only to those doctrines that have been authoritatively decided upon by the church. Pelagius himself was not a heretic since the church had not yet rejected the notion of merit independent of grace. Thomas himself taught doctrines which the church later defined differently, notably the Immaculate Conception. Well-intentioned theological inquiry, even if it leads sometimes to erroneous teaching, is never condemned by Thomas. What makes a heretic is a 'choice [of belief] in contradiction to the teaching of the church' (ST 2/2.2 ad 3). One must persist in one's erroneous belief, holding it while knowing that the church has defined a doctrine that it denies or distorts. If I were to teach others my heretical beliefs, Thomas argues that I should be given a chance or two to recant them, and then, if I remain obstinate, I should be put to death. The reason for this is that if I preach a false opinion about God (which Pelagianism amounts to), then those who followed me would not really know God; they would have the wrong object for their faith and worship and for their intended final end (ST 2/2.10.3). My erroneous preaching would be likely to deny them their salvation, especially if I led them to reject the church's teaching knowingly (ST 2/2.11.1). Loss of eternal life is obviously worse than anything else, so my offence as a heretical or sectarian preacher would be much worse than any other offence that in Thomas's day was thought to deserve capital punishment, such as forgery (ST 2/2.11.3). If someone should refer to Matthew 18:22, where Jesus tells Peter that sins are always to be forgiven, Thomas replies that Jesus's saying applies only to sins against oneself. 'It is not left to our discretion to forgive' those who sin against one's neighbor and against God, if the neighbor's good or God's honor demands appropriate punishment (ST 2/2.11.4 ad 2).

For some people this will smack of authoritarianism or worse, but an analogy with modern science may modify first impressions somewhat. Suppose that I accept the beliefs about the universe shared by modern scientists. As one who is not a trained physicist, I must accept many of my beliefs as an act of will, even, one might say, as an act of obedience, in that I willingly trust the authority of those who know about matters which I cannot investigate for myself. Scientists may agree that time travel is theoretically possible (for the sake of the example, let us assume so). I may find the notion impossible to accept. If, upon my inquiry, I find that time travel is regarded as an uncontroversial theoretical possibility by all those who know about such things, for me to persist in withholding my belief would be irrational. Were I to make the effort to understand the scientists' theoretical arguments, and yet still continued to reject their assertion without good counter-arguments of my own, then I would be no doubt pitied by the scientists as a fool. And if I taught science in the school system, they might regard me as a menace to my students, because I would be likely to teach those in my charge a false understanding of the universe.

At a deeper level, we recall that, for Thomas, obedience to the will of God is transformative. Staying with one's own personal beliefs about God is to stay closed up in oneself and untransformed by the salvific truth and goodness that comes from God. Again, the parallel with science applies, perhaps with any form of intellectual inquiry. Most of us would consider unfortunate those who are so dull of mind that they refuse to open themselves up to the wonders of the universe discovered by science, and persist instead in the errors of what seems to them to be common sense. Faith is the first step in a much greater transformation, the first shift in orientation away from our limited 'natural' views of God and reality. Faith initiates the lifelong training that is at the core of the Christian life, the ongoing struggle to become someone other than the sinners that we are, to become those who prepare for the life of glory.

In my example, the scientists and I have sufficiently broad areas of agreement to permit us to hold a discussion and formulate arguments and counter-arguments. Were I not to accept the modern scientific conception of the universe, we would have little to argue about in the first place. The equivalent with regard to faith for Thomas is its opposite, unbelief. Unbelievers cannot be heretics; they have never accepted Christian faith and the church's teachings, so they cannot reject them. Unbelievers are of two kinds. An unbeliever may never have heard of Christianity. The Inuit of a millennium ago were not responsible for their lack of belief in Jesus Christ, so they did not sin. Rather, their unbelief is a punitive consequence of original sin. It will deprive them of salvation because there is no salvation without faith; without faith we are not justified, and unless we are justified, we cannot do meritorious works (ST 2/2.12.1 ad 2). The unbeliever may, however, be able to do deeds that are 'generically good' in that they conform to natural reason, such as building cities and raising their children. So unbelievers do not sin in everything they do. However, a second kind of unbelief is sinful because it results either from a refusal to listen to the Gospel preached or from actively despising it (ST 2/2.10.1).

Thomas contends that even though faith is necessary for salvation, unbelievers should not be forced into the church. This is, he says, particularly the case with regard to the Jews, since their religion foreshadowed Christianity, and so it still manifests truth about God. Throughout the church's history there have been occasional attempts to baptize the children of Jews without their parents' assent.[6] Thomas condemns this for two reasons. First, it is not unlikely that such children will be persuaded by their parents to revert to Judaism once they are free to do so. They would then reject the faith to which they had submitted before they had attained the age of reason. Second, to take children away from the custody of their father is against natural justice (ST 2/2.10.12). Both reasons reflect the 'danger to faith' of compulsion rather than persuasion. Faith is *free* assent; only those, such as heretics and apostates, who have at one time freely accepted the faith of the church can be compelled to submit to the church by threat of punishment.

Although faith is never reducible to generic belief in God, Thomas does allow various forms of faith, provided that they all involve belief in Christ in some way. 'Belief of some kind in the mystery of Christ's Incarnation was necessary at all times and for all persons, but this belief differed according to differences of times and persons' (ST 2/2.2.7). Christians have explicit faith about the central matters; they must all be aware of and willingly accept the articles of the Creed as true. For the unlearned, faith may be implicit about some of the more secondary matters about which they have not been taught. Such folk would be willing to believe such things were they to be told about them by the church. Those who lived before Christ could not, of course, have any knowledge of the articles of the Creed. If they lived prior to the Fall, their faith involved belief in the future coming of Christ, though not in his Passion, since it was not yet necessary. After the Fall, the just people of the Old Testament believed in the coming incarnate Word and his Passion, too, as the remedy for sin. Thomas submits that the sacrifices of the Old Testament are evidence of such faith since they prefigure the Passion, which the learned among the Israelites believed in explicitly, the ordinary Israelites implicitly. He is willing to go yet further, suggesting that simple belief in a mediator was sufficient for the salvation of some people. Thus certain pagans could be said to have had a kind of faith in Christ because 'they believed that God would deliver humankind in whatever way was pleasing to God', and thus they could be said to have believed in divine providence (ST 2/2.2.7 ad 3).[7]

Hope

Faith begins our salvation by transforming our intellect, turning our minds towards God as our proper end. Likewise, hope begins our movement to-wards God by transforming and turning our will so that we long for God, rather than created things, as our final happiness. Like 'faith' and 'love', which have non-theological as well as theological meanings, 'hope' may refer to any 'future good, difficult but possible to obtain' (ST 2/2.17.1). We may hope for relatively good things like a better job or that the world will survive the threat of global warming. As an infused virtue, though, theologi-cal hope enables us to desire the perfect good, which is 'nothing less than God, since God's goodness, whereby good things are imparted to creatures, is no less than God's essence' (ST 2/2.17.2). Hope, like faith, is a virtue of the *viatores* rather than the *comprehensores*. It is a 'stretching forth' of ourselves to God, a movement of longing that must remain hope until we attain our desire in the next life. Those who are blessed with the vision of God will no longer hope, for they will have all they could ever want. The punishment of the damned is their certain knowledge that they have no hope whatsoever of attaining eternal happiness. Only those in purgatory may continue to hope, for they are wayfarers, too (ST 2/2.18.3).

Hope always involves fear because we fear the non-attainment or loss of that for which we hope. The psalmist says, 'fear is the beginning of wisdom' (Ps. 110:10), which indicates for Thomas that fear of the right kind is a vital element of the Christian life, since theological wisdom is necessary for us to direct ourselves to our proper end. Thomas notes that some people do what they are told is the right thing to do, not because they want to, but out of a fear of punishment; they fear the adverse consequences for themselves of not doing what they should. As a husband, I 'fear' to distance myself from my wife by inappropriate behavior with other women. I might avoid such behavior because I fear my wife's anger or I care about its effect upon my reputation. My concern in such a case would be less with our relationship than with the adverse consequences of my behavior for myself. This would be an example of what Thomas calls 'servile fear', the fear of one, like a slave, who acts under compulsion rather than willingly. If I am obedient to God's will from a fear of being punished, my hope is distorted, for I obey God under compulsion rather than freely and out of love.

Servile fear, then, lacks the loving concern for the other for their own sake. I act appropriately as a husband because I love my wife and do not want to offend or upset her. This Thomas calls 'chaste fear', a concern about our relationship rather than about what might happen to me. The analogous fear of God, which is the kind of fear that begins wisdom in us, is called 'filial fear'. True hope is imbued with the fear of losing the love of God by sin and stupidity. It is exemplified perfectly in the filial fear of Christ himself, the Son of God who seeks to obey his Father in charity. Indeed, in its essence, filial fear is charity itself, the love of God (ST 2/2.19.9 ad 3). That is not to deny that the two fears may be present at times in the same person. What Thomas calls 'initial fear' combines filial and servile, and may be found especially when one has not developed far in the Christian life.

Theological hope thus sets our affections and desires in the right direction and enables us to act with the most fitting motives. Our hope for God prompts us to move forward on the way of Jesus Christ. Without hope, we may fall into its opposite, which is despair. We may believe that our sins are too many or too great to be pardoned. This is sinful because it doubts the power of the forgiveness of sins that Christ has given to his church (ST 2/2.20.2). Another counter to hope is 'worldly fear', through which we may love, and therefore fear to lose, some created good, such as our possessions, our reputation or the object of our distorted desires. Worldly fear makes us love a created good more than God, and so we turn away from God in mortal sin (ST 2/2.19.2 ad 4).

Charity

Both faith and hope differ from charity in that they have as their object that which cannot be attained in the present life, namely the vision of God and eternal life. In contrast, charity is the attainment of a loving fellowship with

God, a union which, while always imperfect in this life, is none the less genuine. Charity is a term of art for Thomas that has little or nothing directly to do with giving money to the poor. It can be translated as 'love', but it is love of a supernatural kind, beyond our natural capabilities, so that, 'though charity is love, yet love is not always charity' (ST 1/2.62.2 ad 3). Moreover, charity is 'not love simply, but has the nature of friendship' (ST 2/2.25.2; ScG 3.95.5; see John 15:15); it is 'the fellowship of the spiritual life, whereby we arrive at happiness' (ST 2/2.25.2 ad 1). Charity is thus fundamentally a relational concept with ontological and practical consequences. It unites us with God as it transforms us and enables us to act meritoriously; in fact, charity *is* union with God, for it is 'a participation of the Holy Spirit' (ST 2/2.23.3 ad 3). Unlike our knowledge of God, which moves first through created things, our love of God is unmediated. We know God as unknowable; but God is essentially lovable, and we love creatures through our love for God (ST 2/2.27.4 ad 2). Charity is therefore the analogy in graced humanity of the personal union of Christ's humanity, which is united with the Son at the most intimate level possible. Our union with God is by the infusion of charity in the power of the Holy Spirit through which we become truly 'friends' of God or, to change from John's to Paul's metaphor, sons and daughters of God by adoption.

Peter Lombard had argued that charity and the Holy Spirit are largely synonymous. Thomas rejected this, not, to be sure, by denying that the very person of the Holy Spirit enters into us, but on the grounds that it is more fitting to understand the role of the Spirit as making it possible for us, on our part, to make a genuine response to God's love. If the Holy Spirit were to work in us without having any effect upon us that enabled us to love God in return, then it would not be we who have a friendship with God, but the Holy Spirit alone. At most we would be an instrument of the Spirit, compelled to love. Real friends freely and joyfully love one another; to become a friend of God we must be transformed rather than simply moved. This is not to say that charity becomes something like an ordinary virtuous habit in us that could increase the more we act charitably or decrease if we do not use it often enough. The transforming movement of charity 'depends neither on the condition of nature nor on the capacity of natural virtue, but only on the will of the Holy Spirit' (ST 2/2.24.3). However, a meritorious response to charity is likely to result in an increase of charity and to our being disposed to that increase. The more God wills to give us charity, the more 'the likeness of the Holy Spirit … [is] perfectly participated by the soul' (ST 2/2.24.5 ad 3).

Charity is a virtue that is oriented towards action, 'a habitual form superadded to the natural power, inclining that power to the act of charity, and causing it to act with ease and pleasure' (ST 2/2.23.2). It brings to us that 'spiritual joy' which is our delight both in God as such and in our participation in God's life (ST 2/2.28.1, 2). Charity must inform all the other virtues for them to work towards our salvation, since 'neither nature nor faith can, without charity, produce a meritorious act' (ST 2/2.2.9 ad 1);

hence all the virtues 'depend upon charity in some way' (ST 1/2.62.2 ad 3). Indeed, strictly speaking, without charity, no other virtue is possible at all, if by virtue we mean the principle of a good action, for only acts done in charity are truly good. Thus it is our participation in the Holy Spirit through charity that enables us to lead a Christian life, to follow Christ obediently as members of his body and to attain eternal life. 'Perfection consists in following just this man, and such perfection is through charity' (*Sup. Matt.* 4:20, n. 373). As the soul is the form of the body, and thus the principle of life without which the body is not really a human body, so charity is the form of faith and hope which enlivens them. 'It is charity which directs the acts of all other virtues to the last end, and which, consequently, also gives the form to all other acts of virtues' (ST 2/2.23.8).

Virtues without charity are therefore unformed, lifeless and distorted. Faith alone cannot save us; even the damned believe in God, though without hope or charity, for they do not see God yet they acknowledge that God has judged them (ST 2/2.18.3 ad 2). Some members of the church may have faith but lack charity; as a result they act with deformed hope and servile fear. They may do generically good works because God has commanded them, not because their filial fear and love of God prompts them to want to do them. Without charity, their attempts to follow Christ obediently cannot be free. They act under compulsion, their reason not in accord with their will. If to be human is to be rational and free, then only in charity can we act in a completely human way, for only 'where the Spirit is, there is freedom' (2 Cor. 3:17). Obedience to Christ, then, may indeed be 'perfect freedom', provided that it is formed by charity.

> Those who avoid evil, not because it is evil, but because of God's commandment alone, are not free; but those who avoid evil because it is evil, they are free. Now it is that which the Holy Spirit brings about, who perfects the interior spirit of humanity by means of a good habit, such that we do by love what the divine law prescribes. We are thus said to be free, not because we submit to the divine law, but because we are prompted by our good habit to do what the divine law ordains. (*Sup. II Cor.* 3:17, n. 112)[8]

The work of charity is to love, and its precepts are that of the great commandment – to love God and to love one's neighbor as oneself.[9] Thomas points out that this means that in one sense we must love ourselves more than our neighbor. If, to save my neighbor, I would have to sin mortally, my friendship with God must take preference over my neighbor's life (ST 2/ 2.26.4). Obviously this is a special case; it is not at all to suggest that we should place our own earthly concerns above those of our neighbor (ST 2/ 2.44.7). 'Neighbor' refers to anyone, not specifically those who live next door, although Thomas acknowledges that we are likely and with reason to care more for those who are closer in distance and better known to us. All people are our neighbors because they are like us in that they have been created in the image of God and with a 'capacity for glory' (ibid.). Thus our neighbor includes the sinner and our enemy, too.

Gifts of the Holy Spirit

The theological virtues are not of themselves sufficient for the Christian life. In addition to the second movement of the Holy Spirit, we need two other groups of things. First, we must acquire the natural virtues, duly transformed by their relation to the theological virtues. (These I will discuss in the next chapter.) Second, we need the seven gifts of the Holy Spirit, which are derived from the theological virtues, following a traditional spiritual interpretation of the list of Isaiah 11:2f. The gifts are wisdom, knowledge, understanding, counsel, fortitude, piety and fear. Since Isaiah spoke of seven 'spirits' rather than gifts, Thomas considers the seven to be infused in us rather than acquired. They are promptings from the Spirit within us, making us 'amenable to the divine inspiration' (ST 1/2.68.1).

It is not necessary to go through all seven here since many of them are in effect supernatural enhancements of the natural virtues. We have already discussed the gift of filial fear that comes with hope. The theological understanding that comes with faith is an infused supernatural light that enables one to penetrate into the heart of things to gain a 'sure grasp of what is proposed for belief' (ST 2/2.9.1). Such understanding, in this life, enables us to acknowledge God as exceeding all that we can think, as one who is known to us only as one unknown (ST 2/2.8.7). Its opposite is dullness of mind, a lack of interest in thinking about spiritual things that may lead to false assumptions about God. Theological knowledge is the ability to make right judgments about what we should or should not believe. Unlike ordinary knowledge, this gift does not involve discursive reasoning but is a simple infused intuition.

Wisdom is a word used by Thomas in a variety of ways. Wisdom in general is distinguished from understanding in that it has to do with the highest cause (ST 1/2.57.2). Theological wisdom is distinguished from philosophical wisdom in that it is an infused gift by which we are brought to participate in divine wisdom, which is the 'Son, who is the Begotten Wisdom', so that we 'participate in the likeness of the only-begotten and natural Son of God'. Uncreated wisdom 'unites itself to us by the gift of charity, and consequently reveals to us the mysteries the knowledge of which is infused wisdom' (ST 2/2.45.6 ad 1 and 2). Theological wisdom is that gift which enables and completes the link between the moral and the ontological, between our action and our being, a link that is made possible by charity. Wisdom orders all aspects of our lives so that we act to bring ourselves to our proper end according to the first principles of wisdom, which are the articles of faith (ST 2/2.19.7). Wisdom is thus our link with divine law, for it creates in us a 'sympathy or connaturality for Divine things' (ST 2/2.45.2).

Conclusion

At this point Thomas's analysis of charity becomes increasingly concrete as it turns to consider particular kinds of actions and their context in human institutions. These I will discuss in the next chapter. In this chapter we have traced the movement of grace from its origin in Jesus Christ, through the work of the Holy Spirit, to us, as it prepares us for the life of the *viator*, for our journey towards the Father and eternal happiness. Thomas's understanding of the Christian life is evidently thoroughly Trinitarian. The Son and the Holy Spirit bring us back to the Father in the ways appropriated to each person. Thomas's term for this movement – 'grace' – is abstract for the sake of clarity and in deference to the kind of witness on the matter in Scripture. By careful analysis of theological language, Thomas rules out any notion that we may merit salvation apart from the work in us of the Holy Spirit, yet he strongly affirms that our meritorious actions are, by the grace of God, truly *our* actions, free, rational and thus realizing our humanity at a level beyond our nature. The Word and the Spirit elevate, transform and perfect what they have created, rather than make us something other than we are.

In the next and final chapter, I begin by discussing the church and its sacraments. This is the social and material vehicle of grace, and the institutional context for the struggle which constitutes the Christian life as Thomas understood it.

Notes

1 At least, so it could be argued. More recent interpreters, concerned with the perceived individualism of modern life, would have liked Thomas to have stressed this more. Thomas did not share their concern, of course, so he does not address the matter. Yet since his moral theology also relies heavily upon life within community, both ecclesial as well as natural, this would seem to be a reasonable interpretation. I discuss Thomas's ecclesiology further in the next chapter.
2 See Wawrykow (1995) for an excellent account of the development of Thomas's thinking on grace from the perspective of the merit question, together with a good overview of the recent literature. Wawrykow's study includes a good bibliography on the subject, too.
3 Thomas makes little distinction between sanctification and justification, and it is important not to read the debates of the Reformation back into his treatise on grace. Nor should his treatise be read in terms of the controversies among the various Roman Catholic schools of theology of the sixteenth century. Of course, this is not to deny that Thomas's theology of grace may be brought to engage – on its own terms – with any other theology of grace.
4 There is a development in Thomas's thinking on merit from his earlier *Commentary on the Sentences* to the ST. See Wawrykow (1995), esp. pp. 74–8.
5 Thomas also organizes a summary of Christian doctrine according to the three theological virtues in his *Compendium of Theology*, though he finished only faith and part of the way through hope.
6 The well-known case of Pius IX and the six-year-old Jewish boy he took away from his parents is still a cause for scandal in the Roman Catholic church. For an account of the

affair, see David I. Kertzer, *The Kidnapping of Edgardo Mortara* (New York: Knopf, 1997).

7   By the time he came to write the ST, Thomas seemed unwilling to consider the case of a contemporary who had never or only partially heard of Jesus Christ. For some discussion of Thomas's position in the history of the question of the salvation of non-believers, see Francis A. Sullivan, SJ, *Salvation Outside the Church?* (New York/Mahwah: Paulist Press, 1992).

8   I owe the reference to Torrell (1996b), pp. 269f.

9   For a good introduction to Thomas's ethics oriented around the concept of charity, see Wadell (1992).

Chapter 6

Life in the Body of Christ

To be a Christian is to follow obediently and freely the way of Jesus Christ to the Father in the power of the Holy Spirit. The previous chapters have discussed Thomas's understanding of the theological context of the Christian life and how the triune God makes that life a possibility for us. In this concluding chapter I turn to consider the response of those who seek to be obedient to Christ. As one might expect, the focus is on Thomas's moral theology, but its scope must be broader than that, for Thomas believes that the theologian should consider all aspects of human action *vis-à-vis* both God and neighbor, including worship and prayer. I will begin with some general remarks on his notion of moral inquiry,[1] and then discuss his theology of law. The chapter concludes with a brief account of the church, its sacraments and the cardinal virtues, within the context of Thomas's understanding of the Christian life.

Universal yet Particular

The discipline of moral or ethical inquiry has changed significantly since Thomas's day, not least in that it now often forms an area of expertise distinct from systematic and biblical theology or, yet more frequently, an area divorced from theological inquiry altogether. Moral inquiry since Kant (at least) has usually been concerned with discerning the principles and formal rules of right action that are accessible to all and apply to all people everywhere. Kant claimed that one needs nothing other than the wit to think for oneself to appreciate his categorical imperative, which is 'to act that the maxim of your will could always hold at the same time as a principle establishing universal law' (Kant, 1985, p. 30). Anyone with a little disinterestedness can apply the universal principle and ask themselves whether the precept that guides their action in a particular case is one which should apply to all people. At least in theory everyone can have the good will to know and intend what he or she decides is the right thing to do. For Kant and many later moral philosophers, traditional or religious knowledge is unnecessary, even obstructive, and should have no bearing on moral decision-making either generally or with regard to a specific case.

Thomas, of course, does not think of moral inquiry in this way.[2] He believes that human activity should be oriented, not to the present life, but to eternal life with God: 'all human affairs are ordered for the end of beatitude, which is everlasting salvation' (ST 3.59.4). Our present lives are 'on the way', we are *viatores*, so our inquiry as to how to live rightly is teleological, ordered to our proper end or telos, which is God. God and our relation to God bear upon all aspects of moral inquiry, so the 'moral virtues ... are about matters that are ordered to God as their end' (ST 2/2.81.6). Only subsequently – though necessarily – do they relate us to our neighbor. Thomas's inquiry is universal in the sense that for him the Christian life is the only true and salvific form of life. There is no other way to complete happiness than by faith and hope in Christ and obedience to him in charity, by which alone we are justified and elevated so that we may act meritoriously. Yet, as we have seen, Thomas acknowledges that not everyone has been given the grace to enter upon that life, and even fewer will persevere in charity to its completion. Thus Thomas makes a universal claim about the uniqueness of a particular and more or less restricted way of life, something that not a few moderns would find irrational, even morally unjustifiable.

Thomas's notion of moral inquiry is also unlike that of many moderns in that he is less concerned to find ethical rules and principles than he is to describe the transformation that is necessary for us to prepare ourselves for, and earn, our salvation. Acting morally is not in the first place a question of making the right moral decision, perhaps by simply following the appropriate rule or by finding and acting upon the correct answer to a given moral quandary. We have seen that obedient and morally correct action is not of itself necessarily meritorious even if one has faith, since one may act under compulsion or with servile fear. To become a Christian and, even more, to become one who is united as a friend of God and neighbor in charity, is primarily a matter of becoming a certain kind of person. Only as we are elevated and transformed by grace and the infused virtues can we obey God's will freely and filially. 'The act of faith inclines believers' minds so that they believe the author of the law to be one to whom they owe submission' (ST 2/2.22.1). But that is only the beginning. The Christian life is a life of freedom; obedience to Christ is the law of the Gospel, which is a law of love, not servitude. Through charity we are elevated beyond our natural capacities so that our obedient act is truly free and rational and human: 'the supreme dignity of people is that they are not led by others, but by themselves, to what is good' (*Sup. Rom.* 2:14, n. 217). Moral inquiry is therefore concerned with how we may progress in our friendship with God.

There is a second reason for thinking of moral inquiry in terms of becoming a certain kind of person. Thomas believed that knowledge of rules and principles, although often useful as a guide, is no guarantee of itself that we will make the right decision. Knowing rules and principles is one thing; applying them prudently is much more difficult. Rules and moral precepts are general and abstract. They must be applied to the particular case, but there are no rules to tell me which rule to follow or which principle to apply in the concrete circumstances in which I must act, since these circumstances are contingent and varied and cannot be foreseen (ST 1/2.18.3; 1/2.19.10 ad 1). We recall, furthermore, that the principle of obedience to Christ overrides all other principles and rules, including such basic principles, for Thomas, as evangelical poverty. Deciding whether wealth and obedience to Christ conflict or not in a particular case requires wisdom and prudence.

Thus to live the Christian life well we must be trained for it. We need to acquire the appropriate virtues that will enable us to make sound moral judgments and dispose us to receive more charity and gifts of the Holy Spirit. Through training we acquire prudence and the other moral virtues, and as these are enhanced by grace we become wiser in our decisions and more readily and successfully orient ourselves and our actions to our proper end. This is a life-long and demanding process. The virtues are all about stretching ourselves to our limits in doing something we find difficult; indeed, what is difficult and what is good are the same thing in an act of virtue (ST 2/2.129.2). Thomas forcefully asserts the struggle involved to live as a Christian: 'it is a great thing to perform a miracle, but an even greater to live virtuously' (*Sup. Matt.* 10:8, n. 819). We will frequently fail and sin. Yet the Christian life can be one of great joy, too, since the acquisition of good habits disposes us to good actions, often making them a pleasure, and forgiveness is readily available. So we 'must delight in God for God's own sake, as being our last end, and in virtuous deeds, not as being our end, but for the sake of their inherent goodness which is delightful to the virtuous' (ST 1/2.70.1 ad 2).

The Christian life is one that must be lived within community, for we cannot acquire virtues of any kind by ourselves, nor can we receive forgiveness except at the hands of those appointed to administer this gift. It is not enough to read Scripture by ourselves and pray long and hard in isolation. We need the company, the gifts and the counsel of those who are more skilled than we are in following Christ obediently. Thomas did not live at a time when people were worried about individualism, so he does not explicitly stress the communal aspects of the church as such. But it is quite clear that for him the Christian life requires our active participation in the fellowship of other *viatores*, in the body of the congregation of the faithful (*congregatio fidelium*), as he calls the church on earth.

Moral inquiry for Thomas is therefore a particularistic and communal inquiry. It is based upon the distinctive account of human action and its relation to God proclaimed by the church in accordance with its Scriptures and the apostolic tradition. If Kant's ethics is an autonomous and secular ethics, and thus a matter of purely philosophical inquiry, Thomas's is a theonomous ethics of grace, a matter primarily of theology, though, for purely theological reasons, it is a theology that can and does make use of philosophical tools. Any consideration of Thomas's moral theology must therefore include some account of its communal setting, the life of the church. But the church itself is too complex an entity to be described without distortion unless we locate it within the larger scheme of God's redemptive plan for all creation. So I turn first to the larger scheme, namely Thomas's account of law.

Law

Thomas uses the concept of law analogically to tie together the divine and human action that constitute the *reditus*, the return of all things to the Father in the Son by the Holy Spirit. Law, as such, 'denotes a kind of plan directing acts towards an end' (ST 1/2.93.3). Law of every kind directly or indirectly regards the final end, which is eternal life with God. Because law is ordered to the common good of all, its end is universal happiness (ST 1/2.90.2). Law is thus the equivalent term for God's prudential governance of all creation. God governs all things in every creature by imprinting in them their particular manner of operation. Each creature participates in its own way in God's providential plan as each follows the law God gives it. Rational creatures like humans and angels fulfill God's plan by directing themselves according to their own plan by the use of their reason. So they can be said to have their own derivative kind of providence and their own kind of law within God's law. Thus, as we saw with the similar issue of the divine *concursus* and the interior movement of grace, one should not think that law is primarily coercive. 'The proper effect of law is to make those to whom it is given, good' (ST 1/2.92.1). Especially for those rational creatures who are in the state of grace, the function of law is their transformation in view of their supernatural end.

Different Kinds of Law

God's providential plan is the first and all-encompassing law, the eternal law. The 'very idea of the government of things in God the ruler of the universe has the nature of a law', and the final end of God's law is nothing other than God (ST 1/2.91.1). We recall that all things are created as God knows God in the divine wisdom, in the Son in whom are the ideas of all creatures. As with existence, so with operation: we consider the Son himself to be 'the eternal law by a kind of appropriation' because 'all the actions and movements which are to be found in each single creature' are present eternally in the Son as the wisdom of God. While all things are subject to the eternal law, God is not. God transcends the law because God, in the Son, *is* the eternal law (ST 1/2.93.1, 4, and ad 2).

We participate in the eternal law initially by means of a second kind of law, the natural law, which is given us as part of our basic equipment as creatures, and which contributes to our 'natural aptitude for virtue' (ST 1/2.95.1). Thomas argues that the basic precept of the natural law is self-evident and indemonstrable. In speculative reasoning, which is concerned with being and truth, we know self-evidently that we cannot at the same time affirm and deny the existence of a thing (the principle of non-contradiction). In practical reasoning, which is about action and the good, we know as self-evident that 'the good is that which all things seek after'. Hence the first precept of the natural law is that 'good is to be done and pursued, and evil is to be avoided' (ST 1/2.94.2). This principle reflects certain key inclinations that come to us naturally, namely to preserve human life and ward off its obstacles; to propagate and educate the species; and 'to know the truth about God and to live in society' (ibid.). From there, Thomas suggests, one can reason to a few very general precepts, such as our obligation to preserve life and to avoid offending those with whom we must live. These constitute the natural law.

The place of the natural law in Thomas's thought remains a point of contention. Thomas does not extend the scope of the natural law any further, nor does he spend much time discussing it (only a single question, one which is considerably shorter than his treatment of the Christological orientation of the ceremonial laws of the Old Testament, for example). Some of his interpreters have tried to develop the natural law further so that it yields some guidance about more detailed matters. This may not be an unreasonable line of inquiry, for Thomas contends that a third kind of law, human law, must be shown to conform to the natural law. Human laws are, like all laws, for the common good. Their force depends upon their justice and their justice depends upon their being 'derived' from the natural law. Their derivation may be as a conclusion from natural law principles. A law that prohibits killing people is evidently such a conclusion. Or the human law may be a 'determination' of the natural law, for example a law that specifies the penalty for breaking the law, which follows the principle of the natural law that an evil-doer should be punished (ST 1/2.95.2). If it is a direct conclusion of the natural law, a human law has the force of natural law and cannot be abrogated. But the kinds of punishments and other determinations of the human law can be changed, depending upon the needs of the society in which they are enacted. A society may decide to give up imprisoning debtors, for example, or replace the stocks or a whipping by a fine.

Thomas makes it clear that he considers it often quite difficult to decide upon the implications of the natural law for human action. He notes that thinking about moral questions is logically more cloudy than thinking about scientific issues:

> the speculative reason is busied chiefly with necessary things, which cannot be otherwise than they are, [so] its proper conclusions, like the universal principles, contain the truth without fail. The practical reason, on the other hand, is busied with contingent matters, about which human actions are concerned: and consequently, although there is necessity in the general principles, the more we descend to matters of detail, the more frequently we encounter defects. Accordingly, then, in speculative matters truth is the same in all people ... But in matters of action, truth or practical rectitude is not the same for all, as to matters

of detail, but only as to the general principles: and where there is the same
rectitude in matters of detail, it is not equally known to all. (ST 1/2.94.4)

Circumstances and details matter in judging the rightness of an action: 'all
acts of virtue must be modified with a view to their due circumstances' (ST
2/2.31.2; 1/2.73.7). Moreover, the natural law is by no means entirely self-
evident. Some of its precepts may be known only to the wise, and not every
society is gifted with wise people. As Thomas notes, 'custom has the force
of a law, abolishes law, and is the interpreter of law' (ST 1/2.97.3), so if one
lives within a society whose customs permit its members to be 'perverted by
passion, or evil habit, or an evil disposition of nature', the natural law will
be proportionately obscured. Thomas cites the example of some German
tribes who at one time, according to Caesar, believed that theft was not
wrong (ST 1/2.94.4). Furthermore, from quite another side of the matter,
Scripture makes it plain that an action which may appear quite obviously
against the natural law can in fact be good. Theft (Exodus 12:35), adultery
(Hosea) and the killing of anyone, innocent or guilty (Abraham's sacrifice
of Isaac), may all be committed without any injustice, if in obedience to
God's direct command (ST 1/2.94.5 ad 2; ST 2/2.104.4 ad 2).

   In light of these difficulties, it seems reasonable to think that Thomas sees
natural law largely as a reference to that place within human nature where
our activity is connected with the eternal law. Rather than forming the basis
for an extensive set of rules and precepts, our knowledge of the natural law
indicates that we are created in order to participate in God's plan by our own
efforts and through our societies' legislation.[3] Our redemption and salvation
are not unnatural, nor are they discontinuous with our better tendencies, for
'just as grace presupposes nature, so must the divine law [which draws us to
an end beyond our natural capacities] presuppose the natural law' (ST 1/
2.99.2 ad 1). We recall that the knowledge we can gain about God through
our natural reason alone is utterly inadequate for our salvation. So, too, with
the knowledge about practical matters we gain from the natural law. Our
lives are oriented towards a goal beyond our natures; the natural law is
inadequate to that goal (ST 1/2.91.4 ad 1).

   Thomas moves on from natural and human law to consider a fourth kind
of law, the divine law. The main purpose of this law, which he treats in
much more detail than the others, is 'to establish humanity in friendship
with God'. Friends must be similar to one another if their friendship is to
persist and be mutually beneficial. Although God derives no benefits from
us, the divine law enables us to become good and so achieve a kind of
likeness to God, who is the Good (ST 1/2.99.2). The divine law differs
from human law in that it is concerned to promote not only justice between people but also their better relation to God. It is concerned not
merely with external actions, but with the goodness of our interior dispositions, which God alone can judge. The divine law is also distinguished
from all the other kinds of law, including the eternal law, in that it is

promulgated by God and made known to us now through the witness of Scripture. Accordingly, it is divided into two parts, which Thomas calls the old law and the new law of the Gospel.

The old law was given to the people of Israel alone. It foreshadows Jesus Christ and prepares Israel for him. Thomas divides the old law into three parts. The moral precepts of the old law are given in the Decalogue and developed and expanded in the remainder of the law of Moses. The moral precepts are essentially natural law; they derive their force from natural reason, and so they apply to all people, including Christians. Thomas is clear, however, that not all the precepts are self-evident to unaided reason. Some are, such as the prohibitions against killing and stealing. Others, especially those precepts having to do with God, such as the law against graven images, need to be made known to us by divine revelation. The Sabbath law, which Thomas treats as a quasi-moral precept since it 'commands us to give some time to the things of God', requires infused faith for it to be understood by the wise as in accord with reason (ST 1/2.100.3 ad 2). Some of the precepts outside the Decalogue can be seen to be derived from the natural law and the Decalogue only after reflection upon the latter. The second part of the old law consists of the ceremonial precepts which were given to the Israelites so that they might worship God rightly. Like Scripture more generally, they should be interpreted according to the fourfold senses (ST 1/2.102.2), and Thomas spends time explicating their spiritual – i.e., Christological – meanings in considerable detail. Finally, the judicial precepts are, like the human law, 'determinations' of the eternal law, since they refer to the ways by which justice is to be maintained among people. Unlike human law, the juridical precepts are divinely instituted. Examples of these precepts are the laws governing the treatment of strangers and servants, the payment of wages and the treatment of criminals. They, too, are figurative, referring forward to Christ, and are annulled with his coming, like the ceremonial precepts (ST 1/2.105).

Besides its primary function of preparing the Israelites for Christ, the divine law was given because they, like everyone else, were easily confused about the precepts and implications of the natural law. Our unaided reason is hard pressed at the best of times to derive appropriate human laws from the natural law. With the loss of natural integrity upon the fall into sin, the natural law became even more difficult to discern. Thomas notes that while we may come to some kind of knowledge of truth even while in a state of sin, that is not the case with regard to the good: 'human nature is more corrupt by sin in regard to the desire for good, than in regard to the knowledge of truth' (ST 1/2.109.2 ad 3). To see why, I need to pause briefly in my account of law to consider Thomas's understanding of sin and human action more generally.

Sin and Human Action

According to Thomas, an account of human action must be considerably more complex than an account of the way in which other creatures act. In part this is because our actions not only must conform to our natures, they should be directed towards our supernatural end. Unlike non-rational creatures like dogs, flowers and rocks, we cannot orient ourselves to, nor achieve, our proper end by our natural capacities alone. We are distinguished from such creatures, too, in that our actions must be rational and free if they are to be fully human. At the same time, we are also distinguished from the higher, 'separate substances', the angels, in that our actions involve our bodies, unlike their actions, which are purely spiritual.[4]

Our bodiliness must be reckoned with theologically for Christological reasons, too. We recall that the primary purpose of Christian existence is to follow Christ obediently. Christ's life was an active one. Rather than withdrawing from the world to seek God in solitary contemplation, he went out into the world to serve the needs of others. His ministry, his Passion and his Resurrection display for us the way to achieve our salvation in him, a way that, like his, is necessarily embodied. While our interior actions, our intentions and good will, are the primary concern according to the new law, for an action to be complete and meritorious it should usually be more than mental. An action involves the whole of the person, body and soul, if it is to be a fully human and successful action. Accordingly, Thomas rejects what he takes to be the Platonic view, which treats human action as if it were second-rate angelic action, better accomplished the less it involves the body. We are animals, so our bodies are constitutive of all our action (ST 1.75.7). But we are rational animals, because our soul is an intellectual soul. We are midway, then, between angels and animals, partaking of aspects of both.

Thomas draws upon a modified form of Aristotle's philosophy for his account of human persons and their action. For Aristotle, all things are constituted by matter and form, i.e., by what is potentially something and by that which makes what is potential into an actual thing. The human soul is the form of the body; the body is the matter. By informing or animating the matter, the soul makes the body a human body. Together, as a composite, soul and body constitute the person (ST 1.75.4). The human soul does not exist without the body, for we are not purely immaterial forms like the angels. Without the soul, the body is no longer human; it is just a corpse. Without the body, the soul cannot function in a human way. Even in heaven we will need our bodies, though, to be sure, there they will be somewhat different than they are now. To be a human person, then, is to be an embodied soul or, to say the same thing, a soul-informed body. For Thomas, materiality or bodiliness cannot be identified with creatureliness, as if our spiritual aspects are (quasi-)divine. We are created as ensouled bodies. Our souls are immortal by nature, for they are pure form; having no matter, they do not decay, as a person does, into matter and form. The angels are naturally immortal for the same reason. Yet souls and angels are created, and all created things have only participated and contingent existence. Unlike God, their essence is not identical with their existence; their existence depends upon God. Souls cease to exist as soon as God ceases to maintain them in a created relation to God.

Everything about a person is embodied, including our minds. Non-bodily activity is certainly possible, for we can think internally without any bodily movement (according to Thomas). However, our minds need our bodies in order to get data for thought. Our knowledge is not innate; it must come through our senses (ST 1.84.3). Each of us has one soul rather than multiple souls, but our soul operates in multiple ways and so can be said to have different kinds of 'powers'. The powers having to do with our reason are the highest, for it is our intellect which differentiates us from all other animals. Our souls are fundamentally intellectual even though they must deal with bodily matters, too. Thomas rejects the notion that there are two kinds of reason, one concerned with eternal matters and another concerned with temporal or earthly matters. The reason must be one, even though it operates in different ways, for it is only as we think about created and earthly things that we can have some knowledge of the eternal God (ST 1.79.9). Similarly, speculative reason, which considers necessary truths, and practical reason, which considers what we are to do, are different operations of the same reason (ST 1.79.11). One may infer that Thomas rejects these hierarchical distinctions because of his belief that practical reasoning about earthly matters is as significant for meritorious action as contemplation of the divine, as Christ himself revealed in his active and engaged manner of life.

A second power of the human soul is the will or the 'intellectual appetite'. By 'appetite', Thomas means that aspect of our souls which moves us to desire or avoid an object, to treat it as a good or an evil. In having a will, we are different from irrational animals. Their appetites are determined by their natures; they cannot help but desire what accords with their natural end. We have free will because we must use our reason and the knowledge we have gained through it to make decisions about what to do. We, like irrational animals, must of necessity will our final end, the perfect good, but since our end is perfect happiness, the necessity of willing it is not inconsistent with our freedom (ST 1.82.1). Our free will comes into play as we choose the means to that final end, means which include penultimate ends. The term 'free will' (*liberum arbitrium*) is used by Thomas in a way somewhat different from contemporary usage. For Thomas, having free will does not simply mean having the freedom to choose between various options; nor is it reducible to freedom from coercion. Free will is not a neutral choice; I do not exercise it well if I choose to drink myself into a stupor rather than do something else, whether the other thing is good or evil. I choose with genuine freedom only when I act in accordance with my reason, and to drink too much clearly fails this criterion in most circumstances. Thomas admits, though, that what constitutes perfect happiness, as well as the means to it, are both things about which we cannot be certain until we are presented with perfect happiness in the vision of God in heaven (ST 1.82.2). Deciding on means and ends is, therefore, the task of both our will and our intellect, a task often very difficult to accomplish well.

The third power of the soul is the 'sensitive appetite', so called because it is moved by what it apprehends through the senses rather than through the intellect. Its movements are called passions because we are moved passively by something other than ourselves, unlike the operations of the intellect, which are more active than passive. We may be moved in two ways. The passions of concupiscence move us 'to seek what is suitable, according to the senses, and to fly from what is hurtful'. Concupiscence has therefore to do with natural needs such as food and sex and avoiding harm, and its primary passion is love. The irascible appetite, by contrast, moves us to respond to an object that is 'arduous'. Its passions, particularly hatred and anger, prompt us to resist something that is not suitable for us or which hinders or obstructs us in gaining what we desire (ST 1.81.2).

Thus for a human action to be good, it must be a product both of the successful operation of the powers of the soul as well as of the proper order among them.[5] The will freely and rightly chooses the means that are in accordance with reason; the reason correctly discerns the means and penultimate ends that are suitable, in these particular circumstances, for moving towards our ultimate end; together the will and the intellect subdue the passions that hinder the proper choice and its achievement in action.[6] All this, to repeat, is frequently difficult to do, and the difficulty is markedly increased by the fact of sin.

A sinful act is one that lacks the proper order among the powers of the soul. It may therefore be termed an unnatural act in the sense that, when we sin, the natural order among our powers is distorted (ST 1/2.71.1) as a result of 'our desire for some mutable good, for which we have an inordinate desire, and the possession of which gives us inordinate pleasure' (ST 1/2.72.2). To sin is also, of course, to fail to conform to the eternal law and is thus an offence against God. If the offence involves a deliberate turning away from God, which is the primary meaning of 'sin', the sin is mortal and merits damnation. If it does not, and if it can be 'repaired' in that the disorder of the particular action does not too adversely affect our orientation towards our supernatural end by depriving us of charity, it is a venial or pardonable sin (ST 1/2.88.1).

Sin is not only a disordered action, it is a disordered state, a corruption of our souls – though not our bodies – passed down from generation to generation ever since Adam's first sin (ST 1/2.83.1). As a state, original sin is the consequence of the loss of that original justice given to Adam and Eve which enabled the powers of their souls to operate in harmony and in due order, and made their wills freely subject to God's will (ST 1/2.82.3). Actual sins are caused by the corruption of the three powers of the soul following the loss of original justice. The intellectual powers may fail to discern that a given course of action is sinful. It may be that I am brought up in a culture whose customs obscure the natural law so that I do not know that it is wrong to commit usury, for instance. Or it may be that I am unaware of the facts of the matter. To use Thomas's example, I do not commit the sin of parricide if I do not know that the person I am killing in battle is my father (ST 1/ 2.76.1). Ignorance in such cases may be 'invincible ignorance' if there is nothing that could have been done to acquire the necessary knowledge. If so, my act is sinless because it is essentially involuntary; I did not sin because I did not know I was doing wrong. Ignorance, though, may be more or less deliberate. I might be negligent in thinking the issues through, or I might have failed to make suitable inquiries about the members of the opposing army. To the extent that I am negligent, I sin because I have freely chosen not to do something I know I should have done, which is a sin of omission (ST 1/2.76.2). Thomas's response to the question of committing a sin when drunk is interesting. Because I cannot think clearly when drunk, I become ignorant and therefore my drunkenness diminishes – though it does not erase – the sinfulness of my action. But I have committed two sins, namely being drunk and committing the sin, so I deserve a double punishment rather than leniency (ST 1/2.76.4 ad 4).

Because sin may be caused by a failure of the intellect, it is a possibility not only for rational creatures who have bodies but for purely intellectual creatures, too. Angels could sin because they, having reason and free will, could (and some did) make decisions that were not in accordance with the eternal law, of which they were not ignorant (ST 1.63.1 ad 4). Sin, to repeat, is a matter of the soul, not the body: 'sin is the spiritual death of the soul' (ST 3.79.6). But for embodied souls, the body may often contribute to the soul's sin. This is especially evident when the sensitive appetite leads the reason and will astray. Thomas is no Stoic; as bodily beings, we are moved by concupiscent and irascible passions which in themselves are perfectly good and necessary for our existence.[7] The passions do not need to be eliminated, but they must be controlled. In a state of sin this has become especially difficult, though not impossible (ST 1/2.82.3). The passions have been corrupted so that the 'fomes', the movement of the passions that prompts us to sin, is sometimes overwhelming. We may be swept away by sudden sinful impulses before we have had time to think. Or the passions may make it difficult for us to reason well or direct our will freely to choose the means suitable to our supernatural end. Not infrequently, the passions may make us act contrary to the knowledge we actually have (ST 1/2.77.2). This is especially evident with regard to those passions associated with concupiscence, since our self-loving desire for food and sex, and the money and power that enable us to satisfy these and other desires, may be very strong (ST 1.81.2; 1/2.77.5). Again, though, the involvement of the passions may diminish the sin to the extent that they render our action involuntary (ST 1/2.77.7).

Finally, the will may be responsible for sin by 'malice', through which one knowingly and purposefully chooses an evil rather than a good. This is more likely when one has a vice, an evil habit which accustoms one to make a malicious choice (ST 1/2.78.1). This is distinct from an evil choice prompted by passion, however, since passions may overcome good habits and be repented quickly, while sins occasioned by malice are likely to be persistent and more voluntary. Thomas is far more forgiving to those who give way thoughtlessly to passion, and who repent quickly after their sin, than he is to those who sin through malice (ST 1/2.78.4).

Old and New Law

Sometimes, then, we are led astray by our passions, our vicious habits, our confusion or our ignorance, so that we do something that does not conform to the eternal law. The gift of the divine law is therefore intended to help us overcome these obstacles so that we may live in obedience to God's will and begin to establish friendship with God. The old law was thus a remedy for sin as well as a preparation for Christ. Its moral precepts at least partly clarified the natural law; its ceremonial precepts turned us towards God and gave us ways to offer worship and praise that foreshadowed Christ; its judicial precepts appropriately determined our relations with one another. With the revelation of the old law, the Israelites were given a body of rules to live by that would help them better discern good from evil, restrain concupiscence and more readily acquire the virtues necessary to fight against sin (ST 1/2.98.1).

The power and effect of the old law were quite limited, however. It helped its adherents prepare themselves for justification and the reception of grace, but it could not justify them or give them grace. And because the old law cannot be fulfilled without grace and charity (ST 1/2.100.10 ad 3), the law in effect revealed our sinfulness, even encouraged it, as much as it helped us to avoid sin (ST 1/2.98.1 ad 2, citing Romans 7:11). Christ submitted to its ceremonial precepts, by his circumcision, for instance, and he complied with the judicial precepts by giving and exemplifying the counsels of perfection (ST 1/2.107.2; 3.40.4). Having been fulfilled and transformed by Christ, the old law gave way to the new law of the Gospel, for though the old law was 'perfect for its time' it is now 'weak and useless' (ST 1/2.98.2 ad 1, 2). The coming of Jesus Christ has made obsolete those parts of the old law which only prepared for and foreshadowed him, especially the ceremonial precepts. Thomas remarks that our faith in Christ is 'the same' as the faith of the people of the old law. But we live after Christ; they lived before. So 'the same faith is expressed in different words, by us and by them' (ST 1/2.103.4). Their words and deeds refer forward; for us to refer to Christ as future would be to deny him and sin mortally.

Unlike the old law, the new law of Christ justifies and sanctifies. It 'consists chiefly in the grace of the Holy Spirit, which is shown forth by faith that works through love' (ST 1/2.108.1). It is essentially a 'law of liberty', with a focus 'chiefly in internal acts', i.e., on having the right disposition and intention, rather than solely on external actions as required by the old law (ibid.). Indeed, to persist in worrying over external acts can be sinful. Thomas distinguishes superstition from genuine faith by the former's overemphasis upon 'externals', upon doing things the proper way at the expense of genuine faith, which worships God internally. He cites Luke 17:21: 'The kingdom of God is within you' (ST 2/2.93.2). The new law is much less burdensome than the old law, for it has far fewer rules and adds 'very few precepts to those of the natural law'. Yet in another sense, following Christ is much more difficult than obeying the old law because it demands internal transformation (ST 1/2.107.4).

Life in the Church

We have seen how Thomas uses law to bring together those elements of his theology that bear upon human action. The various forms of law enable him to make connections and distinctions between concepts such as nature and grace, sin, justification and meritorious action. Law is also used to connect yet distinguish the activities of the members of the body of Christ: those who follow after Christ in grace; the people of the old law, for whom he is future; and those who have only natural and human laws. All the varied efforts of humanity are thereby located in their distinctive relation to the eternal law, the providential plan of God. With this background in place, we can now focus on the life of the Christian as a member of the community of the new law: the church which is *in via*, on the way of Jesus Christ.

Definitions

Thomas did not write a treatise on the church, nor does he dedicate a single question to the church in the ST. Neither he nor his contemporaries nor the tradition before them thought it necessary to discuss the church as a separate topic of theological inquiry. He and they mention the church more or less in passing as they discuss some other topic. We have seen an example of this in the previous chapter, where we looked at one of Thomas's texts which perhaps most nearly approaches a discussion of the church, namely the question of the headship of Christ (ST 3.8). There, we recall, Thomas discusses the church in terms of the various ways humanity may be in relation to Christ, but he leaves the concept of the church undefined and somewhat vague. One may assume that Thomas had a more or less clear idea of the church's nature and functions, and it is possible to piece together some of that idea, particularly with regard to function, from the texts that refer to the church. But we cannot expect to discern Thomas's ecclesiology from such an approach, since he might have cast the matter differently had he thought of considering it directly and systematically.

It has become customary in the last fifty years or so to discuss any given ecclesiology in terms of a particular model, an image or concept that expresses what is thought to be the church's essential characteristic (Dulles, 1974/1987). Whatever the merits of this procedure for modern ecclesiologies, it is less than helpful when applied to Thomas's theology. As George Sabra has shown in his excellent monograph on the subject, Thomas's concept of the church was 'manifold, non-univocal and primarily theological' (Sabra, 1987, p. 33). To focus upon one element as more basic than another distorts his complex understanding of the church. That said, Sabra is also correct in contending that 'Thomas's ecclesiology is to a very large extent simply a moment of his Christology' (ibid., p. 84; also Dulles, 1982, p. 155). But this can be misunderstood. It has sometimes been said by later Roman Catholic theologians that the church is in its essence the continuation of the incarnate Christ. In his *De Veritate*, Thomas himself says that 'Christ and his members are one mystical person' (DV 29.7 ad 11), but what he means by this is not obvious. We recall that 'church' may be a very broad concept for him, and 'Body of Christ' even broader. Moreover, he frequently distinguishes between the earthly church and the heavenly church. The members of the church on earth are *viatores*, still on the way, so we must expect that part of the church to be different in significant respects from the heavenly church. Clearly, it is sinful, for one thing (ST 3.8.3 ad 2). Only the church of the *comprehensores* completely realizes the perfection of life in Christ.

I suggest that one approach to Thomas's conception of the earthly church is to think of it as the community of the new law of Christ, the gathering together of those who, through the Gospel and the gifts of grace, live in Christian freedom.[8] Accordingly, the unity of Christ and the church on earth lies not so much in identity of being as in unified activity, which Christ makes possible for us through the Holy Spirit. We are one with Christ because we have joined ourselves to the apostolic mission. Christ lived an active life engaged with those around him, rather than retiring to solitary contemplation. He went off by himself on occasion, but only to come back enriched by prayer to serve the needs of his friends and followers. He relied upon the traditions of the people of Israel, without which he could not have accomplished his mission. He understood himself and his work in terms of his people's Scripture and gathered around him a group of disciples whom he trained to continue his mission in obedience. The church's function is to continue that mission, primarily through its preaching and witness.

Thomas often calls the earthly church the *congregatio fidelium*, the gathering of those who seek to be faithful to Jesus Christ. The church of the faithful *viatores* does not exist for its own sake. Unlike some modern theologians, for whom the church community is highly valued as a bulwark against the perils of individualism, Thomas does not dwell on the benefits of the church community as such. He takes them for granted, concentrating more on the benefits of church membership for the individual Christian. The three main benefits for the individual Christian are the church's preaching and teaching, much of which has already been discussed, the sacraments, and its training in the life of obedience to Christ.

The Sacramental Church

All seven of the sacraments are in a significant sense prior to the church. The church did not institute them; it arose from them. The sacraments derive from Christ's Passion rather than from the church as such, because grace comes from no other source than Christ's merits achieved in the flesh. From the pierced side of the crucified Christ flowed the blood and the water which were the signs of baptism and the Eucharist (ST 3.62.5). One becomes a member of the Christian church by one's act of faith in Christ. Faith has always been necessary for salvation, for 'at no time, not even before the coming of Christ, could people be saved unless they became members of Christ' (3.68.1 ad 1), and we become justified members by faith alone. Faith is required for baptism, either one's own faith or, if the one baptized is an infant, the faith of the church as a whole, which is applied by the operation of the Holy Spirit 'who unites the church together and communicates the goods of one member to another' (ST 3.68.9 ad 2). Faith is the basis for baptism and for membership in the church, so the church 'is built on faith and the sacraments of faith' (ST 3.64.2 ad 3).

We have been given the sacraments for two main reasons, namely to worship God and to bring about our sanctification. The sacraments of the new law are a vital means by which we obtain those special, 'sacramental' graces which, in addition to 'ordinary' grace, help us live the Christian life. They are also the means by which supernatural virtues and gifts are infused in us. They imprint upon those receiving them a certain spiritual 'character' which marks them as separate from the servants of the devil. All Christians, whether lay or clerical, are distinguished by their having been 'deputed to the Christian worship' which belongs primarily to Christ. So to receive the sacramental character is to be 'likened to Christ' and thus to participate in Christ's own priesthood (ST 3.63.3 ad 2).

Since grace is the consequence of the meritorious actions of Christ in his humanity, the seven sacraments 'derive their efficacy from the incarnate Word himself' (ST 3.60 prol.). They are Christ's sacraments, instituted by him as rules for the reception and 'right use' of grace so that we may achieve our proper end, eternal life in him. With regard to baptism and the Eucharist, institution by Christ is obvious. The sacrament of orders began with the 'institution of the apostles and the seventy-two disciples', while confirmation comes from Christ by his promise to send the Holy Spirit. Penance, 'indissoluble matrimony' and healing of the sick also originate with Christ (ST 1/2.108.2). Some of the sacraments, though not all, were prefigured in the old law, for example matrimony by ordinary marriage and baptism by circumcision.

The sacraments are signs which make use of ordinary things to lead us to spiritual things. They direct our attention away from created realities to God, our eternal happiness (ST 3.61.1). In this they reflect the way we come to knowledge of God, for it is 'proper to discover the unknown by means of the known' (ST 3.60.2), and we also find that 'in Scripture spiritual things are set before us under the guise of things sensible' (ST 3.60.4). In addition, Thomas draws upon the analogy between natural ends and our proper end. 'The Church's sacraments are ordained for helping people in the spiritual life. But the spiritual life is analogous to the corporeal, since corporeal things bear a resemblance to spiritual' (ST 3.73.1). Thus baptism corresponds to spiritual birth, confirmation to spiritual growth, and the Eucharist to spiritual food (ibid.).

The sacraments, then, are sensible signs which, like other signs, point or refer to something other than themselves. The sacraments or ceremonies of the old law did that, too; they were signs of the faith that justified the people of Israel (ST 3.62.6 ad 3). The sacraments of the new law are distinctive in that they also effect the spiritual realities they signify. A sacrament is not only a sign of grace; it is also a cause of grace for the one receiving it in faith and charity. Thomas argues against those theologians who thought that grace is conveyed to the soul merely at the same time the sacraments are given, without any real causality on the part of the sacraments. According to this view, God would give the grace while the sacraments would be the signs of that grace, but there would be only a coincidental relation between the two. Against this Thomas contends that a sacrament is an efficient cause of grace; it actually does something to bring grace to the recipient. It is not, of course, the principal cause of grace, since only God can transform us so that we participate in the likeness of the divine nature. But the sacrament is truly an instrumental cause (ST 3.62.1). When a carpenter uses a saw, the saw has a kind of power of its own as it cuts through wood. So, too, with sacraments: they have 'a certain instrumental power of bringing about the sacramental effects' (ST 3.62.4).

Something similar may be said of those who administer the sacraments. They, too, act instrumentally in that they do not themselves confer grace, since they have been given no power of their own to do so. If they are good people who act in charity, they are living instruments, freely contributing to the sacramental act. If they lack charity, they are merely lifeless instruments and thus not unlike the carpenter's saw (ST 3.64.5 ad 2). But even if they are wicked or heretics, or even unbelievers and unbaptized, as long as they go through the proper procedure their instrumental effect is sufficient, due to the fullness of the power of the principal agent, Christ.

Baptism

Baptism is the most necessary of the sacraments. If a priest is not available, even laypeople (women, too, if a man is not available) and those who have not themselves been baptized, such as pagans, may baptize those who are in danger of dying without the benefit of baptism (ST 3.64.6 ad 3; 3.67.4). Baptism is necessary because it is only in baptism that we receive the capital grace of Christ that transforms us so that we may begin the journey of further transformation that constitutes the Christian life. In baptism we are justified, re-established in a right relation to God. We die to our old selves, who were born in the state of sin, and rise with Christ into the state of grace. Our past sins and the punishment we owe for them are washed away as 'the pains of Christ's Passion are communicated' to us inasmuch as we are made 'members of Christ' (ST 3.69.2 ad 1). To be sure, we still have natural bodies in which we can suffer, but it is only as embodied souls that we are able to join with Christ's suffering, as we suffer for his sake. Our bodies are still subject to the effects of sin, too, so our children will be born with original sin, we will all die, and throughout our lives we will have to fight against concupiscence (ST 3.68.1 ad 2). Baptism, though, is a rebirth and a genuine transformation that, since it confers a permanent character, cannot be repeated.

As he does with regard to a number of the sacraments, Thomas distinguishes between the sacramental sign, the reality and the sacrament, and the reality alone. Baptism uses water as a sign, but the water itself is not the sacramental reality as such, nor is it of itself the instrument of grace. It is only as the water is used in the rite of washing that it becomes not only a sign but also the sacramental cause of the reality that is signified. It is through the rite – water, washing and the proper words – that the reality of the sacrament is achieved. That reality is the 'inward justification' consequent upon baptism (ST 3.66.1). The water cleanses the body in the usual way, but the cleansing is used by God, the principal agent, as the means by which the soul is cleansed from sin.

While baptism is necessary for salvation, the effects of baptism may be had without the actual sacrament. Thomas follows Augustine to say that those who desire baptism but cannot receive it because of something beyond their control may be given its effects by their desire alone (ST 3.68.2). This is a general principle that applies to penance and even to the Eucharist. Provided one desires these sacraments and would willingly partake of them if it were possible, their effect is accomplished, though usually without quite the same amount of grace (*Sup. Ioan.* 11:44, n. 1562). Intention can be sufficient because the sacraments of the new law pertain, we recall, to interior acts rather than solely to exterior. There are other kinds of baptism, too, through which one may be justified and saved. One kind is baptism by repentance, whereby those who are moved by the Holy Spirit to repent of their sins and to believe in and love God have the effect of baptism without the sacrament. The best kind of baptism, however, is the baptism of blood, i.e., martyrdom, for it reflects the highest degree of fervor and love for Christ (ST 3.66.11f.).

Thomas argues that baptism should be preceded by Christian education so that those who are baptized have the right faith. However, in his day as in ours, many people were baptized in early infancy, in part because of a fear of eternal damnation if they died without it. So for baptized infants, their sponsor promises to teach them as soon as they are able to learn (ST 3.71.1 ad 3). The custom of infant baptism is reflected in Thomas's understanding of confirmation, the sacrament which brings one 'to mature spiritual age'. In confirmation, 'the Holy Spirit is given to the baptized for strength' (ST 3.72.7), enabling one to 'do those things which pertain to the spiritual combat with the enemies of the faith'. Sanctifying grace is given in addition to that given at baptism, 'for growth and stability in righteousness' (ST 3.72.7 ad 1). Pursuing the military analogy, Thomas says that confirmation makes one a soldier of Christ, a 'front-line fighter' (ScG 4.60.1); hence it is fittingly performed by the bishop, who is the commander of the Christian army (ST 3.72.10 ad 2). As a sacrament oriented towards distinctive action, confirmation imprints a special character (ST 3.72.5).

Eucharist

The Eucharist is both a sacrament and a sacrifice. Though performed count-less times, the Eucharist is only a single sacrifice because each performance is 'an image representing Christ's Passion, which is his true sacrifice' (ST 3.83.1). By our eucharistic participation in Christ's sacrifice we also partake of the fruit of his Passion and are thereby drawn up into him. The Eucharist is 'the sacrament of ecclesiastical unity', but not because it is a celebration of something that we have here on earth, such as our togetherness or our love for one another. Rather, the sacrament turns us away from ourselves by signifying that our unity 'is brought about by many being one in Christ'. It signifies not that we are one so much as that we are one *in him* (ST 3.82.2 ad 3; *Sup. Ioan.* 6:52, n. 960).

This orientation towards Christ bears upon Thomas's explanation of the presence of Christ in the sacrament. The doctrine of the Real Presence – that Christ is truly there in the bread and wine – was well established by his day. Thomas cites the case of Berengar of Tours, an eleventh-century monk who, to clear himself of accusations of heresy, famously had to subscribe to the notion that he literally crushes Christ's body when he chews the sacramental bread (ST 3.75.1). Thomas certainly accepts the doctrine of the Real Pres-ence, but not in such a materialistic way. He develops an alternative line of thinking (perhaps suggested by his reading of John Damascene) that distin-guished between two ways in which Christ can be said to be present in the sacramental elements. One is reflected in Berengar's statement, namely that Christ is there in person, in what Thomas calls his 'proper species'. The problem with this view is that, after his Ascension, Christ took his rightful and permanent place in heaven, from which he sends the Holy Spirit. Jesus is and remains in heaven in his proper species, as the Son who, body and soul, is united personally with divinity (ST 3.75.1 obj. 3, premise not de-nied). Therefore he cannot be present in the elements dimensively or in terms of location; nor can the sacrament be said to bring Christ down to us by bodily movement. Rather, it must be that the sacrament in a sense raises us up to him. Christ is indeed really present, but in another way, namely sacramentally or 'substantially'.

Thomas explains sacramental presence in his teaching on the doctrine of transubstantiation, which uses some Aristotelian concepts in a way that Aristotle would no doubt find quite incomprehensible. According to Aristotle, the being of a thing may be divided conceptually, though never in reality, into two elements, its substance and its accidents. Bread may come in all kinds of different shapes, sizes, smells, colors and tastes. These are its accidental qualities, the variations among which do not affect the fact that any given piece of bread is substantially (or hypostatically) bread. The reality that underlies the contingent qualities is the bread's sheer 'bready' substance, so to speak, that which makes it bread. That substance remains invisible to us since, like any substance, it is accessible to us only conceptually. That substance is taken away by the prayer of consecration, leaving only the bread's accidents, such as the wafer-like quality, the off-whiteness, dry taste, and so on – the things available to our senses that tell us we are eating bread. But although these indicate that we are eating bread, we are not in fact, for the substance of the bread is replaced by Christ's substance. Christ is present substantially, though not with his accidents, so there is nothing quantitative or dimensional about his presence. We have, that is, the reality of Christ, a more than conceptual reality, but one which is inaccessible to us in every way except conceptually (and that only by distorting Aristotle). Christ is not crushed in our eating of the bread because the crushing occurs to the accidents of the bread that remain, not to his accidents (ScG 4.65.2). Christ is not present in his proper species, which would include accidental qualities of place and dimension and other accidents, only in his sacramental species (ST 3.77.7 ad 3).

If transubstantiation seems next to impossible, it is; the sacrament is entirely supernatural (ST 3.75.4). Nor will Thomas accept what may appear to be more reasonable, namely the notion of consubstantiation, according to which the substance of Christ is *added* to the substance of the bread, which remains after consecration (ST 3.75.6). No, the bread is no longer really bread at all; it is really Christ. Yet, too, the sacramental reality we have in the elements is distinctly different from the reality of Christ in heaven. Christ is really present in the elements in a way that strengthens our relation to his heavenly presence, drawing us closer to him, that is, provided that we take the sacrament fittingly. Thomas draws the distinction between sacramental eating and spiritual eating. The former is available to anyone or anything that eats a consecrated host, including mice, dogs, unbelievers and those in mortal sin. They all eat Christ because the reality of his sacramental presence cannot be reduced to a mere psychological phenomenon; it is objectively real. Nor is there anything undignified about this, since Christ suffered much greater humiliation on the Cross (ST 3.80.3 ad 3). However, no one eats Christ to their advantage unless they eat spiritually, because the sacrament is 'ordained to the enjoyment of heaven' and must therefore be eaten in faith, after having been absolved of one's sins (ST 3.80.2 ad 1).

Penance, Orders and Marriage

Absolution is achieved through the sacrament of penance. Thomas has no doubt that everyone will need this sacrament because all will sin after their baptism. Penance is like a kind of spiritual medicine that keeps us healthy (ST 3.84.5) by 'spiritual healing of a sort' (ScG 4.72.1). Unlike the two sacraments just mentioned, there is no element that is consecrated. Rather, the concern is to take our sins away and recover the infused virtues we have lost or deadened by our sin. The grace that flows from this sacrament depends upon the penitents' actions, which are themselves consequent upon prevenient grace. They must be contrite, wanting to atone for their sins; they must confess their sins, thereby submitting to the judgment of the church in the person of the priest; and they must give satisfaction by their subsequent actions (ST 3.90.2). The priest is empowered to grant absolution by the power of the keys given by Christ to Peter (Matt. 16:19) and subsequently handed on to the apostolic church. The sacrament of orders confers that power with other spiritual powers, particularly the power to administer the Eucharist. The priest is thereby able to function instrumentally by his participation in Christ's power (ScG 4.74).[9] Once again, because he has special duties, a special character is imprinted on the priest at his ordination.

The sign in the sacrament of marriage is the union between the man and the woman. This signifies – though it obviously does not effect – the union between Christ and the church. Since the latter is indissoluble, so also is sacramental marriage. One reason for matrimony is that the church needs new generations until the end of the world. But marriage is not merely 'a function of nature'; it is 'the sacrament of the union of Christ with the church' (ST 1/2.102.5 ad 3). Thomas makes an interesting point when he considers the marriage of Our Lady. She was, he contends, truly married to Joseph, even though her marriage was not consummated. The marriage was true in the most important way, namely in the perfection of its form, which 'consists in a certain inseparable union of souls' (ST 3.29.2). That perfection is of more significance than the second perfection, namely the perfection of operation, which is the propagation and upbringing of children. Clearly for Thomas, marriage is far more than a matter of biology or even the natural law. The union of souls is the primary sacramental reality of marriage, fittingly so in light of the union of church and Christ.

While the seven sacraments are vital for the life of the church, the church is not centered upon them in Thomas's thinking. The sacraments are but beginnings and strengthenings and orderings of the activities of the *viatores*; they are never ends in themselves. There is no suggestion in Thomas of the kind of sacramentalism which asserts that when the Eucharist is celebrated the church achieves its most profound being and somehow anticipates the heavenly church. Certainly the Eucharist transforms, but only as part of the whole gamut of ways in which the Christian is aided in following Christ obediently. The sacraments are given us to help us live the Christian life as we seek to draw closer to God along the way of Jesus Christ. Action is required of the earthly church; we live in a different sphere from the blessed in heaven, who have only to contemplate God (ST 2/2.181.1). Membership in the earthly church is therefore less a question of a distinctive kind of being than it is a distinctive kind of activity (albeit an activity based upon prayer and contemplation).

Thomas and Virtue Theory

Thomas's moral theology has recently received considerable attention not only from those who seek his support for a natural law ethic but also from those who are attracted by his emphasis upon the virtues. Thomas devotes considerable space in the ST to the virtues, both infused and acquired. By appropriating and modifying Aristotelian virtue theory he is able to flesh out his understanding of the Christian life as something that has more to do with internal transformation than following a complex system of rules and principles. Treating the Christian life in terms of the virtues thus enables him to develop his account of the new law of the Gospel.

Virtue theory has become attractive to some contemporary theologians for somewhat similar reasons, but it may be that there are a couple of significant differences. Perhaps the most important thing to say about Thomas's moral theology is that the point of being a Christian is to work towards eternal life with God. It is not, as it seems to be for some contemporaries, primarily to become a particular kind of person, namely a good Christian. Thomas agrees that it is our virtues that make us good. But being good, while certainly a goal, is only a penultimate end for Thomas. In his discussion of the Beatitudes, Thomas remarks that being a peacemaker, for example, is not the blessing; it is only a means to the blessing. The blessing is not something about us and our perfection; it is God. *Deus est praemium eorum qui ei serviunt*: God is the reward of those who serve God (*Sup. Matt.* 5:2, n. 412). We are not united to God by our work or by what we become, but by God alone as we are drawn up into God through the grace of Jesus Christ (*Sup. Matt.* 5:7, n. 407).

A second reason why virtue theory is attractive for some contemporaries is that it offers useful ways of talking about Christian witness that go beyond preaching and teaching doctrine. A visible community of Christian people who display distinctive Christian virtues is, so it is quite reasonably argued, a good form of witness. But Thomas himself does not seem to share this concern. He says nothing to indicate that he thinks that we can attract non-Christians or unenthusiastic Christians by our manner of life. Rather, our manner of life is worth living because it leads us towards our proper end. What attracts others to Christianity is the operation of the Holy Spirit in the first movement of grace that convinces them of the reasonableness of making an act of faith. One can speculate that were Thomas to be asked about this, he might point out that some of the monks of his time were splendid Christians with obvious virtues, yet their virtue had no appreciable effect upon the commitment of ordinary folk to Jesus Christ. What is of more significance than being a virtuous person is to be a preacher and teacher, a Dominican friar or a bishop engaged with the world. Certainly, preachers need virtues, but they need them – as do all Christians – in order to become the kind of person who can readily obey Christ as they turn to serve God and our neighbor. The virtues are all about our action, for 'virtue is a habit by which we work well' (ST 1/2.56.3); they are 'productive of good works' (ST 1/2.55.3).

The Cardinal Virtues

Earlier we examined Thomas's discussion of the infused virtues of faith, hope and charity. Charity, we recall, brings us into union and friendship with God and is oriented to meritorious and loving action. After his discussion of charity in the ST, Thomas goes on to examine the actions with which charity is especially associated, such as acts of mercy, almsgiving and fraternal correction, as well as those actions which are opposed to charity, such as discord, war and sedition. From there, he turns directly to the four cardinal virtues: prudence, which in Thomas's usage has little or nothing directly to do with later connotations of caution or carefulness; justice; fortitude (or courage); and temperance. He organizes a long section (102 questions) analyzing a multitude of actions, good and bad, in terms of one or other of these four virtues. It is difficult to summarize this section, nor is it really necessary to do so, for its details are often comparatively less significant for Thomas's theology. What is significant is that the section is there at such length in the ST, which indicates Thomas's concern to extend his theological inquiry to include the complexities of obedient Christian action. Here I will very briefly discuss the cardinal virtues, though only in terms of their place and function within Thomas's theological scheme.[10]

The link between the theological virtues and the cardinal virtues is prudence, which is necessary for the exercise of any acquired virtue. Prudence is a virtue that draws upon both the reason and the will. The reason is involved because the prudent 'consider things afar off, in so far as they tend to be a help or a hindrance to that which has to be done at the present time'. Put more abstractly, one who is prudent applies universal principles to make decisions about a particular course of action. Since prudence is concerned with action towards a goal, it involves the will, too, for the will moves us to act in ways that bring us towards our proper end (ST 2/2.47.1 ad 2 and 3). The virtue of prudence thus comes very close to one of the gifts of charity, wisdom, which Thomas treats as the last of the effects of charity, just before he turns to prudence. It is because of their lack of charity, and thus their lack of infused wisdom, that the wicked lack prudence. They may have some knowledge of the universal principles of action, but they will not be able to apply their knowledge wisely or prudently to make a good decision about a particular action (ST 2/2.51.3 ad 2).[11]

We recall that Thomas acknowledges how it can be sometimes difficult both to decide what to do as well as to follow through one's decision. There are no rules about how this is to be done. One learns how to choose and act well habitually, by practice, as one acquires the appropriate virtues. Virtues are acquired by watching those who live well and by heeding their counsel as we make our own decisions and act upon them. The virtues are necessary because one cannot simply obey the prudent or follow them blindly. Our actions are to be *ours*. Each one of us, in Thomas's view, is on our own, as it were, in that each of us must act freely and rationally, from filial rather than servile fear, if we are to act in grace and in accordance with our humanity. We must make decisions for ourselves; that is what we do as rational animals. Our freedom is our gift, but it is also, of course, one reason – besides the supernaturalness of our proper end – why we need grace and the sacraments. The function of all four virtues – indeed, of the sacraments and the infused virtues and gifts, too – is to give us the dispositions to act well as we face the contingencies of the Christian life *in via*. It is by virtues like prudence and temperance that we control those passions which may lead us to act badly. The virtues work to keep our will in accordance with our reason so that we make good decisions and then act upon them (ST 1/2.56.4; 2/2.141.1).

The Christian life is lived over time. For those who are successful Christians in the sense that they have been elected to receive grace sufficient to act meritoriously, it is a journey of transformation towards ever greater obedience. No one is given a sudden, perfecting enlightenment. Each particular action has therefore only a relative significance. While any human action may be sinful or generically good or, through charity, meritorious, a single act does not make one a good or an evil person. It is by possessing virtues that people are good; if they have vices, they are evil. The cardinal virtues and their opposing vices take time to acquire and time to lose. If I commit an evil act I do indeed commit a sin and, if it is grievous, I may immediately lose charity. But if I have acquired countervailing virtues and I quickly and truly repent and confess my sin, this may have little bearing upon my virtue and goodness. The same applies to the contrary with regard to the vicious person who does a single good act. And if I cease to exercise a particular virtue, like any unpracticed habit, the virtue will likely diminish over time (ST 1/2.52 and 53). Christians therefore must practice their faith in charity so that they acquire and strengthen the virtues they need to enable them to make good decisions and act in obedience to Christ in the future. But this is an ongoing struggle. If we do not maintain our vigilance and if we act badly too often, we will lose the virtue and become more prone to evil; we will become vicious. The prudent may become imprudent, or their prudence may be distorted into guile or craftiness (ST 2/2.55.3). Once that happens, it will be all the more difficult to turn back to follow Christ.

'It belongs to virtue to safeguard a person in the good of reason … [which] consists in the truth as its proper object, and in justice as its proper effect' (ST 2/2.124.1). Justice is that virtue which makes it possible for us to perfect our relations with others in all the varied circumstances of our engagement with them. It inclines us to give the other person their due, to act in accordance with their right (*ius*) (ST 2/2.57.4 ad 1). To be just is therefore not so much a question of having the intellectual ability to decide what is just in a given case. It is that in part, but as a virtue it is a disposition, an inclination that becomes second nature to the just person to act justly in any given circumstance, even sometimes without much thought (ST 1/ 2.58.5).[12] The virtue enables us to will to act constantly and voluntarily, as a habit (ST 2/2.58.1). To act justly requires prudence, of course, for there are many cases where giving everyone their due is complicated by competing rights and complex circumstances. And we will need temperance, too, so that our judgments are not distorted. Temperance is that virtue which controls the passions of concupiscence. It 'moderates those passions which denote a pursuit of the good' (ST 2/2.141.3) so that we are not swept away by earthly desires and pleasures. As in every virtue, Thomas seeks the mean. He rules out the notion that we should so completely subdue our passions that we no longer feel anything. Passions are a vital part of the moral life; anger can be righteous. To become so temperate that one becomes insensitive and passionless is to become vicious (ST 2/2.142.1).

The Christian life requires fortitude. The virtue of fortitude complements temperance, for it deals with those irascible passions that lead one to be disinclined to act in accordance with reason because of some difficulty (ST 2/2.123.1). We recall that the life of virtue, the Christian life, is an arduous one, by definition (ST 2/2.129.2). Jesus Christ displayed for us the way to eternal life, and his way is evidently not easy.

> A Christian is one who is Christ's. Now people are said to be Christ's not only through having faith in Christ, but also because they are actuated to virtuous deeds by the Spirit of Christ … Hence to suffer as a Christian is not only to suffer in confession of the faith, which is done by words, but also to suffer for doing any good work, or for avoiding any sin, for Christ's sake, because all this comes under the head of witnessing to the faith. (ST 2/2.124.5 ad 1)

The Christian life, as Thomas sees it, is difficult and costly. It takes courage to follow Christ in a life of poverty and humility, devoting oneself to preaching and teaching. We need the virtue of fortitude, which can be acquired in part through practice, so that we gain firmness in the good and can endure greater difficulties. Again, keeping to the middle between extremes is important: fortitude has little to do with aggression or foolhardiness. Rather, it is endurance that is 'the principal act of fortitude' (ST 2/ 2.123.6). Through the power of fortitude we can stand firm even unto martyrdom, which is the most perfect act if done in charity. In martyrdom, the full strength of endurance is displayed, for it 'consists essentially in standing firmly to truth and justice against the assaults of persecution' (ST 2/2.124.1).

The Church as Teacher and Guide

It is evident that for Thomas the church *in via* is less a place of rest and peace than it is the scene of activity and struggle. The church's central function is to serve its members as they seek to conform themselves to Christ. Through their various gifts the members of the Body of Christ help one another to follow their head obediently. The faithful require not only the grace and gifts the sacramental church brings to its members; they also need guidance and counsel from those more skilled in the way of Jesus Christ. The primary forms of guidance are preaching and teaching, which are finally of more significance for Thomas than the sacramental aspect of the church. As George Sabra rightly notes, '[t]here are rather clear indications in Thomas's writings that he assigns greater importance to the role of the word and a higher status to its ministry than he does to the sacraments and their ministry' (1987, p. 152). This preference is reflected in occasional comments about the relative importance of priests, bishops and theologians. Thomas compares to 'manual workers' those priests who are restricted to ministering the sacraments and caring for their parish. In contrast, the bishops are 'superintendents', as are the teachers of theology like Thomas, for their service has greater scope. Not only do they minister; they also 'inquire and teach how others ought to procure the salvation of souls' (Qd 1.7.2).

Grace flows from Christ to his members 'in various ways, for the perfecting of the body of the Church', resulting in a diversity of roles. This reflects what we know of an 'earthly commonwealth', where it is helpful for the general peace when more are involved, in diverse ways, in public life (ST 2/ 2.183.2). People need governance, though, and the best form of governance is by one person. The pope's role, which is derived from Christ's charge to Peter, is to maintain the unity of the church amid these diverse activities so that the church may serve its members better (ScG 4.76). However, there are clear checks and balances upon the power of the pope and the bishops. The apostolic witness controls the hierarchy, rather than vice versa: 'The apostles and their successors are God's vicars in governing the church which is built on faith and the sacraments of faith. Wherefore, just as they may not institute another church, so neither may they deliver another faith, nor institute other sacraments' (ST 3.64.2 ad 3). Nor do theologians have any special authority to interpret Scripture. 'The teaching of the catholic doctors has its authority from the church; it is better, then, to maintain the custom of the church than the authority of Augustine, Jerome or some other doctor'

(Qd 2.4.2). The custom of the church generally trumps all challenges unless it can be shown that it is disobedient to Christ. Again, the vital principle of the Christian life is to follow Christ, the principle of the new law which overrides all human laws and authorities.

Conclusion

The church's way of life is authorized by the apostolic witness of Scripture to Jesus Christ. Scripture displays Christ and the apostolic life (*vita apostolica*) as normative examples of virtuous obedience which Christians are to emulate. However, to be truly obedient, the church and its members are to follow Christ in ways appropriate to their own times, places and circumstances. That is because the new law of the Gospel is the law of freedom rather than a set of rules that apply apodictically.

Over the centuries, through its intellectual, moral and spiritual efforts at submitting all that it does to the judgment of Christ, the church has developed guidelines and norms in its customs, practices and doctrines. Its preachers and teachers convey to the congregation of the faithful the fruits of the church's contemplation, as they seek ever anew to approach the 'high, full and perfect' vision of John the Evangelist. The church's teaching, complemented by its sacramental ministry, helps the faithful to be transformed by grace and the virtues so that they may act meritoriously in faith and charity. If they are given grace to persevere to the end of their lives, they may achieve their proper supernatural end and participate, in Christ, in the life of the triune God. The church strengthens the *viatores* in their struggle on the way of Christ, mediating to them his grace and the charity and gifts of the Holy Spirit. As they pursue their life-engaging adventure, Christians cannot do without such strengthening and guidance. Living in the earthly church is difficult, in part because it is a life in the world, in active engagement with those around one, following the example of Christ and his apostles. Like them, too, Christians always have an eye upon their goal, upon God, the vision of whom is to be their eternal happiness in the life to come. Then, as *comprehensores*, they will no longer need any virtue but charity, for their work will be done and they will rest in the vision of God.

Notes

1 Interpreting Thomas's moral theory is always controversial and there is a massive literature on the subject. I present his account of the Christian life – the term is already an interpretation, since some would say that his moral theology is largely a matter of moral philosophy – in as uncontroversial a manner as possible, consistent with what I have suggested is his inherently evangelical and Trinitarian theology. But it should be clear that others would disagree with my interpretation here.

2 One of the ways Kant displays his genius is in his imaginative appropriation of many

elements from the Christian tradition for his own program. As a consequence, there are a number of areas where parallels with Thomas can be found, and some modern ethicists sympathetic to both Kant and Thomas have exploited these. The difference between the two thinkers is too radical, however, for such parallels to be more than superficial, in my view.

3   See Bowlin (1999), p. 123. Bowlin suggests with some reason that the concern for natural law reflects modern worries about how to ground morality in an age of skepticism. Among Roman Catholics who advocate a natural law ethics, it may be, too, that there is a concern with the particularist tendency of Thomas's account of the Christian life and a desire to show the reasonableness of Catholic morality to those who are not Christians. It seems unlikely that Thomas was so concerned. A good account of Thomas's notion of natural law is that of Pamela Hall (1994).

4   My account of the human person and human action is comparatively brief compared with more philosophically oriented interpretations of Thomas's thought. I limit the account to what is necessary and useful to know for understanding his theology.

5   'Good' here can mean generically good, the goodness we can achieve without grace, and thus without merit. For an act to be meritorious, grace and the second movement of the Holy Spirit are also necessary.

6   Again, this is a highly compressed summary. Thomas expends considerable effort in unpacking the complexities of the human action in ST 1/2.1–48.

7   Thomas acknowledges that his disagreement with the Stoics may be merely linguistic, since they can be understood as concerned to rule out those passions that are not in accordance with reason, a notion with which Thomas agrees. See ST 2/2.123.10.

8   This is an 'approach', not a model, for it does not attempt to determine Thomas's idea of the essential character of the church; quite the contrary, it in effect rules out such a move even by way of a summary concept. Thomas himself does not directly character-ize the church in this way. It is my attempt to set his understanding of the church within the larger context of his view of the Christian life as one that is intelligible only in terms of its relation to God's eternal law and the redemptive work of Jesus Christ and the Holy Spirit.

9   The ST ends before completing the discussion of penance and the remaining sacra-ments; hence I draw more upon the ScG, though the treatment there is comparatively brief. Editions of the ST usually draw upon the early *Commentary on the Sentences*. I have chosen not to, in part because the remaining sacraments are not central to Tho-mas's theology.

10 Thomas's account of the moral virtues is subtle and complex and cannot be justly treated in a brief account. McInerny (1982/1997), Bowlin (1999) and Porter (1990) are all good and should be consulted, though they partly diverge in their interpretations.

11 The wicked, like all people, have knowledge of universal practical principles by means of 'synderesis', which is a 'natural habit' that parallels the natural knowledge of the first principles of reason. See ST 1.79.12.

12 It may help to avoid confusion if I point out that Thomas treats the virtues in two places in the ST, in 1/2 and in 2/2. The first is a general overview; the second is more detailed. It so happens that the question numbers referring to the two different parts are very close, as here and in the next reference.

References

All references to Thomas's works in Latin are to the Marietti Edition, Turin. References to the Scripture Commentaries use the following abbreviations:

Super Evangelium S. Matthaei Lectura (1951), ed. P. R. Cai, OP
    (*Sup. Matt.* chapter:verse number)
Super Evangelium S. Ioannis Lectura (1952), ed. P. R. Cai, OP
    (*Sup. Ioan.*)
Super Epistolas S. Pauli Lectura, 2 vols (1953), ed. P. R. Cai, OP
    (*Sup. Rom*; *Sup. I Cor*; *Sup. Titus*, etc.)

References are to the following translations (with their abbreviations):

Summa Theologiae (1981), trans. Fathers of the English Dominican Province, Westminster, MD: Christian Classics. (ST)
Summa contra Gentiles (1975), trans. Anton Pegis and others, Notre Dame and London: University of Notre Dame Press. (ScG)
The Disputed Questions on Truth (1954), trans. R. W. Schmidt, SJ, Chicago: Henry Regnery. (DV)
Quodlibetal Questions 1 and 2 (1983), trans. Sandra Edwards, Toronto: Pontifical Institute of Mediaeval Studies. (Qd)
Compendium of Theology (1952), trans. Cyril Vellert, SJ, London and St Louis, MO: Herder.

Other Works

Barth, Karl (1975), *Church Dogmatics*, 1/1, Edinburgh: T. and T. Clark.
Booth, Edward (1983), *Aristotelian Aporetic Ontology in Islamic and Christian Thinkers*, Cambridge: Cambridge University Press.
Bowlin, John (1999), *Contingency and Fortune in Aquinas's Ethics*, Cambridge: Cambridge University Press.
Buckley, Michael J., SJ (1987), *At the Origins of Modern Atheism*, New Haven, CT: Yale University Press.
Chenu, M.-D., OP (1997), *Nature, Man and Society in the Twelfth Century: Essays on New Theological Perspectives in the West*, eds and trans. J. Taylor and L. K. Little, Toronto: University of Toronto Press.

Corbin, Michel (1972), *Le Chemin de la théologie chez Thomas d'Aquin*, Paris: Beauchesne.

Cross, Richard (1999), *Duns Scotus*, New York: Oxford University Press.

Davies, Brian (1992), *The Thought of Thomas Aquinas*, Oxford: Clarendon Press.

Dulles, Avery, SJ (1974/1987), *Models of the Church*, expanded edn, New York: Doubleday.

Dulles, Avery, SJ (1982), *A Church to Believe In: Discipleship and the Dynamics of Freedom*, New York: Crossroad.

Emery, Gilles, OP (1995), *Trinité et Création dans les Commentaires aux* Sentences *de Thomas d'Aquin et de ses Précurseurs Albert le Grand et Bonaventure*, Paris: Vrin.

Emery, Gilles, OP (2000), 'Essentialism or Personalism in the Treatise on God in Saint Thomas Aquinas?', *The Thomist* **64**, 521–63.

Emery, Kent, Jr and Wawrykow, Joseph (eds) (1998), *Christ Among the Medieval Dominicans: Representations of Christ in the Texts and Images of the Order of Preachers*, Notre Dame: University of Notre Dame Press.

Farthing, John L. (1985), 'The Problem of Divine Exemplarity in Saint Thomas', *The Thomist* **49**, 183–222.

Goering, Joseph (1998), 'Christ in Dominican Exegesis: The Articles of Faith', in Emery, Jr and Wawrykow (1998), pp. 127–38.

Hall, Pamela M. (1994), *Narrative and the Natural Law: An Interpretation of Thomistic Ethics*, Notre Dame: University of Notre Dame Press.

Hibbs, Thomas S. (1995), *Dialectic and Narrative in Thomas Aquinas: An Interpretation of the* Summa contra Gentiles, Notre Dame: Notre Dame University Press.

Horst, Ulrich, OP (1998), 'Christ, *Exemplar Ordinis Fratrum Praedicantium*, According to Saint Thomas Aquinas', in Emory and Wawrykow (1998), pp. 256–70.

Jenkins, John I., CSC (1997), *Knowledge and Faith in Thomas Aquinas*, Cambridge: Cambridge University Press.

John, Helen James, SND (1966), *The Thomist Spectrum*, New York: Fordham University Press.

Kant, Immanuel (1985), *Critique of Practical Reason*, New York: Macmillan.

Lash, Nicholas (1996), *The Beginning and the End of 'Religion'*, Cambridge: Cambridge University Press.

Levering, Matthew (2000), 'Wisdom and the Viability of Thomistic Trinitarian Theology', *The Thomist* **64**, 593–618.

Lovejoy, Arthur O. (1964), *The Great Chain of Being: A Study in the History of an Idea*, Cambridge, MA: Harvard University Press.

Lubac, Henri de, SJ (1998a), *Medieval Exegesis: Volume I: The Four Senses of Scripture*, trans. Mark Sebanc, Edinburgh and Grand Rapids: T. and T. Clark and Eerdmans.

Lubac, Henri de, SJ (1998b), *The Mystery of the Supernatural*, trans. Rosemary Sheed, New York: Crossroad Herder.

MacIntyre, Alasdair (1990), *Three Rival Versions of Moral Enquiry: Encyclopaedia, Genealogy, and Tradition*, Notre Dame: University of Notre Dame Press.

Maritain, Jacques (1956), *Existence and the Existent*, trans. L. Galantière and Gerald B. Phelan, New York: Image Books.

Marshall, Bruce (1987), *Christology in Conflict: The Identity of a Saviour in Rahner and Barth*, Oxford: Blackwell.

McCabe, Herbert, OP (1987), *God Matters*, Springfield, IL: Templegate and London: Geoffrey Chapman.

McCool, Gerald A., SJ (1989), *From Unity to Pluralism: The Internal Evolution of Thomism*, New York: Fordham University Press.

McCool, Gerald A., SJ (1994), *The Neo-Thomists*, Milwaukee: Marquette University Press.

McInerny, Ralph M. (1982/1997), *Ethica Thomistica*, Washington, DC: Catholic University Press.

Milbank, John and Pickstock, Catherine (2001), *Truth in Aquinas*, London and New York: Routledge.

Narcisse, Gilbert, OP (1997), *Les Raisons de Dieu: Argument de convenance et Esthétique théologique selon Thomas d'Aquin et Hans Urs von Balthasar*, Fribourg: Éditions Universitaires.

Newhauser, Richard (1998), 'Jesus as the First Dominican? Reflections on a Sub-Theme in the Exemplary Literature of Some Thirteenth-Century Preachers', in Emory and Wawrykow (1998), pp. 238–55.

O'Meara, Thomas F., OP (1997), *Thomas Aquinas Theologian*, Notre Dame: University of Notre Dame Press.

Porter, Jean (1990), *The Recovery of Virtue; The Relevance of Aquinas for Christian Ethics*, Louisville, KY: Westminster/John Knox Press.

Rahner, Karl, SJ (1982), 'Remarks on the Dogmatic Treatise "De Trinitate"', *Theological Investigations*, vol. 4, trans. Kevin Smyth, New York: Crossroad.

Rogers, Eugene F., Jr (1995), *Thomas Aquinas and Karl Barth: Sacred Doctrine and the Natural Knowledge of God*, Notre Dame: University of Notre Dame Press.

Sabra, George (1987), *Thomas Aquinas's Vision of the Church: Fundamentals of an Oecumenical Theology*, Mainz: Mathias-Grünewald-Verlag.

Schmidt, Margot (1998), 'The Importance of Christ in the Correspondence between Jordan of Saxony and Diana d'Andalo, and in the Writings of Mechthild of Magdeburg', in Emery and Wawrykow (1998), pp. 100–112.

Smalley, Beryl (1952), *The Study of the Bible in the Middle Ages*, Oxford: Blackwell.

Stevenson, William B. (2000), 'The Problem of Trinitarian Processions in Thomas's *Roman Commentary*', *The Thomist* **64**, 619–29.

Tanner, Kathryn (1988), *God and Creation in Christian Theology: Tyranny or Empowerment?*, Oxford: Basil Blackwell.

Torrell, Jean-Pierre, OP (1996a), *Saint Thomas Aquinas: Volume I, The Person and His Work*, Washington, DC: The Catholic University of America Press.

Torrell, Jean-Pierre, OP (1996b), *Saint Thomas d'Aquin: Maître Spirituel: Initiation 2*, Paris: Cerf.

Torrell, Jean-Pierre, OP (1998), *La Somme de Saint Thomas*, Paris: Cerf.

Torrell, Jean-Pierre, OP (1999), *Le Christ en Ses Mystères: La Vie et L'Oeuvre de Jésus selon Saint Thomas d'Aquin*, Paris: Desclée (two vols, consecutive pagination).

Tugwell, Simon, OP (ed.) (1982), *Early Dominicans: Selected Writings*, New York: Paulist.

Wadell, Paul J., CP (1992), *The Primacy of Love: An Introduction to the Ethics of Thomas Aquinas*, New York/Mahwah: Paulist Press.

Wawrykow, Joseph P. (1995), *God's Grace and Human Action: 'Merit' in the Theology of Thomas Aquinas*, Notre Dame and London: University of Notre Dame Press.

Wawrykow, Joseph P. (1998), 'Wisdom in the Christology of Thomas Aquinas', in Emery and Wawrykow (1998), pp. 175–219.

Weisheipl, James A., OP (1983), *Friar Thomas d'Aquino: His Life, Thought and Works*, Washington, DC: The Catholic University of America Press.

Williams, Rowan (1999), *On Christian Theology*, Oxford: Blackwell.

Williams, Rowan (2001), 'What Does Love Know? St Thomas on the Trinity', *New Blackfriars* **82**, 260–72.

Wippel, John F. (2000), *The Metaphysical Thought of Thomas Aquinas: From Finite Being to Uncreated Being*, Washington, DC: The Catholic University of America Press.

Index

DATE DUE

AUG 0 2 2013	
SEP 3 0 2013	

DEMCO, INC. 38-2931